On the Theory of Descriptive Poetics:
Anton P. Chekhov as story-teller and playwright

DUTCH STUDIES IN RUSSIAN LITERATURE | 4

On the Theory of Descriptive Poetics: Anton P. Chekhov as story-teller and playwright

Essays by

JAN VAN DER ENG, Amsterdam

JAN M. MEIJER, Utrecht

HERTA SCHMID, Amsterdam/Bochum

LISSE
THE PETER DE RIDDER PRESS
1978

ISBN 90 316 0155 1

Printed in The Netherlands by Academische Pers bv, Amsterdam
Typesetting done by Mondeel bv, Amsterdam

Table of contents

ON DESCRIPTIVE NARRATIVE POETICS

JAN VAN DER ENG

On Descriptive Narrative Poetics

I. THE REQUIREMENTS FOR A NARRATIVE MODEL

Descriptive narrative analysis has lately developed a tendency to concentrate itself upon a narrative model, a general pattern, forming the basis of concrete narrative structures. This model rests upon a series of invaribale components of the action and their specific sequence. The action-components are mostly designated by noun-derivatives from verbs: prohibitions and violations of them, transgressions. Their sequence is dictated by 'natural logic'; in the terms of Propp: theft cannot precede the forcing of doors (Propp, 1928, izd. 2e 1969:25). I will not go into the inadequacies of this sequential logic in the 'volšebnaja skazka', worked out by Propp: Claude Bremond has justly remarked that from a logical point of view a choice can often be made between several sequential alternatives and that Propp's design is largely dependent on cultural conventions: a fight does not necessarily lead to victory, as it does in Propp's scheme, but may lead to both victory and defeat, or to neither of the two (Bremond, 1964:15-6). At this moment I am concerned only with the fact that in these narrative models the action is of central importance. Such a presupposition has its consequences for the rôle the characters play. Roland Barthes states that structural analysis avoids the definition of a

character as a 'being', a 'psychological entity'. Instead, characters acquire their identities from their participation in the
various actions. Their descriptions are not based upon 'what
they are', but upon 'what they do'. Hence the name 'actants',
which we find in the classification suggested by Greimas:
Sujet/Objet, Donateur/Destinataire, Adjuvant/Opposant.
Barthes does acknowledge the fact that in renowned narrative
texts the principal characters are complete individuals from
the outset. In "War and Peace" Nikolaj Rostov is from the
very beginning a good man, loyal, courageous and arduous.
Prince Andrej constantly shows his lineage, his desillusionment
etc. What happens to them illustrates their personalities, but
does not create them (Barthes, 1966:16-7).

The conclusion that may be drawn from this, is obvious:
narrative models may very well be centered upon the action,
but in many texts the characterization will prove to be more
important: a person's being, his or her psychological idiosyn-
cracies will be the center of the story. In such texts the principal function of the action is to exemplify the character(s).
Outside the circle of the French structuralists especially the
characterization-issue is taken up in critical remarks.
Bremond's model is strongly criticized for instance by Lidija
Ginzburg. She points out that the narrative texts of Tolstoj,
Dostoevskij and Čechov – contrary to Bremond's model – do
not show a straight correspondence between the rôles of the
characters and their 'functions', their behaviour. The relation
between them is sometimes paradoxical, sometimes even
downright inconsistent.

She states that in the psychological novel of the 19th
century the behaviour of the characters is unpredictable,
which makes Bremond's model inapplicable: a structurally
significant element in these novels is the discrepancy between
the characters' rôles and their functions. The rôle of a character has become more complex: traditionally in literature the
rôle of a character was based upon a well-organized pattern of
behaviour, rooted in aesthetical laws. In the later development
of literature these aesthetical rules ceased to be all-conclusive
and social, psychological and biological constituents became

determining elements. To a character could be allotted more rôles than one; intimations of them are mostly given in the exposition. Sometimes, however, we find a continued exposition later on in the text, introducing a rôle that clashes with the previous one. In *Anna Karenina* Vronskij is first presented as a popular officer of the guards, a Russian gentleman, then as a frustrated, egotistic career-hunter. The latter rôle he hides behind a posture of proud independence, of self-sufficience, of a man, who wants one thing only: to be left alone, a man who does not blame anyone for anything.

Lidija Ginzburg concludes that in complex literary structures there is no such thing as a fixed relation between an invariable rôle and the consequential behaviour, though the traditional typological outlines can still be discerned in them (1973:376-88). Lidija Ginzburg does not indicate how 'these elementary typological profiles' — in her opinion of great importance for the recognizability of a character — are expressed in these complex literary structures. We might suppose that Vronskij's different rôles agree with the possible change of rôles in Bremond's scheme (possible interchanges between the functions 'amélioration' and 'degradation': the 'beneficiaire' of some generous deed or profitable act may feel obliged to do his benefactor a good turn, or, if he refuses to acknowledge the obligation he is under, he may do so in many ways, he may even become aggressive towards his former helper).

In the case of Vronskij we may say that at first there is a 'processus d'amélioration': the winning of Anna. This could have been the end of the novel: "Un processus d'amélioration, en arrivant à son terme, réalise un état d'équilibre qui peut marquer la fin du récit" (Bremond, 1966:71). When the narrator wants to continue his story at such a point, he can do so, for instance, by unfolding and developing certain evil elements, which have been present in his story, but as yet have not been explicitly stated. In Bremond's terms this is called: "développer des germes nocifs laissés en suspens' (72). The winning of Anna's affection turns Vronskij into a 'bénéficiaire': he is the one who enjoys her love and surrender. The same goes, of course, for Anna: both are each other's 'bénéfici-

aire' and 'aide', completely in accordance with Bremond's
scheme: "l'aide est reçue par le bénéficiaire en contrepartie
d'une aide qu'il fournit lui-même à son allié dans un échange
de services simultanés: les deux partenaires sont alors solidaires
dans l'accomplissement d'une tâche d'intérêt commun ...
l'amélioration est obtenue grâce au sacrifice d'un allié dont les
intérêts sont solidaires de ceux du bénéficiaire" (66). The
seeds of destruction which are developed later on in the novel,
are connected with Vronskij's social ambitions, which are
hampered by his own misjudgement. When he starts living together with Anna these ambitions crash altogether. Their living
together even robs him of the glamour of having seduced an
important official's wife: up till then this glamour was a kind
of compensation for his frustrated ambitions, it strengthened
his rôle of the independent officer, indifferent to promotion.
In Vronskij's social circle his living together with Anna de-
prives their liaison of its luster, turns it into what in Bremond's
terms is called a 'dégradation'. Gradually Vronskij comes to
see Anna's demands upon him as 'agression' (the term is
Bremond's), and himself as 'agressé'. He tries to revise the basis
of their relation: en négociant une révision du contrat (74).
Seen from Anna's perspective this means he observes his
obligations towards her inadequately. In her turn she comes
to feel herself 'agressée', and more and more she opposes
Vronskij's propositions and deeds of 'agression'. In the end she
resorts to vengeance: la vengeance, qui consiste, non plus à
restituer à la victime l'équivalent du dommage subi, mais à in-
fliger à l'agresseur l'équivalent du préjudice causée (75). Her
vengeance is her appalling suicide.

The above selection of examples shows that Bremond's
model is in some ways applicable to the structure of *Anna
Karenina*. The various rôles Vronskij plays and the various
functions connected with them can be explained with the help
of the model. It is more difficult for the model to cope with
the two series of 'dégradation', which become characteristic of
the relation between Vronskij and Anna: for both of them
their relation develops from bad to worse. In a case of two
characters with opposed interests, where both of them partici-

pate in the same series of events, the model presupposes a combination of 'dégradation' and 'amélioration': "la dégradation du sort de l'un coïncide avec l'amélioration du sort de l'autre" (Bremond, 1966:4). In their liaison, however, both Anna and Vronskij seem to be losers. In order to make the model applicable it is necessary to assert that the losses they suffer in a certain situation are not as great as those in later situations. In every situation there is something worth fighting for which turns out to be lost in the next: therefore the preceding situation is a (relative) 'amélioration' in comparison with the next. This is an application of the model which Bremond gives himself: "il existe des récits dans lesquels les malheurs se succèdent en cascade, en sorte qu'une dégradation en appelle une autre. Mais, dans ce cas, l'état déficient qui marque la fin de la première dégradation n'est pas le vrai point de départ de la seconde. Ce palier d'arrêt – *ce sursis* – équivaut fonctionnellement à une phase d'amélioration, ou du moins de préservation de ce qui peut encore être sauvé. Le point de départ de la nouvelle phase de dégradation n'est pas l'état dégradé, qui ne peut être qu'amélioré, mais l'état encore relativement satisfaisant, qui ne peut être que dégradé" (Bremond, 1966:63). (The same holds, of course, for two series of progressive 'amélioration': the preceding phase is related to the phase following as an 'amélioration' which leaves something to be desired, and is therefore equivalent to a phase of 'dégradation' (63).) The 'dégradation' in the relation between Anna and Vronskij, which both experience as growing worse, now seems to fit into Bremond's model. I say 'seems', because Bremond does not explicitly show such an applicability. A condition for the applicability of the model is the presupposition of distinctive phases in the 'dégradation': that sometimes Anna, sometimes Vronskij is the greater loser, and that consequently one of them always has the position of 'amélioration' in comparison to the other. This way of looking at the struggle between Anna and Vronskij shows the model's union of 'amélioration' and 'dégradation'.

Thus Vronskij's and Anna's alternating modes of behaviour correspond with successive rôles and fit into Bremond's scheme. The model becomes inapplicable, however, when Anna's behaviour shows certain features that are characteristic of more than one rôle: after her departure with Vronskij to Italy Anna's function towards Karenin is that of 'agresseur'. The narrator, who restricts himself to Anna's view, expresses this by way of a metaphor: "The thought of the wrong she had done her husband aroused in her a feeling akin to revulsion, like the feeling a drowning man might have, who has shaken off another man clinging to him in the water. The other was drowned. It was wicked, of course, but it had been the only hope of saving oneself, and better not to brood over such horrible details." At the same time Anna's behaviour shows elements which are part of the function 'sacrifice'. This, too, is expressed explicitly in the text: "I have inevitably made that man wretched", she thought, "but I don't want to profit by his misery. I, too, am suffering, and shall go on suffering: I am losing what I most cherished – my good name and my son. I have done wrong, so I don't want happiness, I don't want a divorce: I shall go on enduring my shame and the separation from my son". On the one hand Anna's behaviour may be characterized as successful 'agression' = 'amélioration', on the other hand we find sacrificial elements (she does not seek a divorce, she accepts the separation from her son, she accepts her loss of respectability) = 'dégradation'.

It is questionable whether Bremond's scheme here still holds. His model precludes the possibility that one series of events, connected with one person can be characterized as both 'amélioration' and 'dégradation' (Bremond, 1966:64). It would seem that Bremond's scheme is applicable in narrative texts where the action is of primary importance and where the characters are subordinated to the logical pattern of that action according to the scheme 'amélioration'-'dégradation'. The model does not seem appropriate, however, in narrative texts where the characterization takes the central place and where the characters play more than one rôle at the same time – rôles which are mutually exclusive in Bremond's scheme. A narrative model, that can be pertinent to the psychological novel, should include psychological patterns as well as action patterns. In a psychological novel the action patterns must be looked upon as dependent upon the psychological patterns, whereas a possible consequence may be the disruption of the action's logic. In an action-novel the psychological patterns must be considered to depend on the action and the possible consequence here may be a simplification of the psychology. In other words: in the first type of novel the characterization may be considered to be dominant, in the latter the action.

In 1928 Edwin Muir published his suggestions for the classi-fication of novels; they were based upon a specific relation be-tween action and characterization. One of the classes of novels he distinguishes is the action-novel, in which the peculiarities of the characters depend solely upon the action: Trelawny in *Treasure Island* must be incapable of keeping a secret, because otherwise the pirates would never have known he sailed out to find treasure, etc. The action dominates and the descriptions of the dangers and successful escapes are given in their chrono-logical order. They form a mere series of successive events, narrated according to the simple principle 'and then, and then'. In Šklovskij's words: "there has been a time when people were not interested in the hero of a literary work. The hero was merely a chip of wood on the waves of the sea, which was only there to show the movements of the waves". (1927: 50).

As a second class Muir mentions the character-novel. Here the action is subordinated to the characterization, it functions to portray the characters, i.e. it traces their static existence in relation to their social environment. The action has no logical necessity, it does not advance towards a finale, but consists of incidents, like a dinner, a theater-play, an unexpected meeting, or something more drastic like a death, etc. The incidents demonstrate the unchangeability of the characters: the scenes change, but the characters always remain the same. In Forster's terminology such characters are called 'flat', i.e. they are unchangeable, their peculiarities can be comprised in one sentence. (See Forster, 1958:65, etc.)

A third class is what Muir calls the 'dramatic novel'. Here the action has, as Muir says it, 'a strict interior causation'. The

specific characteristics of the participants in the story determine the action and the action in its turn influences and
changes its participants, and turns them into 'round' characters
(the term is Forster's again). 'Round' means they are dynamic,
they act unpredictably, one sentence is not enough to describe
their personalities. The term does not imply the absence of
certain invariable distinctive qualities, such qualities remain
the basis for their identification. 'Round' does imply that a
character may change his/her attitude towards him/herself,
others, life in general, etc.

In his description of the various classes of novels Muir does
not neglect the greater or lesser importance of the social
setting. In his opinion it plays a very important part in the
character-novel. He explicitly states that this type of novel is
situated 'in space'. 'Space' comprises a great variety of social
circles. Talking about this variety Muir remarks: "we will be
shown by the character novelist ... that Queen's Crawley is a
very different place from Russell Square, and that there is an
inexhaustible diversity of places and states of life in the Five
Towns" (Muir:67-8). The function of the 'plot' therefore, is
not solely the introduction of as many characters as possible,
but also the introduction of as many places as possible, and it
shows the characters in relation to these settings: "When we
think of Thackeray's characters, we think of them in the
costume and against the background of their time; their
clothes, the houses they live in, and the fashions they observe,
are part of their reality; they exist in their period as in a
suddenly fixed world" (Muir:66). We may very well imagine a
type of novel in which the emotional and intellectual make-up
of the characters and their doings are determined by their
social circles, or, to be more exact, by the interaction between the specific, physiologically conditioned 'tempéraments'
and the environment: the latter determines the way in which
the 'tempéraments' reveal themselves.

We may think of the naturalistic novel à la Zola, in which
Zola himself considers the environment to be dominant. He
does so, for instance, in his notes for the novel *l'Assommoir*
(1877): "Montrer le milieu peuple et expliquer par ce milieu les

moeurs du peuple, comme quoi, à Paris, la soûlerie, la déban-
dade de la famille, les coups, l'acceptation de toutes les hontes
et toutes les misères viennent des conditions mêmes de l'existence ouvrière ...'". Inherent to this dominance of a determinative social environment is the frequent occurrence of descriptions. Zola defends this aspect of his narrative style in the
following, more or less apologetic passage: "Nous estimons
que l'homme ne peut être séparé de son milieu, qu'il est com-
plété par son vêtement, par sa maison, par sa ville et sa province; et, des lors, nous ne noterons pas un seul phénomène de
son cerveau ou de son coeur, sans en chercher les causes ou le
contre-coup dans le milieu. De là ce qu'on appelle nos éter-
nelles descriptions" (Zola, 1880:228). Generally speaking
we may say that especially in the French realistic and naturalistic novel the main accent came to rest upon descriptions of
the social environment. The importance attached to the
environment reduced the scope of the action and conditioned
the events that remained.

In a letter of June 25/26, 1853 Flaubert wrote about
Madame Bovary that he was working on a novel 2/3 of which
consisted of descriptions: "J'ai déjà deux cent soixante pages
et qui ne contiennent que des préparations d'action, des expo-
sitions plus ou moins déguisées de caractère (il est vrai qu'elles
sont graduées), de paysages, de lieux. Ma conclusion, qui sera
le récit de la mort de ma petite femme, son enterrement et les
tristesses du mari qui suivent, aura soixante pages au moins.
Restent donc, pour le corps même de l'action, cent vingt à
cent soixante pages tout au plus" (129). After les Goncourts
Zola reduced the dramatic element in his novels even further,
to a point where changes in the conditions of life, in the
environment, changes in age, came to take the place of the
changes which in other narratives are effected by the actions
of the characters. The point at issue here is, that it seems
logical to base narrative models upon ànd the action ànd the
characterization ànd the geographical and social setting. For
the classification of novels the hierarchical relation between
these three narrative levels seems to be of vital importance. It
is the narrator who determines this hierarchy, not only in his

explicit function of narrative medium, but also in his implicit
composing function. In the former function he chooses the
degree of knowledge with which he tells the story (varying
from all-knowing to nothing-knowing), in the latter he is in-
obtrusively present, arranging and grouping the ingredients of
his story. Of course these two functions are complementary.
The general categories of narrative presentation (vision 'par
derrière', vision 'avec', vision 'du dehors', transitions from the
one to the other) are all connected with the degree of knowledge the narrator chooses to exhibit. This provides him with
an opportunity to blend his information with contradictions,
misunderstandings, gaps, inaccuracies and paradoxes. By
means of these paradoxes, gaps, contradictions, etc., the narrator directs the reader's attention to the central thematic issues:
these may be intriguing, dark events, or fascinating aspects of
somebody's psychology, or disturbing influences of the social
situation. This dosing of the information falls within the
boundaries of the composition, the arrangement of a narrative
text. Moreover, narrative presentation is characterized by a
variety of phraseological forms, which correspond with as
many differentiations in the emotional or intellectual approach. This phraseological diversity is of course an excellent
means to bring out the arrangement and the relationship between the components. The narrator, the explicit and implicit
source of information, determines the 'type' of his narrative
with the devices he uses: story of adventure, or a psychological
or realistic novel, etc. To remain in control of his narrative, he
employs three categories of devices: devices of selection from
the thematic material and devices of its arrangement and
phraseological expression. These are the well-known categories
which are of central importance in Tomaševskij's poetics. They
are to be found in the chapter 'stylistic elements' at the beginning of his book, and in 'thematic elements' at the end of it
(1928:9-68 and 131-205).

   Their importance is also stressed in Žirmunskij's article
"Zadači poètiki" (1921). The three categories are interlinked.
A specific selection from the thematic material leads f.i. to
specific forms of arrangement and specific modes of expres-

sion: when exciting details of the action are singled out as
central elements in a narrative, this will have an influx upon
the descriptions of nature. The same happens, of course, when
psychological, geographical or social details prevail. In the
Formalist movement this has been recognized by Tynjanov in
the following words: "... from our vantage point in a particular
literary system, we would be inclined to reduce nature descriptions in old novels to an auxiliary rôle, to the rôle of making
transitions or retardation; therefore we would almost ignore
them, although from the vantage point of a different literary
system we would be forced to consider nature descriptions as
the main, dominant element. In other words, there are situations in which the story simply provides the motivation for the
treatment of 'static descriptions'." (1929:36-7; transl. 1971:
70).

Apart from the internal system of thematic motivation
there are two more (external) determinators of selection,
arrangement and phraseology: a) the relationship of a literary
text with what Tynjanov in the above quotation calls a literary
system; b) the relationship with other textual systems and
with human reality in its immediate manifestation. A literary
system is a complex phenomenon. It consists of several con-
temporaneously operative literary subsystems, one of which is
dominant, while the others remain in the dark. In Puškin's
time the peripheral systems were Deržavin's tradition (which
was continued by Kjuchel'beker and Griboedov), the Russian
vaudeville-tradition, and many other traditional systems, such
as, for instance, the novel of adventure after the manner of
Bulgarin (Šklovskij, 1925:163). A further enlargement of
this phenomenon is the fact that the scope of a literary artist is
not necessarily restricted to active literary movements but it
may encompass currents of bygone ages which are no longer
active. The latter may ferment his work most strongly. In
other words: the artist decides upon the relationship between
his work and other text-systems, he decides how to build his
semantic structure with the help of supplementary information, derived from other text-systems (cf. the concept of the
'minus-device' in Lotman, 1968:49, 53, 55, 174). The prin-

ciples of selection, arrangement and phraseological expression
cannot be but influenced by the correlation with − or the
reaction to − other narrative texts that belong to one or more
literary movements. The influx of human 'reality' upon these
principles is, according to Tynjanov, reduced to social conventions (byt). And "social conventions are correlated with literature first of all in its verbal aspect" (1929:42; transl. 1971:
73). The verbal performance of a given time, however, carries
specific information about that time: about the human reality,
the social, psychological, religious and philosophical aspects of
the period. In many cases the information conveyed has a
universal value, is unconditioned by time-relationships.

In fact Bremond's model is based upon invariable action
patterns, upon invariables of human behaviour: "Aux types
narratifs élémentaires correspondent ... les formes les plus
générales du comportement humain. La tâche, le contrat, la
faute, le piège, etc. sont des catégories universelles" (Bremond,
1966:76). It seems, however, that this model can only prove
its universal value when the logical action patterns are not
complicated by psychological or social elements. According to
Bremond such elements merely diversify the invariable action-
patterns, as do cultures, periods, literary genres and styles. Do
we agree with him in this respect? Or do we think that his
model must be enlarged with certain invariable psychological
and sociological constituents? In which case these may be
supposed to complicate the action-pattern to such an extent
that − contrary to Bremond's supposition − 'dégradation' and
'amélioration' will both become characteristic features of an
action-pattern with one actant only. (Cf. Anna's attitude
towards Karenin after her departure with Vronskij: she takes
the part of the aggressor and that of the victim.) Shouldn't we
at least consider a possible dominance of the characterization
or the social setting? Raising the question of dominance (or,
to be more precise, the question of hierarchy in the thematic
levels): shouldn't we assign a more important rôle to the
narrator? Shouldn't we even consider the narrator to be
ultimately determinative of the type of narrative (thinking of
his devices of selection, arrangement, modes of expression, and

the consequent relations to human reality and other texts in his narrative)?

All these questions lead us to a conception of a narrative model based upon a set of fundamental narrative attitudes, in its relation to a set of fundamental narrative systems and a set of fundamental anthropological data. The fundamental narrative attitudes concern the transmission of information: the intellectual and emotional attitude towards it and the extent of knowledge about it. As I have said we may in general distinguish three narrative attitudes: all-knowing, knowledgeable as to one character only, pretended ignorance. The narrator may, of course, interchange these three attitudes or he may combine them: he may be all-knowing in some respect, ignorant in others, etc. The possibility of combining and interchanging these attitudes is recognized in the model without any further specifications. Such a task would be enormous, and useless, because it would have to deal with individual differentiations (and, consequently, with a widely different phraseology and narrative arrangement). (For linguistic differences between the narrative attitudes, cf. Doležel, 1967; cf. also Schmid, 1973: 41-2.) The fundamental narrative systems rest upon specific relationships between the thematic levels and upon the dominance of one of them. This dominance is effected by the chosen narrative attitude (or the chosen mixture of attitudes) together with the devices of selection, arrangement and phraseological expression. The fundamental anthropological constituents concern the universal aspects of the thematic levels (i.e. the action, the characterization and the (social) setting). It is these universal elements that determine the comprehensibility of the narrative world (even of 'dated' facts that are no longer valid and have proved to be ephemeral). Thus the narrator must, implicitly and explicitly, 'tune' his fiction to the outer world. An example of such explicit tuning would be a sentence like: "Something strange happened, something you wouldn't believe to be possible ..." or "Water was a tabu here. Dirt was fought against with special electric cleaners ... Thirst seemed to be non-existent ..." Implicit tuning can be found in almost every narrative fragment, because every action, every aspect of the setting etc. is always dealt with fragmentarily, and thus always asks for a supplementation from reality. In the words of Benjamin Hrushovski: "We have to use the 'world' in order to be able to understand literature and, in general, to connect meaning in language" (1974: 16-17).

I have suggested earlier that a narrative model should be based upon three interrelated sets: a set of narrative attitudes, a set of narrative systems and a set of anthropological data. This suggestion is not inconsistent with Lubomír Doležel's conception of a narrative model: "I assume that a complete model of narrative structure will consist of four 'blocks': the block of the story, the block of characters, the block of setting and the block of interpretations" (1972:56). The block of interpretations (commentaries, evaluations) seems to be absent in the scheme I have proposed. In my opinion, however, this is not a separate block, but an integral part of the set of narrative attitudes: the narrator may evaluate his fictional world in directs statements, or he may do so indirectly, using the devices of selection, arrangement and phraseological expression. When he resorts to the latter devices, the consequently effected dominance of one thematic level functions within the system of comments and evaluations. Within the scope of this level a greater or lesser importance may be assigned to the characters. This results in a greater or lesser impact of their pronouncements. The characters may thus have their share in the comments and evaluations, but it is the narrator who is the controlling operator, and therefore they operate within his province. In this rôle the narrator functions of course as the 'arranging' authority. Sometimes a distinction is made between this function and his narrative function, characteristic of which are the frequent changes in his approach and professed knowledge: Schmid calls the 'arranging' author 'der abstrakte Autor', Booth 'implied author' and Todorov speaks of 'image du narrateur' (Schmid, 1973:34, Booth, 1961:75, Todorov, 1966:146). In my opinion the two narrative functions coalesce: the many forms of the direct narrative presentation will be shaped in such a way that they fit into a network of relationships; the — emotional and intellectual — dosing of the information in these forms is based upon the existing interdependency between them: the narrator's direct information is attuned to the indirect information by means of the arrangement. Thus the many forms of direct narrative presentation are an integral part of the compositional arrangement. Such a concept of 'arrangement' makes a rephrasing of Bachtin's notion of a polyphonic type of novel (as created by Dostoevskij) possible, if not desirable. Characteristic of this type of novel is, as Bachtin says, the equal importance of the voices of the prominent characters and the narrator's voice (Bachtin, 1963:8, cf. Schmid, 1973:14, 34). I assume, however, that even statements made by characters which are considered irrefutable by Dostoevskij himself (in his letters, note-books, etc.), may be toned down in the construction of a novel. Let me give an example. Dostoevskij states in his note-book for the novel *The Brothers Karamazov* that Ivan Karamazov's negation of 'the meaning of life' is based upon an indisputable argument (the unanswerable question why children must suffer). This may be the truth, but it cannot be denied that Zosima's attitude towards life is diametrically opposed to Ivan's and as such emphasized in the novel. A letter of May, 10th, 1879 (and some other letters as well) shows that Dostoevskij considered Zosima's antipodal attitude to be very important and he realizes its representation in his arrangement of the novel. In Zosima's philosophy we find the same themes as in Ivan's, which induces the reader to compare both men — not only in their philosophies, but also in their lives and actions. From the ethical angle the reader will consider Ivan Karamazov's attitude to be ambiguous (to say the least). The narrator's explicit comments on Ivan are sometimes given from a view-point which seems to be Zosima's, sometimes the narrator's wording even reflects Zosima's speech. An illustration of the use of this device is the narrator's explanation of Ivan's inner distress after he realizes that he cannot but feel guilty of his father's murder. The description is correlated with Aleša's state of feeling towards the hallucinations of Ivan: "He began to understand Ivan's illness: «The agony of a proud decision — a

deep-seated conscience», God in whom he did not believe, and
truth had gained a hold over his hearth, which still refused to
give in" (771). We do not find, however, any such superior
comments upon Zosima which reflect Ivan's opinions or
speech. In short: in Dostoevskij's novels, as in other novels, we
find a narrator who explicitly and implicitly conveys his own
views. The theory of Dostoevskij's 'polyphony' finds its origin
in the fact that he delegates comments, interpretations and
evaluations to his characters. And sometimes he allows them
to make statements which from a rationalistic point of view
are irrefutable, though as a result of the novel's arrangement
they prove to be intenable in their psychological, emotional
and ethical consequences. We cannot say, therefore, that the
voices of the characters carry the same weight as the narrator's
voice. In other words: it means that the narrator arranges the
different view-points hierarchically.

I fully realize that in a narrative model, such as I have
proposed, the distinction between 'histoire' and 'discourse' has
been left out. Todorov and other French theoreticians do
make this distinction (Todorov, 1966). In fact, this brings us
back to the old dichotomy of content and form. In his narrative model Bremond states with some emphasis that the construction of a narrative structure is not connected with a
privileged outlook (the hero's or the narrator's), the scheme is
based upon the perspectives of the characters, which are considered to be of equal importance (1966:64). As I said before,
I doubt whether the perspectives of the characters always
move between 'dégradation' and 'amélioration' and whether it
is impossible for both these qualities to be present. Moreover,
I believe that the perspectives of the characters function as
constituents of the characterization, and that as such they fall
within the boundaries of the narrator's arrangement (as do the
constituents of the action and the setting). The narrator shows
them in different lights and evaluates them, which implies a
possible 'amélioration' from a character's perspective and a
possible 'dégradation' from the narrator's. Since the narrator is
the one who selects, arranges, chooses the word-formulas, he is
the principal story-forming factor in a narrative text. He deter-

mines the type of narrative (depending on the dominance of the characterization, the setting or the action). Bremond's model is based solely upon universal, anthropological data, valid for the logic of the action only. Its usefulness is limited, especially when it is applied to present-day narratives, but it may be interesting to trace its residues, and analyze the way in which these are used.

Doležel's study about narrative 'modalities' provides Bremond's model with a far greater applicability (1976:129-151). These narrative modalities are connected with a wider scope of universal anthropological data, with 'modal logic', which may be studied outside the realm of narrative structures. Doležel introduces four modal systems that regulate human actions and situations: the deontic system, formed by operators of permission, prohibition and obligation; the alethic system, formed by operators of possibility, impossibility, and necessity; the axiological system expressing modal concepts of goodness, badness and indifference; the epistemic system comprising modal concepts of knowledge, ignorance and belief. Doležel mentions only these four, but he does not deny that there may be more modal systems. He connects these modal systems with narrative structures by introducing the concept of atomic stories (A-stories). When we "define a story as a string of narrated states (static motifs) and narrated events (dynamic motifs), then an A-story is defined as a string of motifs, characterized by the property of modal homogenity. This means that an A-story is governed by operators of one, and only one modal system. If in a string of motifs modal formulas occur with operators of two or more different modal systems, the string will be interpreted as a compound (molecular) story (that is, as manifesting two or more A-stories)" (p. 144). Doležel uses the modal systems in the first place at the action-level. When applied to narrative structures the deontic system may be characterized as 'acquisition of freedom of acting', the axiological system as 'acquisition of value', the alethic system as 'acquisition of possibility', the epistemic system as 'acquisition of knowledge'. Inherent to all these possible 'acquisitions' is the possibility of 'loss'. Doležel points out that the antonymical pair 'acquisition-loss' shows a strong resemblance to Bremond's pair of 'amélioration/dégradation'.

I may here recall my objections to Bremond's scheme: I am of the opinion that in some narrative texts a character shows both 'dégradation' and 'amélioration' in the relation with his/ her partner. The example I gave was Anna Karenina's attitude towards her husband after she has left him. Using Doležel's terminology, it can be said that in this text-segment acquisition and loss of freedom occur simultaneously (Anna's leaving Karenin, her elopement with Vronskij vs. her self-imposed punishment: not to seek a divorce, to accept the separation from her child). The underlying presence of a second modal system: the loss of value (the evil that is done) seems to be connected with the loss of freedom. If this is true, the basic structure of many narrative texts might be a combination of A-stories, in which the presence of different modal systems can be discerned and both the properties 'acquisition/loss' of one modal system in relation to one agent and one string of motifs. I am not quite sure whether Doležel supports such an interpretation. In the already given quotation, it seems he does (at least inasfar as the simultaneous occurrence of more than one modal system is concerned): "If in a string of motifs modal formulas occur with operators of two or more different modal systems, the string will be interpreted as a compound (molecular) story (that is as manifesting two or more A-stories)". Doležel assumes that in contrast to factual human action – which is controlled by jointly operating modalities – stories can be based upon a single modal system (1976a:7). This may be true for many stories, for many others it is not. As a specimen of a more complex ('molecular') story, Doležel has analyzed Wolfgang Borchert's *Die Hundeblume*. This story shows a combination of deontic and axiological A-stories. The deontic story presents only the end-state of what has happened to the protagonist: imprisonment. There is no specification of the actional part leading to this loss of freedom: the state of the character's deprivation continues from the beginning until the finale of the story. The second half of the narrative consists mainly of an axiological story. The core of this A-story is the protagonist's taking action to acquire a thing of value (a dandelion). The acquisition of this precious thing to him means the return of the smell of the earth, the sun, the sea, of honey, tenderness and warmth, etc. Doležel speaks of a concatenation of two atomic stories, linked in such a way that the switch from one modal level to another does not endanger the coherence of the story (1976b:471). In other words, the two A-stories are played off against each other in a contrastive balance and each of them fulfils the requirement of modal homogenity. The question arises whether modal systems in compound stories are always so relatively easy to distinguish. This seems to apply especially to the second type of combined A-stories, mentioned by Doležel. In this type the combination is based on a modal synthesis (imposing two or more jointly operating modal constraints) (1976a:7). If several modal systems are operative in the same string of motifs, how will the several A-stories and the modal homogenity in each of them be demonstrated? And how will this complex of A-stories be linked with the texture, constituted by formulas representing two or more modal systems? An analysis of a molecular story of this second type should make the procedure clear.

What is very important in my opinion and what is missing in Doležel's article, is the question of hierarchy: he does not introduce the concept of hierarchy with respect to the modal systems that are present in certain narrated facts, nor does he speak of it in respect of the different interpretations of loss vs. acquisition, which seem to be operative within one underlying modal system. A solution of the problem of hierarchy again asks for the introduction of the narrator into the system (or better: of the narrator's rôles). The narrator controls the impact of his information by the use of a variable degree of knowledge and understanding of what is going on. He may accept the opinions of one of his characters completely, or he may take a superior attitude towards them (resulting for instance from his being better informed). Two extreme narrative attitudes can be found in the beginning of *Crime and Punishment*. This implies that in this novel two deontic systems are operative, or, to be more exact, two narrative approaches to the deontic system: in the first freedom is acquired, in the second it is lost. Raskol'nikov considers — and at this point of the story his view is taken over by the narrator — that his killing of the old money-lender just proves him to belong to that superior class of men for whom the distinction good-evil is not made: the murder is the supreme proof of his freedom. For the narrator — superior in understanding — the murder signifies obsession: loss of freedom. This narrative attitude is dominant and therefore every uncertain step Raskol'nikov takes towards his freedom, is a step towards obsession, a loss of freedom from the superior narrator's point-of-view (Van der Eng, 1973a:85).

Raskol'nikov's actions may be connected not only with these two approaches to the deontic system, but also with the same two approaches to the axiological system: acquisition of value and loss of value. Raskol'nikov — and the narrator, limited by his hero's point of view — look upon the murder of the usurer as the removal of an evil element from society. In Raskol'nikov's eyes his deed is completely in accordance with the nihilistic philosophy of how to reach a desirable social state. The narrator, who is superior in knowledge and understanding, however, deplores the loss of a moral value upon which human society is built. Such an attitude does not necessarily find its expression in direct comments by the narrator. In *Crime and Punishment* it is apparent in the descriptions of Raskol'nikov's loneliness, of his incapability to keep contact with his family and his friends, etc. The presence of more than one modal system in the same narrative segments, and the conflicting properties of loss and acquisition within a string of motifs of one modal system is not a rare occurrence I think.

The occurrence of two narrative approaches to one modal system may very well confuse the reader, if the narrator does not give any specific clues as to which attitude is dominant. Sometimes, later on in the story a narrative medium is introduced that pronounces a final judgement upon previously related facts, thus forcing the reader to a reinterpretation of f.i. axiological modalities (has an ethical value been acquired, or has it been lost?). Sometimes, the narrator refrains from interfering directly: he may subtly present the opinions and voices of the characters and leave it to the reader to decide which one of them is the most reliable, the best informed. Sometimes, the narrator may choose an ambiguous approach as to loss or gain. Here, the term 'hierarchy' seems no longer applicable, unless we allow this notion to include the varying degrees of uncertainty about the outcome of a system. Such a broadening of the concept 'hierarchy' seems justifiable since ambiguity may be connected with a narrative medium that is superior to other manifestations of the narrator: thus, ambiguity can have the same structural importance and the same effect as a narrative approach which provides new, irrefutable and unequivocal evaluations of previous facts. Moreover, the narrator's ambiguous approach may find its expression in several passages and it may show as many varieties as there are passages: hence, it is possible to distinguish a hierarchical ordering of the more or less ambiguous bits of information. The same can be said about a narrator who presents all the elements of his story in a farcical way, which is − according to Èjchenbaum − characteristic of Gogol's *The Overcoat*. The overall punning quality here is connected with the view-point of a superior narrator that can be discerned behind, or in addition to, the modal formulas that express acquisition or loss. Moreover, there are gradations in the mocking attitude that runs through several passages. From time to time a touch of seriousness creeps into the narrator's puns, which make certain specific human qualities of the hero stand out against the other characters, and perhaps against humanity as a whole. In short, it may be supposed that the hierarchical patterning of narrative positions is an important and perhaps essential element in the semantic make-up of a story, and consequently in its modal structuring. This patterning may display changing − and even contradictory − appreciations of a given modal system. A definite and dominant (possibly sophisticated or even idiosyncratic) view-point of the narrator will, however, ultimately stand out.

The conception of modalities as the governing principle of narratives will have to account for yet another intricate property of stories and tales. This is, again, connected with the narrative attitude. I have said before that the author effects a specific hierarchical order between his thematic levels: the characterization, the action and the social setting. When effectuating this order (by means of − often − implicit comments) he will mostly keep down two levels in favour of the third. The dominance of a thematic level implies not only the subordination of the other levels, it also implies that their significative components support the dominant level. Action-elements may, for example be only of secundary importance to the action and of principal importance to the characterization. Elements of the setting, of the social environment may tell more about a character than about the setting. And, again, this may not become obvious until much further on in the narrative: the narrator may arrange his text in such a way that at first such elements will seem to be relevant to their own level only. Later on they will appear to have psychological features too, and these will gradually come to be predominant.

In Doležel's concept the modal systems are particularly applicable to human actions. He uses the notion 'action' in a rather broad sense: physical action (changes of physical states − Ivan killed the dragon), mental actions (changes of mental states − John became angry), social actions (changes of social states − the judge sentenced Meursault to death). All these 'events' fall within the group 'actions of narrative agents'. Next to this group he distinguishes supernatural, natural and social processual forces. According to him, stories are based mainly upon 'interaction of narrative agents', or 'interplay of processual forces and narrative agents'.

In A-stories with more than one agent, the modal operators are relevant to each agent: we may speak of a modal accord if the operative modal systems are identical and are centered round a mutual object of effort or ambition (alliance), of modal discord when this is not the case. Doležel does acknowledge, however, that modalities may be applied to f.i. a deontic or axiological system, characteristic of a particular setting. The latter may then have a relationship of accord or discord with the 'world' of the agents.

When modal conceptions are thus related to a wide range of 'events', it would seem possible to register narratives under such headings as: stories of physical action (travel, fight, etc.), or of mental action (spiritual search), of social action (social or national progress), etc. Stories, however, often show subtle combinations of physical actions, mental actions, social actions and processual forces. (Sometimes the word 'situation' will be more adequate than 'action'.) The relationship between these components is hierarchical. Features of physical actions sometimes exemplify a state of mind. Raskol'nikov's physical and mental actions in the beginning of *Crime and Punishment* are symptomatic of his pathological predicament, of his obsession (cf. Van der Eng, 1973a). A complicating element is that the narrator does not provide an explanation, does not forthwith present Raskol'nikov as a pathological case. The narrative medium is complex: the information is given in many different ways and is carefully dosed. Several 'voices' are speaking in the narration so that it is difficult to decide which is the most authentic one. Hence it is hard to trace the hierarchical order of the 'ingredients' of the information given.

Thus, generally speaking, in a narrative text we may be confronted with many voices i.e. variations in the degree of knowledge and in the intellectual and emotional approach of the narrative medium; each 'voice' provides us in its own way with information (about the characterization, the action or the setting), each speaks with its own measure of reliability. The occurrence of different modal systems and the occurrence of the aspects 'loss' and 'acquisition' in the same textual elements may very well originate in the very presence of these voices. In that case the modal systems and their relevance to the thematic levels ('blocks' in Doležel's terminology) could be ordered hierarchically, depending on the hierarchy of the voices. The problem is, however, that the hierarchical order of the voices can often not be decided upon until further on in the story (when the authentic narrative attitude is finally exposed).

As an example of this I have mentioned Anna Karenina's departure from Russia; at first we are allowed to look upon this 'event' in two ways: she may have acquired freedom, or she may have lost it. Eventually the narrator provides us with information that leaves only the latter possibility. Gradually the loss of value proves to be even more important than the loss of freedom. The clues leading to this modal system, are at first only given implicitly: thus, we are confronted with a regressive orientation upon a second modal system, which ultimately proves to be predominant.

I will not try to work out a narrative model that combines and elaborates Doležel's views and my own (as I have mentioned them earlier). What I wanted to demonstrate was the inadequacy of the now available models to cope with the intricate semantic structure of a narrative text. More attention should be paid to the dynamic construction of narrative texts, to the fluctuating thematic dominance in the arrangement of the events, of the specific features of the characters and of the spatial and social circumstances (which cannot be valued hierarchically until the whole text has been read), to the fluctuations of the modal systems that have a bearing on the same text-elements (and that do not show a hierarchical order till the end of the story) and above all to the manifold manifestations of the narrator (in his explicit and implicit rôles) which lie at the root of these hierarchically ordered dynamics.

In the next part of this essay I will concentrate on the dynamic aspects of narration as they can be found in the narrator's dosing of the information, in his presentation of the story-components, in the interrelations between these components. I shall first explain the procedure I have chosen and some important aspects of my descriptive method. Then I will discuss the way in which Čechov in *Dama s sobačkoj* has arranged the various constituent elements into a dynamic network. I will not go into the incorporated relations with other (narrative) texts, or the references to human reality. I shall indicate them at those places where the author specifically draws attention to them, or where the originality of the structure of his story necessitates a comparison with more traditional structures.

II. THE DYNAMIC AND COMPLEX STRUCTURE OF A NARRATIVE TEXT

1. *Intratextual and extratextual elements of the semantic construction*

The semantic construction of a narrative text is based upon a set of signs which refer to three correlated levels: the action, the characterization and the social and geographical setting (the social milieu). This correlation can take several forms: the three levels may occur simultaneously and condition one another. Sentences often show such an interdependence of actional, personal and spatial data. If there is no simultaneity, we may find continuity and causality in the interactions of a fixed number of characters in one and the same place: a succession of sentences and paragraphs often shows this kind of correlation. Moreover, one of the levels will mostly dominate over the other levels. As a result of this type of correlation an element of the action may appear to be more relevant to the characterization of a personage than to his/her actions. In the same way, an element of the setting may often reveal more about a character than about the particular setting. The primary function of a characterization-element may be the motivation of an action and not the delineament of an individual.

1.1 This narrative structure becomes complex because of the fact that important aspects of a certain level (f.i. the characterization of a personage X) are not presented in an uninterrupted sequence of fragments: the relevant fragments are scattered all through the text. And it is possible that their meaning is not restricted to the characterization of X, they may contain some information about setting Y, etc. Consequently, one and the same fragment may at one or more levels show references to any number of passages. The complexity of the semantic structure is more intricate yet, because the text may deal with more than one character, more than

one action, more than one setting and these may very well be
as such unconnected, but be subject to comparison on the
basis of striking similarities or dissimilarities between them.
An instance of this is Tolstoj's short story *The Three Deaths*,
This story consists of three independent parts, each describing
a way of dying.

1.2 We are not finished with the intricacies of the semantics
of narrative structures: the comprehensibility of a story is
based upon a projection of human reality (or better: upon the
reader's supposed conception of it). This projection, however,
is directed by the narrator in a round-about way: in between
the narrative text and human reality he places other texts (in
the first place texts belonging to the same literary system).
These other texts (or 'text' as the case may be) function as
points of reference: the narrative under discussion either con-
forms itself to this/these other text(s), or shows some striking
differences. The conformity and the difference (whichever the
case may be) may both have the effect that the 'reference-
text(s)' come(s) to be an essential source of information.
Perhaps it is better to speak of a 'source of omitted (though
tacitly included) information'. Think f.i. of the marked absence or romantic stereotypes in Puškin's *Stories of Belkin*.
Jurij Lotman refers to phenomena like this as 'minus-priemy'
(1968:174). On the other hand Puškin does use certain types
of stereotypes in these stories, but he distinctly connects them
with other thematic ingredients in order to present a complex
picture of the characters and their actions, which deviates
from the literary point of reference. Think f.i. of the heroine's
impersonations (as a sheperdess, etc.) in Baryšnja-krest'janka.
These are based upon sentimental stereotypes and function as
decoys to an exciting amorous play. The use of such structures
to describe characters and events is widely different from the
use of simple, straightforward structures à la Karamzin: the
'badinage' springs mainly from the deviations from the latter,
and the reader will be aware of that, provided he knows the
point(s) of reference (Van der Eng, 1968:23 ff.). The relations
between a narrative text and reality are furthermore often

brought forward by non-narrative other texts: religious, philosophical, political, publicistic texts, etc. It is easy to give a few examples of this: parallels can be found between some of the religious teachings of starec Zosima, as written down by Aleša, and the writings of Tichon Zadonskij (Nadejda Gorodetzky, 1951:184). The stoic ideas as they are represented in Strachov's essay "The inhabitants of the planets" have their echoes in the Devil's words to Ivan Karamazov (Tschiževskij:6). Nečaev's terroristic program (laid down in the pamphlet *Obščie pravila organizacii*) is carried out by Petr Verchovenskij in *Besy* (see Dolinin's commentaries in F. M. Dostoevskij, Pis'ma II:483-5). The reflections of court minutes can be found in many novels by Dostoevskij (see Dorovatovskaja-Ljubimova). The number of examples is countless. Literary criticism relates the works of every famous author to a wide variety of manifold scriptures.

1.3 The continuous relations of a literary text to human reality — whether they are established directly or via other texts — in themselves form a continuous complexity. It is a relationship that is only fragmentarily indicated in the narrative text, and it is left to the reader to fill in the gaps from his own experience. Some texts of course demand more from the reader than others. Writers like Isaac Babel and Ernest Hemmingway always demand a great activity from the reader in this respect. Still, every reader must complete every story himself, must be a co-creator of it. There is always more in a good story than meets the eye: much of it goes without saying, is implicitly understood, sous-entendu. The first sentence of Čechov's *Lady with Lapdog*, seems to inform the reader only of a new arrival at the boulevard: a person characterized by one simple attribute. But it is possible to deduce from the sentence, that it confronts us with a typical sea-resort community with its limited, narrow range of interest. The sentence is as follows: "It was said that at the boulevard someone new had appeared: a lady with a lapdog". It will be clear that the elements of a narrative text become semantically complicated in many different ways:

1) by a network of intratextual relations between passages scattered throughout the text (while one text-segment can be related to a second in a different way than to a third, emphasizing different thematic levels);

2) by extra-textual relations to human reality;

3) by extra-textual relations to other texts.

These three categories of relations may occur simultaneously in one text-segment. I shall give one example, in which I leave the relevance to the thematic levels out of consideration. At the end of Gogol's story *The Nose*, the narrator comments in a jocular way upon the unlikely events in his story. (See Vinogradov:1921.) This commentary is a paraphrase (both as to its content and its phraseology) of a review of Puškin's *Snowstorm* (another unlikely story). There are, moreover, implicit relations to many other texts with 'nose-puns': both to narrative texts of this type, and to naseological dithyrambic works. There is also a strongly indicated relation to human reality in the narrator's commentary: he says that, all considering, there is some truth in his story. The presented events, he says, may in fact happen, though they will occur rarely. The reference to human reality may be understood by a contemporary reader as an allusion to what is clinically described as 'fear of castration', manifesting itself in the fear of losing one's nose.

2. *Complexity as a means to concretization and visualization of the information*

2.1 The web of relations spun between the text-elements, complicates their meaning and the meaning of the text they set up. And yet I would hesitate to overemphasize — as Jurij Lotman seems to do — the complexity of the meaning that is built by an artistic text (cf. Lotman, 1964:19). The admission that a narrative text is complex, does not imply the admission that it is not easily accessible. The complex semantic structure quite often heightens the comprehensibility, the appeal of a narrative text and its constituent parts. When round a text-element a network of semantic relations is gradually realized, this implies not only that its semantic structure is enlarged and set forth, but also that it is given a more and more concrete form. When a text-element again and again appears to have new semantic relations to other elements, it will automatically come to be more important both to the already narrated text and to the text to come. It will strengthen the grip on the already given information and it will draw the reader's attention to forthcoming information. As to the latter, the reader's expectations will be influenced by the text's connections with other texts. This, too, will induce him to presuppositions about future information. It will be known that Jurij Tynjanov considered the inter-textual relations (that is the relations to the 'systems' of other texts) of primary importance to the intra-textual relations between the text elements, in other words: to the text's semantic structure (1929:30-48). In his opinion deviations from another literary system, or a different handling of certain properties of it, are the only really effective aesthetic determining elements in a text (and hence they are very important to the text's concretion). Viktor Šklovskij has underlined, that such deviations effect a most vivid visualization of the objects indicated by the words. New language structures do away with stereotyped associations with reality — which we recognize without any conscious thought —, they provide fresh associations with, and fresh images of reality (1925:12). Šklovskij's ideas are remarkably in line with the actual practice of those authors, who turned away from the traditional thematic patterns and introduced themes of the social reality of their own time, like f.i. Flaubert and Maupassant. December 12th, 1857, Flaubert wrote to Mlle Leroyer de Chantepie: "Vous me dites que je fais trop attention à la forme. Hélas! c'est comme le corps et l'âme; la forme et l'idée, pour moi, c'est tout un et je ne sais pas ce qu'est l'un sans l'autre. Plus une idée est belle, plus la phrase est sonore; soyez-en sûre. La précision de la pensée fait (et est elle-même) celle du mot ...".

Much later (beginning 1879) he wrote to Huysmans that in his opinion the representation of reality was much more

important than reality itself. "Ni les giroflées, ni les roses, ne
sont intéressantes par elles-mêmes, il n'y a d'intéressant que la
manière de les peindre. Le Gange n'est pas plus poétique que la
Bièvre, mais la Bièvre ne l'est pas plus que le Gange." Even
more outspoken is his letter (from the beginning) of February,
1880 to another representative of the naturalist school,
Hennique: "Il n'y a pas de vrai! Il n'y a que des manières de
voir".

In the preface to *Pierre et Jean* (1888) Maupassant writes
about the lessons of his teacher Flaubert: "Il s'agit de regarder
tout ce qu'on veut exprimer assez longtemps et avec assez d'attention pour en décrouvrir un aspect qui n'ait été vu et dit par
personne. Il y a, dans tout, de l'inexploré, parce que nous
sommes habitués à ne nous servir de nos yeux qu'avec le
souvenir de ce qu'on a pensé avant nous sur ce que nous con-
templons. La moindre chose contient un peu d'inconnu. Trou-
vons-le. Pour décrire un feu qui flambe et une arbre dans une
plaine, demeurons en face de ce feu et de cet arbre jusqu'à ce
qu'ils ne ressemblent plus, pour nous, à aucun autre arbre et à
aucun autre feu."

All these pronouncements refer to the ultimate concrete
form of a narrative, which is established by thematical and
lexical selection, and by a specific phraseology that deviates
from the traditionally accepted one. The main accent falls
upon the tangible aspects of reality.

2.2 Many readers, however, will probably find a narrative
easily accessible and comprehensible, because it gives a concrete form to intangible aspects of reality (or, to put it better:
because it gives a concrete form to a way of looking at reality,
to the sense or lack of sense ascribed to human existence).
Maurice Merleau-Ponty has pointed out that the works of great
writers always rest upon two or three basic philosophical ideas
(as f.i. the presence of the past in the present in Proust's
works). In their novels these ideas are presented as actual
'things', not as abstract philosophies (1948:51). I would like
to specify 'things' as elements of the characterization, the
action and the setting. The various relations between these

three levels are not stated in abstract formulas either, they emerge in the presentation of the thematic levels; the dominant level makes itself known even without explicit indications (i.e. by the implicit correlations it has with the other levels).

3. *The motif and the arrangement*

The predilection for concreteness instead of abstract reasoning, the painstaking efforts to find something new in the old existential data and to express this in unexpected words, are not the only contributors to a story's comprehensibility: it has been said that very important, too, is the network of the manifold relations which a textual element has with other segments of the text. In other words: the arrangement is a powerful means by which the narrative's accessibility may be furthered. 'Arrangement' could be defined roughly as a system of repetitions and changes, drawing the reader's attention again and again to the characterization of a personage and the gradual development in it, to an action-pattern and its characteristic gradual leading towards some climax, etc. In this chapter I will discuss the arrangement of the constituent elements of a narrative structure.

1. I shall first define a 'narrative element', the ultimate thematic particle of a narrative structure.

2. I will then discuss the various types of relations such an element (or combinations of elements) may have with other elements (or with combinations of these) of a narrative structure. I will not discuss the relations to human reality and other texts, which have, of course, their bearings on the arrangement.

3. Then I intend to discuss the fact, that a narrative element (or a combination of them) often functions as a link in a semantic chain of interrelated narrative elements which may occur throughout the text. Such a semantic chain functions to add up to a more or less complete insight into a conflict, an intrigue, the inner and outer characterization of a personage or a setting.

4. Next, I will pay attention to the phenomenon of 'gradation', which is a characteristic of such a semantic chain: its
semantic components may acquire a greater emphasis when
they are repeated again and again, when their possible implications are continuously narrowed down; the semantic implications of the components may come to cover a wider field,
when their inherent semantic properties are actualized by
preceding or following links in the chain, etc.

5. Then I will discuss the fact that one narrative element
may function as a link in more than one semantic chain (f.i. in
a chain resulting in the portrait of a character and in a chain
displaying the development of a conflict). My discussion will
be based upon two specific ways in which narrative elements
may string themselves to a chain: there are series of oppositional narrative elements, separated from one another by intermediate text-parts and there are series of narrative elements in
successive text-parts (these are characterized by a continuity
of places, actions and characters).

6. The next point of discussion will be the thematic change
that may occur in a chain of narrative elements: a series of
narrative elements may seemingly refer to the action but may
afterwards appear to have a principal relevance to the characterization, or vice versa.

7. The last part of this chapter will deal with the sequence
of chains and their hierarchy in relation to the dominant
thematic level. The narrator is the leading director in the creation of such a dynamic semantic structure. He creates it by
carefully dosing his information and by often changing his
emotional and intellectual approach to this information. These
approaches and this dosing are thus decisive of the semantic
structure of the narrative elements and consequently of the
specific relations one such an element may have at different
levels with a third, a fourth element, etc. It is the approach
and the dosing that determine the formation of chains of elements (i.e. elements throughout the text, that share one or
more distinctive aspects) and of the gradation within a chain
of elements. They are also conclusive of the participation of
one narrative element in more than one chain, of changes in

the chain's thematic dominancy (which may or may not be accompanied by changes in the type of the relations within a chain) and of the sequence of the various chains of a narrative and of their hierarchy.

Many literary critics make the rough distinction between an 'abstract' narrator and a 'concrete' narrator (Tomaševskij, 1928:142), an 'auctorial' vs. 'personal' narrator (Stanzel, 1955:23-25), etc. The narrator's knowledge, however, is often as it were 'floating': from a complete knowledge to a limited knowledge, or even to ignorance. We can also think of information, upon which cannot be depended (Booth's 'unreliable' information), or even treacherous, inauthentic information. The intellectual approach may vary in many other ways (the narrative medium may, for instance, display a complete knowledge of what is going on, together with a complete lack of understanding). The emotional approach is subject to even more pronounced changes (though it is obviously often impossible to disentangle the two approaches). These varieties of the narrator's position may be explicitly stated in the given commentaries or they may be hidden in the modes of expression or the different forms of the story's arrangement.

3.1 What I have called a 'narrative element', the 'ultimate thematic particle' of a narrative structure, is often called a 'motif'. Boris Tomaševskij has been, I think, the first to impart to this word another meaning than it has in comparative literature. There, a motif denotes a thematic unity, which has an existence of its own, is independent of any narrative text and may as an independent element fit in with the arrangement of widely divergent narratives. Tomaševskij's concept of a motif is different: he uses the word to denote an untransferable element of a particular narrative text. To him, a motif is the theme of the smallest meaningful unit of a narrative text and he puts it on a level with a sentence. He gives some simple sentences as examples: "night fell', "the hero died", "Raskol'nikov killed the old woman" (1928:137). Vladimir Propp was probably right, when he doubted, whether a motif necessarily coincides with a sentence, whether a sentence necessarily contains only one motif. A simple sentence like: "the dragon carried off the czar's daughter" falls apart in four elements: the dragon, the abduction, the daughter and the czar (Propp:18). In my opinion — as I have said before — a narrative structure is a semantic totality consisting of elements that refer to the action, the characterization and the setting. Every sentence of this totality may contain bits of information on these three levels. These bits of information may each have connections with many other shreds of information in the text, and these gradually complete the thematic level. When we take this into account, a narrative element (a motif) can be described as 1) a text-element of the characterization, the action, or the social setting; 2) a text-element, the semantic structure of which (i.e. its prevailing relevance to one of the thematic levels) is determined firstly by its connection with the sentence and the paragraph; secondly by its connection with one or more other text-fragments. In other words: a motif is an in itself not complete text-element of the characterization, the action or the setting, having a chameleonic pertinence to these levels and being dependent upon the connection with other text-elements. Within a sentence or paragraph a motif may have a principal relevance to the setting (social milieu) even if it consists of words expressing some human feature: think f.i. of a peculiarity of a personage, that is characteristic of a particular society in a particular time at a particular place. Similarly, within a sentence or paragraph, a motif expressing an action-moment may be principally relevant to the characterization of the person performing that action, etc. In its connection with several segments of the text, a motif may, as a result of one of these connections, be pertinent to the social setting, as a result of another connection it may be pertinent to the characterization, a third connection may link it up with the action. The semantic make-up of a motif in a sentence comes from the attitude the speaker (the narrator, the personage) takes towards it. A sentence can be described as an organic unity expressing a perception and consisting of one or more words, this unity being more than and different from the sum total of its parts, showing the speaker's attitude towards what is perceived (see De Groot, 1964:51). Whereas spoken language has the help of intonation to give a concrete form to the speaker's attitude, written language often needs the support of the paragraph to convey the speaker's attitude in a sentence. This adds extra meanings to a sentence-part which expresses f.i. an aspect of the setting. Once more I may refer to the first sentence of *Lady with Lapdog*. In it are the words: 'at the boulevard'. Outside the sentence — and paragraph-context, these words contain semantic components, that will remain unchanged in every possible sentence. But, being a segment of the first sentence of Čechov's story, it contains subtle supplementary components, like: the promenade, where the tourist appears to look and be looked at, where every new person appearing is a subject of discussion. In this particular case, the rest of the text does not supply many additional features: the boulevard becomes the place where the two protagonists meet each other every afternoon; the aspect of recurrency that is connected with the boulevard is to be found again in later text-fragments, where it is associated with 'ennui'; other aspects of the boulevard are the heat and the dust, which are attributes of Yalta as a whole and which figure elsewhere in the text. Throughout the story the boulevard maintains its dominating relevance to situational and social aspects of the setting. For an example of motifs of the setting coming to be primarily relevant to the characterization, I may refer to a passage in Tolstoj's novel *Anna Karenina*: the description of the snowstorm and Anna's struggle with this phenomenon of nature when, at a halting-place, she gets out of her carriage. The snowstorm itself and other aspects of the setting, too, become symbols of her inner turmoil, of her awakening passion for Vronskij. When seen against later text-elements, these aspects of the setting will be understood as symbolizing the both extatic and terrifying love-affair between Anna and Vronskij: i.e. they will function as aspects of the action.

Motifs of the setting may, of course, be directly relevant to the action: this is the case when they are f.i. presented as natural forces, against which man struggles.

3.2 The semantic structure of a motif cannot be fully grasped, when no account is taken of the connections it has with the sentence, the paragraph, in which it occurs, and with other motifs. Its semantic weight is, as it were, 'filled up' by these connections, which are based upon comparable semantic features, often irrespective of causal, logic or temporal links. These connections are laid down by what I have called elsewhere 'oppositional relations' or 'oppositions' (Van der Eng, 1973:38 ff.; forthcoming 1977). Such oppositions sometimes pertain to motifs in successive (causally, temporally or logically linked) text-fragments, sometimes to text-fragments that are not connected by such links. The oppositional motifs are comparable because they share certain aspects of one thematic level. These aspects contain similar and dissimilar features. Either the similarity or the dissimilarity will be dominant. It is the reader, who coordinates the motifs, who finds out the comparable elements, who discovers the dominant features. Let me give an example of this: at the level of the characterization two characters differ greatly in erudition and social position, but show a striking psychological resemblance. This resemblance may be given the greater emphasis by means of the phraseological presentation and the devices of arrangement. It can also be the other way round: two characters show a strikingly similar erudition and social activity, but have totally different personalities. This dissimilarity may be put forward.

Though it is the reader, who realizes the opposition, it is, of course, the narrator who directs the reader's focus. He wishes the reader to discover the oppositional motifs in text-fragments, even if these fragments do not show a causal or temporal connection, and it is he, who brings forth either the dissimilarities or the similarities in the opposition. He will usually confine his most effective phraseological and compositional devices to the prevailing properties. The subordinated properties will pass almost unnoticed, or they will be only implicitly present. It may even be that they can only be inferred from facts narrated elsewhere in the text.

Of course an opposition originates in a strong stimulus of

the text-part that provides the association: this always is the last-read passage. I distinguish different types of oppositions, depending upon the prevalence of either similarities or dissimilarities:

1) analogies (in them the similarities prevail);

2) parallelisms (in them the dissimilarities prevail);

3) antitheses (in these the central dissimilarities have an antinomic character);

4) variations (in these the central similarities prevail; the difference with analogies is that here the dissimilarities have no independent 'status': they merely promote the similarities by presenting them in a different form; in analogies, on the contrary, the dissimilarities have their own 'status' and as such they are indispensable to the similar features: the latter stand out most clearly when set against the former).

Oppositions may be explicitly or implicitly stated (or both). 'Explicit' means that the comparable features are directly stated in words and pertain to the nucleus of the constant significant elements that are connected with these words. 'Implicit' means that the oppositional parts actualize the potential features of one another. In the latter case these features may be hidden behind all manner of thematic and phraseological elements which at first glance do not seem to offer a basis of comparison. Let me give an example: the text provides certain information about the actions of a Mr. X and a Mr. Y. These actions show no relationship whatsoever, they seem to have nothing at all in common. Later on, however, it becomes clear, that the narrator has introduced the descriptions of these actions to display the ruthlessness of Mr. X as opposed to the kindness of Mr. Y. This would be an instance of an (implicit) antithetic opposition at the characterization-level.

There is only a limited number of types of oppositions, though there are probably more than the four I mentioned. The possible varieties of an opposition-type, however, seem to be unlimited. Sometimes two oppositional motifs are segments of one sentence. More often they are parts of different, non-adjacent text-parts. The number of motifs may vary in the

opposed text-parts and not every motif in them is necessarily
relevant to the given opposition (though they may be relevant
to an opposition with other motifs elsewhere in the text).
Though the motifs of the last-read text-passage are always
placed in opposition to motifs of a preceding passage, this does
not necessarily imply a greater importance of the last-read
passage: it may f.i. deal with a secundary character, about
whom is said something that sets forth earlier information
about the hero. The regressive orientation towards a preceding
text-part involves the activation and actualization of the
explicit and implicit semantic properties in that preceding
text-part. This is followed up by a progressive orientation
towards the last-read text-part (with the same effects). These
regressive and progressive orientations have a semantically
'catalytic' effect: the reader's attention is drawn once more
(and possibly more forcefully than before) to the semantic
properties of the text in between the relevant passages (and
sometimes of the text preceding them). These semantic
properties often provide a possible explanation for the
dominance of the similarities or the dissimilarities in the
oppositional motifs. Thus they further the accessibility of the
narrative text: the recurring orientation towards the text
preceding and the text in between the opposition increases the
semantic weight of it and brings out a fuller understanding of
its meanings. Sometimes it is the opposition that fully realizes
important implicit semantic features of the text preceding it.
I will now give some illustrations of opposition-types and their
catalytic effects.

In Gogol's short story *The Nose*, f.i., the action-level confronts the reader with two *analogous* text-parts. In these
passages combinations of motifs are opposed to one another:
Kovalev's visit to the cathedral and Kovalev's visit to the
newspaper office. In both these cases Kovalev for a moment
stops thinking about the loss of his nose, when he notices a
charming woman (a worshipping woman in the cathedral, the
picture of an actress on a poster in the newspaper office).
When thinking of possible approaches to the woman in the
cathedral and the actress, Kovalev realizes the loss of his nose

with renewed dismay and stops considering taking any initiative. The analogy draws the reader's attention to Kovalev's
preoccupation with the other sex (which has been mentioned
in the earlier text) and gives it its specific erotic touch.

A clear example of *parallelisms* at the characterization-level
are f.i. two instances in *Anna Karenina*: the first and last times
Vronskij sees Anna. The description of the last time he sees
her — at the end of the novel — explicitly refers to the first
time he set eyes upon her, when her beauty enthralled him,
seemed to promise him a future full of happiness. When he
sees her for the last time, her beauty is still dazzling, but
overshadowed by her vindictiveness. A great many previous
passages, in which the possibility of happiness and understanding between Anna and Vronskij is annihilated, culminate in
this ultimate description and they are recalled by the given
opposition.

In Čechov's "Na Podvode" we find an *antithetic* opposition
at the level of the social setting, which characterizes the beginning and the end of the story. At the story's beginning we are
told that the past and the present life of the school-teacher are
completely fenced in by her miserable existence as a teacher in
a hole-and-corner-ditch of a village. At the end we are told,
how happiness reaches out for her, how there is a future after
all, how unreal her position as a teacher has become. She even
believes that such a profession has never been hers. The narrator presents these two text-instances as subjective impressions
of his personage, while he takes care to show that only the
first impression is deeply rooted in (the story's) reality. The
opposition sets forth many instances of frustration and priva-
tion in the interposed text and it is these instances that eluci-
date the final illusion.

For an example of a *variation* I will use another story by
Čechov: "Volodja bol'šoj i Volodja malen'kij". The end of this
short story repeats (at the level of the social setting) a number
of motifs of its beginning, a.o. the endless billiard-games of the
two Volod'jas, the carriage tours out of the town. These re-
iterated activities are at the end loaded with semantic properties that reflect the stifling hold that class-conventions exert

upon people. The catalytic effect is that the reader is reminded of the frustrating incident that takes place in between the beginning and the end of the story: Volodja malen'kij's ill-use of Volodja bol'šoj's wife and her desire to break through the vicious circle of her existence.

All these opposition-types are built upon features that are directly connected with the wording in the related passages. I shall use *The Brothers Karamazov* to add one example of a variation, the characteristic semantic properties of which are to be found implicitly in widely different text-fragments. There are two passages in this novel that are characteristic of old Karamazov's personality, in particular of his cynical and derisive attitude towards religion. One passage contains his story about the philosopher Diderot, with whom he identifies himself. This Diderot, as old Karamazov says, became religious and had himself baptized no sooner than he had heard the words of the Bible: "The fool says in his heart there is no God". The second passage deals with old Karamazov's question about a story from the Church Calendar, which, he pretends, has shaken his belief. He asks, whether it is true that one of these stories recounts the beheading of a martyr, and the martyr's subsequent walking away with his head in his hands, kissing it affectionately again and again...

In the same way analogies, parallelisms and antitheses may be hidden in oppositional text-segments. The reader must detect the implicit comparable features in them. I may refer to the earlier given example of an antithesis at the characterization-level, in which nothing is pointed out explicitly (the seemingly incomparable actions of Mr. X and Mr. Y., which come to be relevant since they oppose ruthlessness to kindness).

3.3 The reader's grip on a narrative text is, as it were 'guaranteed' by the fact that oppositions of one type – connected with one and the same thematic aspect – often occur in chains, i.e. they cover more than two text-parts. The formation of a chain of oppositions is based upon semantic features, common to all its segments. Thus, a chain rests upon a number of features, which can be traced in all its oppositional motifs, even when they are not explicitly stated: the common semantic features come to light as a result of the interrelatedness of the motifs, or, to be more precise, these features establish this interrelatedness. In other words: the set of semantic features upon which a chain is built, is realized dynamically, i.e. by the correlation of each oppositional motif (group of motifs) with previous and/or subsequent motifs (groups of them) in the chain. In the first fragments of a chain the semantic components will for the greater part be 'potentially' present: the realization of this 'potential presence' takes place when later links in the chain of fragments are connected with the earlier ones. A clear example of this is to be found in Tolstoj's story *The Three Deaths*. In the introductory passages of this story a servant and her mistress are more than once compared with one another on the basis of their physical characteristics. Both women are young and beautiful. This is as far as the similarities go. The series of oppositions consists of antitheses. Various physical characteristics bring out the dissimilarities between the two women. At one moment mention is made of an anemic, skinny mistress vs. a buxom, ruddy servant. At another moment we are told of a sallow-coloured skin, that has lost its freshness vs. a rosy, blushing face. This description may be opposed once more to a later specification of the mistress: there was something arid and deathlike in the paleness of her skin. A later opposition says the following: the mistress, placing her hands on the seat of her chair, tries to shift herself to a more comfortable position, but she does not have the force to do so – vs. – the servant stood up high on her strong legs and chose a seat further away. The underlying semantic components of this antithetic chain, which opposes heterogeneous physical properties, are illness/weakness vs. health/ vigour. In the first opposition the underlying characteristics of the mistress are actualized at a later point of the story (paleness and thinness do not necessarily imply illness and weakness). It is the connection with later oppositions that introduces these elements into the first, actualizes them. In still later text-fragments the elements life/death are opposed to one another in relation to the mistress and the servant, and the preceding oppositions come to be permeated with these characteristics as well. Consequently, every opposition comes to participate in a set of semantic features which it shares with every other opposition in the chain. Of course, every opposition has specific semantic features of its own in the texture: dull, flat hair vs. springy hair; a shrivelled chest vs. a strong, healthy chest; a pale, wan face vs. a ruddy face, etc. Generally speaking, we may say that: 1) a chain of one-type oppositions consists of heterogeneous oppositional motifs (groups of motifs); 2) each of these motifs (groups), when set against another oppositional motif (group) of the chain, mostly shows explicit comparable features, which are particular to this isolated oppositional pair only; 3) when an oppositional motif is set against all the other oppositional motifs (groups) of the chain, it tends to incorporate a mostly implicit set of comparable features, common to all of them.

3.4 The relationships between the various oppositions in such a chain are endowed with a 'dynamic power'. I have used the word 'gradation' in this respect (see Van der Eng, 1973b; 1977, forthcoming). 'Gradation' means that the features of a set, which is constituted within a chain, are being emphasized with an increasing expressivity. It is often in the last oppositions of a chain that a great many (or all) of these features will be most emphatically expressed to attract the reader's attention. In *The Three Deaths*, for instance, the weakness of the mistress and the energetic vitality of the servant come to the fore most forcefully in one of the last antithetic oppositions: the opposition that describes the mistress's futile attempt to alter her position and the subsequent ease with which the servant takes another seat. The very last opposition introduces the aspect 'death' and thereby underlines the implications of the earlier aspects 'illness/weakness', connects these aspects in a regressive way with death.

3.5 The chain of antitheses with which Tolstoj's story begins, is an example of what I have called a 'frame-work series'

(1973b:45 ff.; 1977: forthcoming). I would now prefer the term 'integrational chain' as opposed to 'dispersive chain'. An integrational chain embraces (integrates) causally, spatially and temporally interlinked motifs of the action, the characterization and the social setting. One of the thematic levels dominates the others. The motifs of the subordinated levels are significant only in as far as they show features that are relevant to the motifs of the prevailing level. A dispersive chain consists of motifs of one thematic level, that are scattered throughout the text without any direct causal, temporal or situational relationships. Think, f.i., of the passages that describe Anna Karenina's beauty: they are to be found all through the novel. The motifs of the ailing lady in the beginning of Tolstoj's short story can be opposed to the motifs of the healthy maid-servant, but also to motifs outside the frame of causal, temporal and spatial connections. Think, f.i., of the motifs that deal with the sickness and death of a cart-driver. These can be correlated with the motifs of the ailing lady — as oppositional elements — and thus constitute a dispersive chain of parallelisms, that emphasizes the differences between two ways of dying. The motifs in the beginning of Tolstoj's story are part of an integrational chain — as antithetic elements. Hence the physical data that oppose the two women, appear in a context which encompasses many other data, thus ensuring temporal continuity and causal and spatial connections. These other motifs are only of secondary importance to the integrational chain and their significance is actualized only in as far as it is relevant to the data of the women's physical states.

Some elements — those of the setting — have practically no relevance at all in this respect, such as the gloomy weather, the dirty road, the cart-driver's exhortations, etc. We can only say that they give an additional emphasis to the wretched physical condition of the mistress, cf. the corresponding gloominess of nature, of the weather, etc. In other cases — when they express aspects of both the inner and outer characterization — these elements may have a greater relevance to the series of oppositions. The visible irritation in the mistress's face, her uncontrolled outburst against the servant may be connected with ill-

ness and pain. It seems, however, that these elements are more
connected with psychological features: they draw attention to
new aspects, aspects no longer of the outer but of the inner
characterization. These new aspects ask for further supplementation, and this is indeed provided later on in the story, outside the integrational chain. The oppositions that are connected with the mistress and the servant are in fact part of a more
or less episodic moment. The servant disappears from the story
later on. The story's basic theme is then narrowed down to the
mistress's fearful resistance to death, to her grudge against
healthy people. In the integrational chain of the story's beginning there were already suggestions and indications of this
development: they had only a secondary relevance to the
physical state of the ailing lady; their main significance did not
fall within the chain. They turned out to mark the transition
to a later part of the story.

3.6 Generally speaking, we may say this: motifs that occur
within an integrational chain, but do not fit into its pattern
(refer f.i. to other thematic levels or to other aspects of the
dominant level), that ask for supplementary information, bring
about the transition to a story's next phase, in most cases to
another integrational chain, in which the desired information
(or part of it) is given. When only part of the desired information is given, it often happens that new secrets, paradoxes,
puzzles etc. present themselves, which in their turn demand an
explication. In my essay on semantic dynamics in narrative
prose, I have used Sinjavskij's story *Pchenc* to illustrate this
(1977, forthcoming). In this story we have an integrational
chain of parallelisms at the dominant action-level: a sequence
of amorous overtures of the female personage vs. wary, parry-
ing reactions of the male personage. He is the central figure in
the story, the reader's interest is primarily drawn to his
actions. It is quite clear that his cautious behaviour springs
from his wish to continue the relationship at a different
footing, he certainly does not want to end it altogether. Exactly what sort of relationship he has in mind, remains an open
question for the time being, as do the reasons he has for his be-

haviour. The reader will gradually begin to wonder what kind of a man the story's 'I' really is. This puzzle becomes more and more intriguing as a result of the 'I' 's observations, which are given in between the oppositions of the combined advances and retreats. They are observations about the possible rôles he might assume to keep the girl at a distance, without losing her altogether. These observations draw our attention more and more to his enigmatic identity; they necessitate the ending of the series, the insertion of an episode that gives us the desired supplementary information. Moreover, the series is interspersed with reflections that have no connection with the interlinked advances and retreats: when f.i. the 'I' believes he cannot possibly evade having dinner with the girl, we are confronted with some passages, that describe his thoughts on culinary sadism in some detail. Extremely curious is his indignation about the way corn is treated to make it fit for consumption: it is said to be tortured by endless beatings. Passages like this, that are not incorporated in the series, draw the reader's attention so forcefully to the 'I' 's identity, that even within the series a change of the thematic level is effectuated: the reader will begin to reread all the oppositions of combined advances and retreats with an eye to their possible implications for the 'I' 's psychology. The above clearly shows that 'gradation' is not limited to oppositional text-fragments of an integrational chain. It shows that 'gradation' plays an important part in the text-fragments that do not completely fit in the integrational chain, fragments that consist of motifs which draw the reader's attention primarily to other thematic aspects.

Thus, in Sinjavskij's story there is an increasing expressiveness on the one hand, which results in a maximum emphasis in the integrational chain of the parallelisms that give a concrete form to the advances and retreats between the girl and the 'I'. On the other hand, there is a gradual increase in the story's cunning perplexity, which is connected with mysterious elements, that function outside the dominant level of the chain and that draw attention to the 'I' 's identity. The series of advances/retreats reaches its culminating-point at the same

time as the increasing mysteriousness about the 'I' 's psychological (and physical) make-up. There is, as it were, a competition between the two informative aspects, that coexist within
the frame of the integrational chain. In the end, these thematic
aspects that partly − or even wholly − deviate from those
upon which the integrational chain is built, ultimately prove to
have a greater significance and effect a thematic change. The
'I' 's mysteriousness comes to be of central importance, it determines the next integrational chain in which, again, the dominant
thematic level is that of the action (until ever stronger thematic
deviations again bring about a thematic change). In this new
chain, the reader's attention is, at first, more or less drawn away
from the 'I' and directed to another personage. The 'I' has been
watching this other person for some time in the story; after his
affair with the girl he sets out to find him and, when he has
succeeded, he tries to make him acknowledge 'something'.
This is described in a series of increasingly aggressive scenes.
The unspecified 'something' brings the central issue back to
the enigmatic identity of the 'I', since it becomes clearer and
clearer that the 'I' thinks to have the 'something' in common
with that other person. So, here again, is a regressive change in
the thematic dominance. Again the reader is confronted with a
chain of action-moments in which his attention is gradually
drawn away from the interaction with another person to the
'I' s identity: here, this is brought about by the secret the 'I'
thinks he shares with the other man, viz. his supposition that
they come from the same land, have the same native language,
etc. The 'I' 's misapprehension − he is wrong in thinking he
has found a kinsman and a fellow-sufferer − together with the
disclosed 'normal', human identity of the other man, reveal
that the 'I' comes from another planet. The reader will now
reconsider the whole chain for the last time on the basis of the
'I' 's information about his identity and the new obscure elements, which that information contains. The story will have to
account for these obscurities. As I have said before, certain intriguing and deficient pieces of information in an integrational
chain are an indication of the information that will be given in
a later part of the story (often again in the form of an integra-

tional chain). The gaps in the information must be 'filled in'.

In the case of dispersive chains, the replacement of one chain by another is brought about in much the same way: complete information about one thematic aspect makes the reader ponder upon – as yet ungiven – information about another thematic aspect. As I have said, a dispersive chain is built upon oppositional motifs or groups of motifs, that are scattered throughout the text. Such a chain is not based upon causal, temporal or spatial connections between its segments. Such connections may, of course, often be inferred with the help of text-parts in between the oppositional fragments. Sometimes this is not possible, as, for instance, in Tolstoj's *The Three Deaths* where three ways of dying are compared with one another. The fact that dispersive chains are not founded upon actional causality and upon temporal and spatial continuity, has as its consequence that in these chains thematically deviating motifs will not occur: the reader's discovery of comparable motifs (groups of motifs) will not be obscured by additional elements that have no – or only a weak – relevance to the thematic aspect of the chain. Does this imply the absence of a much needed property (i.e. deviating motifs), that is essential to initiate a change in the thematic aspect and in the type of opposition? No: there are comparable structural devices that can take over this dynamic function. A leading dispersive chain may become of lesser importance as a consequence of the information given in an initially secondary dispersive chain. This secondary chain may gradually grow more important, when it appears to present more and more thematic data that obscure the information given in the leading chain, turn it into dubious, ambiguous information. When the obscurities, paradoxes, etc. become more and more intriguing, the secondary chain may take over the leading position, provided that it will orientate the reader on a possible solution of the riddles it has brought forward. As a rule such a secondary chain begins to function as the leading one, when in the subsided chain the finishing touch is given to certain specific thematic aspects: this finishing touch, however, must necessarily leave a number of questions unresolved. It is upon these questions that the secondary chain — the prevailing one from now on — will be focused. When, for instance, in a dispersive chain the information about a murder and the possible murderer is completed, and when certain questions which are essential to the reconstruction of the crime remain unanswered, the reader's attention may be drawn to another dispersive chain, which offers an alternative reconstruction. The reader may then be confronted again with a number of motifs, which at first seemed to be only relevant to the possible reconstruction that was presented in the first completed chain. Now these motifs may appear to have an even greater relevance to the alternative reconstruction in the second chain. It will be clear that the reconstruction in both chains may rest upon causal-temporal links. These links, however, must be inferred from causally, temporally and spatially discontinuous motifs and clusters of motifs. We can, of course, imagine an example in which causality is almost irrelevant: we may think of two dispersive chains, each of them built upon statements expressed by widely different personages; one of these chains may inform us about a certain character in a positive way, whereas the other may give negative information about the same character.

It may be noted that there can be a kind of competition between two dispersive chains (just as there can be a competition in an integrational chain between the thematically appropriate and the thematically deviating motifs). Moreover, when the initially secondary dispersive chain has become the leading one, it may effect a change in the thematic function of many elements of the initial principal chain (just as the deviating motifs in an integrational chain may cause a change in the thematic function of many elements of this chain). Let us suppose that the secondary chain is built upon motifs which pertain to the level of the characterization (the inner motivation of some deed), whereas the preceding dominant chain was built upon actional motifs. When the secondary chain takes over the leading position, a number of these actional motifs will penetrate into it, but they will be actualized in their psychological significance. The occurrence of such thematic

changes and the development of new chains does not mean
that the existing semantic webs become altogether disinte-
grated, it means that the thematic functionality changes at a
certain point of the story. Up to that point other thematic
developments will have prevailed: they are the necessary
requisites for the reversal, and as such they are essential to the
dynamic construction of the narrative.

The above remarks, in fact, introduce the problems of the
possible relationships between the various chains (both integrational and dispersive). The problem of the relations between
chains comprises the question: how important is a specific
series for the semantic structure of the narrative text? Or: how
do we discover the hierarchy of the chains in a specific narrative text?

3.7 The hierarchy in the arrangement of the chains are determined by the extent to which they participate in the essential
thematic issues of the specific narrative text. These essential
thematic issues are not identical with the issues that are
presented in explicit terms: in *Pchenc* the central theme is not
the struggle between man and woman, but that, which is
hidden behind that struggle. The essential thematic issues are
concealed behind deficient information. Every new chain
reduces this insufficiency, but at the same time it stresses
certain crucial, unresolved questions: the 'I' in *Pchenc* experiences a sickening disgust when confronted with a female
nude (human bodies in general are repugnant to him). This
explains his attitude towards the girl to some extent, but at
the same time it awakens an even greater curiosity about his
identity. Mostly every new chain supplies the reader with
answers to questions, but at the same time it raises more
questions and complications: therefore every new chain is, as a
rule, more important than the chain preceding. A chain at the
end of a story often answers the questions of the preceding
chains, solves their contradictions, their riddles and mysteries,
etc. When all these answers and solutions have been already
anticipated by the reader, when there are no surprise-elements
in them, such a final chain cannot be considered to be superior

in the hierarchy. When, however, it does provide unexpected answers, when it extricates potential semantic features from preceding chains, when it forces the reader to re-interpret the preceding story, when it establishes an unexpected relationship with other texts and with human reality, then this final chain is undoubtedly superior in the hierarchy.

'Final chain' is a slightly confusing term, because such a chain is based upon a set of semantic components, which may very well be connected with passages throughout the text. Such a hierarchically superior chain runs through all the other chains, supplements their deficient information, actualizes their potential semantic features, sets forth new implications, and thus it ultimately reveals the essential thematic issues and determines the dominant thematic level. In Sinjavskij's story we find an example of such a chain, which shows itself in its full force at the end of the story, when the mysteries have been solved. At that moment it begins to pervade the story in a regressive way: cf. the information about the psychological and physical identity of the 'I', his aesthetic tenets, etc., all of which 'explains' many of his preceding actions and pronouncements.

Čechov's stories constitute such a superior chain in a different way: obviously deficient (withheld) information about central thematic issues plays a less important part in them. Characteristic of the end of his stories is a different opinion about previously narrated facts, which mostly is the result of a different narrative attitude, adapted to the mental view of the principal personage. The resulting new semantic implications of old facts, the new way of looking at them, changes the previous interpretation into deficient information. Thus, a change in the narrator's emotional and intellectual approach may have the same effect as changes in the degree of knowledge the narrator chooses to profess (which wraps up the essential theme in mysteries, secrets and paradoxes, until the disclosure at the end).

III. THE SEMANTIC STRUCTURE OF *LADY WITH LAPDOG**

1. *Some general remarks on the arrangement of the thematic levels*

This discussion of Čechov's story is concentrated upon the principal patterns of the semantic organization at the three thematic levels. These patterns are constituted by different successive chains of oppositional motifs (and groups of motifs) and by the hierarchical relationship that exists between these chains. I do not intend to present a strictly formal analysis. I do not aim at a detailed description of the semantic elements upon which the various chains are based, nor shall I try to state precisely to what extent these elements are realized in the many oppositional text fragments. In some cases the oppositional text parts will speak for themselves well enough, and it will be unnecessary to reduce them to clusters of those semantic components that bring out the similarities or the dissimilarities.

I am concerned with the 'corpus' of the semantic construction in this story as an illustration of the exposition I have given before. In this story of Čechov, the central place is taken by a series of episodes that take place in the hotel room of the female protagonist. These episodes are the result and the fulfilment of the secret wish for an amorous adventure of both the male and the female protagonist. At the same time, however, they mark the beginning of a completely new development.

The action-level in *Lady with Lapdog* consists of text moments that oppose the protagonists Anna Sergeevna and Gurov. The events can hardly be described as manoeuvres for a seduction with obstructions in the form of counteracts and rebuffs by others or by Anna herself. There is hardly any

*The translations of the quoted passages are taken from *Lady with Lapdog and other Stories*, transl. with an introduction by David Magarshack (1964).

resistance or impediment. Anna's husband is a potential hindrance, but he never actually intervenes. The winning of Anna does not need much effort. In the beginning of the story the narrator does hint at a possible resistance and at the tactics that are to be employed in that case: he raises such expectations in the reader's mind by contrasting Gurov's speculation "Esli ona zdes' bez muža i bez znakomych, to bylo by ne lišnee poznakomit'sja s nej" (if she's here without her husband and without any friends, it wouldn't be a bad idea to strike up an acquaintance with her) with Anna's announcement, in its reproduction by the narrator, that her husband may possibly come to Yalta. There is something else, which also leads the reader to expect a conflict: first he is told about Gurov's playboy-like way of beginning an affair, and later on about the painful and bitter way in which he always ends them.

The possibility of the husband's arrival seems to prevent an 'affair' between Anna and Gurov till the second chapter. There are a number of stereotyped indications that his arrival has indeed been an obstacle, and that it will soon cease to be one. These stereotyped indications are: Anna's shining eyes, the nervousness and agitation she shows in connection with that days's last ship (a week has passed by now). The husband does not turn up, and soon Gurov succeeds in having his way. Now the story should, according to the raised expectations, go on with descriptions of the ending of the affair. This affair, however, ends with no difficulties at all, because Anna's husband falls ill and writes her a letter, begging her to come home: she leaves without troubling Gurov with appeals or pleas. Instead of the expected conflicts, the story is filled from then on with Gurov's reflections (in the narrator's representation of them) about the affair and about its being different from his other affairs.

Of great importance in this respect are a number of passages, that refer to previous amorous affairs. The relationship between Anna and Gurov is more than once compared with these other affairs. In this comparison different phases can be distinguished, each of which constitutes a different chain of oppositions. The various phases (chains) represent different attitudes of the narrator, whose approach is nearly always closely connected with Gurov's views (cf. Usmanov on the symbiosis of narrator and character in Čechov: 1969:14 ff., 1971:247-8; Nilsson:91 ff.; Vinogradov:139, 153).

The characterization level is, of course, almost exclusively allotted to the two protagonists. Gurov is more than once characterized by the narrator's direct, authoritative observations; Anna's characterization is mostly handled in a different way: her picture arises from remarks that reflect Gurov's attitude towards her, or, better, from remarks, in which the narrator restricts himself to Gurov's perspective. This is done many times in the observations that accompany the situations in which both the protagonists figure. There are a few text parts that deal with the characterization of Gurov's wife and Anna's husband. The former is characterized by statements of the narrator that reflect Gurov's perspective. Anna's husband comes to the fore in Anna's own words (incorporated in the narrator's representation of Gurov's observations) and in the narrator's observations which reflect Gurov's perspective. Anna and Gurov, Anna and Gurov's wife, Anna and her husband, Gurov and his wife, can often be compared on the basis of similarities and dissimilarities.

Basically, the story is a story on the process of Gurov's coming to know himself. The gradual development of his insight into himself is concealed in motifs of actions (displaying the varying attitudes of Gurov and Anna towards each other). The same applies to motifs of the social setting. It is in this indirect way that the characterization of Gurov — from whose perspective almost the whole story is told — comes to be the dominant theme.

At the level of the geographical and social setting we find text-fragments that picture Moscow, Yalta and the provincial town S. Gurov's mental approach (rendered by the narrator) to the Moscow setting and, to a less extent, to the Yalta setting, is far from invariable. These fragments form a chain of oppositions, that is based upon his changing views (Moscow positive and negative, Yalta positive and negative). A consequence of this is that Moscow and Yalta are being opposed

to one another in different oppositions (Moscow positive –
Yalta negative and Yalta positive – Moscow negative). The
fragments referring to the provincial town S. form a chain of
oppositions that is based upon only one (Gurov's) mental
approach.

The varying attitudes that are characteristic of Gurov's
perspective determine the developments and changes at the
levels of the action and the social settings. Hence the dominant
thematic level is the – mainly indirectly given – characterization of Gurov. From his point of view (paraphrased by the
narrator) Anna is opposed to his wife, the affair with Anna to
other affairs, Moscow to Yalta, etc. The rarely intruding voice
of the authoritative narrator constitutes a certain hierarchy in
the various phases in which Gurov gradually unravels his actual
feelings. In the course of the story the narrator comments
upon Gurov's changing attitude towards his life in Moscow, he
indicates which is the essential phase in the relationship with
Anna. It is characteristic of the story that it does not describe
the end of the love-affair, though it does give an account of
the final phase of Gurov's growing insight into his feelings and
thoughts. This phase is set forth at the end of the story in
some fragments that describe both actual events and Gurov's
reflections. The future development of the love-affair thus
remains an open question, while the process of Gurov's self-
knowledge is brought to an end (cf. Hélène Auzinger, 1960).

2. *The action level*

2.1 The central place at the action level is at first taken by the
episodes that follow the rapidly effectuated liaison with Anna
Sergeevna. Chapter II describes a number of scenes which
connect this liaison with Gurov's earlier affairs ànd, as will
appear later on, with the later relationship with Anna. The
essential components of these clusters of motifs are Anna's
reaction to what has happened just then and Gurov's responses
to it. Anna's reaction is given in her own words and in the
observations of the narrator (whose perspective coincides with

Gurov's). Gurov's response is thus implicitly conveyed; it is also expressed, however, in his own words, and incidentally in the narrator's descriptions of his behaviour. Anna's reaction has two characteristic aspects, the second of which is, as it were, a natural consequence of the first. On the one hand there is her youth and naïveté, on the other hand her moral certainty of having sinned. Her naïve youthfulness at first appeals to Gurov, her − in his opinion − disproportionate and incongruous sense of guilt repels him. It is especially the aspects of repulsion and lack of understanding that stand out in Gurov's replies (and sometimes in his behaviour, cf. the eating of a piece of melon and the subsequent half hour silence). The different scenes create a chain of variations which are connected by a causal-temporal sequence and a unity of time and place. This integrational chain consists of oppositional groups of motifs that repeatedly show a combined set of features, related to her and his attitudes. The recurrent semantic components, upon which this chain is built, are set forth with an increasing expressiveness (gradation). Her sense of guilt and sinfulness is first expressed by the narrator (his perspective coinciding with Gurov's): (1) "... ona zadumalas' v unyloj poze, točno grešnica na starinnoj kartine." (... she sank into thought in a despondent pose, like a woman taken in adultery in an old painting.) Then it is stated in her own words: (2) "Ne chorošo. Vy že pervyj menja ne uvažaete teper'." (It's wrong. You'll be the first not to respect me now." (3) "Pust' Bog menja prostit! Èto užasno." (May God forgive me. It's terrible.) (4) "Čem mne opravdat'sja. Ja durnaja, nizkaja ženščina ..." (How can I justify myself? I am a bad, despicable creature.) (5) "... menja poputal nečistyj." (The devil has led me astray.) Each of these statements is accompanied by Gurov's responses or by observations of the narrator which echo Gurov's reactions. Gurov's lack of understanding, his astonishment and his rejection, in their turn show an increasing expressiveness: (1) the narrator uses words like "stranno i nekstati" (odd and disconcerting), which reflect Gurov's sentiments. (2) The description of Gurov eating a melon, his silence, his subsequent reply: "Otčego by ja mog

perestat' uvažat' tebja? ty sama ne znaeš', čto govoriš'." (But
why should I stop respecting you? You don't know yourself
what you're saying.") (3) "Ty točno opravdyvaeš'sja." (You
seem to wish to justify yourself.) (4) "Ja ne ponimaju, čto že
ty chočeš'?" (I don't understand what it is you want.) (5)
"Polno, polno ..." (There, there ...)

Gurov is captivated by Anna's youth, her naïveté and timidity. In between the (narrator's) description of this, we are
presented with motifs that express Gurov's non-understanding
and astonishment. These two aspects of his attitude finally fall
together in a fragment where the elements of astonishment
prevail, where Anna's naïveté is presented in a negative way:
"Gurovu bylo uže skučno slušat', ego razdražal naivnyj ton,
èto pokajanie, takoe neožidannoe i neumestnoe." (Gurov
could not help feeling bored as he listened to her; he was irri-
ted by her naïve tone of voice and her repentance, which was
so unexpected and so out of place.)

2.2 The chain of variational episodes may as a whole be
opposed to the three categories of women which Gurov distinguishes, when he considers his previous affairs. These three
types of women (and their respective, specific ways of making
love) are presented in a description of Gurov's recollections of
his past experiences. This is a text fragment that immediately
precedes the observations on Anna's reaction to their intimacy: (1) "... sochranilos' vospominanie o bezzabotnych, dobro-
dušnych ženščinach, veselych ot ljubvi, blagodarnych emu za
sčast'e, chotja by očen' korotkoe"; (2) "i o takich, kak,
naprimer, ego žena, − kotorye ljubili bez iskrennosti, s izlišnimi razgovorami, manerno, s isteriej, s takim vyraženiem, kak
budto to byla ne ljubov', ne strast', a čto-to bolee značitel'noe";
(3) "i o takich dvuch-trech, očen' krasivych, cholodnych, u
kotorych vdrug promel'kalo na lice chiščnoe vyraženie, uprjamoe želanie vzjat', vychvatit' u žizni bol'še, čem ona možet
dat', i èto byli ne pervoj molodosti, kapriznye, ne rassužda-
juščie, vlastnye, ne umnye ženščiny ..." ((1) ... he preserved
the memory of carefree, good-natured women, whom love had
made gay, who were grateful to him for the happiness he gave

them, however short-lived; (2) and of women like his wife, who made love without sincerity, with unnecessary talk, affectedly, hysterically, with such an expression, as though it were not love or passion, but something much more significant; (3) and of two or three very beautiful, frigid women, whose faces suddenly lit up with a predatory expression, an obstinate desire to take, to snatch from life more than it could give; these were women no longer in their first youth, capricious, unreasoning, unintelligent women ...)

Opposed to these recollections of old affairs are the observations on how it was with Anna Sergeevna. This results in an (integrational) chain of parallelisms, and the narrator (still speaking from Gurov's perspective) indicates the prevailing differences (the youthful inexperience, the sense of guilt) in his very first sentence: "No tut vse ta že nesmelost', uglovatost' neopytnoj molodosti, nelovkoe čuvstvo; i bylo vpečatlenie rasterjannosti ... Anna Sergeevna ... k tomu, čto proizošlo, otneslas' kak-to osobenno, očen' ser'ezno, točno k svoemu padeniju ..." (But here there was still the same diffidence and angularity of inexperienced youth – an awkward feeling; and there was also the impression of embarrassment ... Anna Sergeyevna ... regarded what had happened in a peculiar sort of way, very seriously, as though she had become a fallen woman ...)

All illicit affairs have, of course, certain elements in common. In this story, however, the prevailing differences do not only stand out against such universal aspects, but also against specific similarities. The latter are subtly used to compare Anna's behaviour with that of the women in some of Gurov's categories. Gurov's non-understanding, his rejection and astonishment bring Anna to a reaction, which reminds the reader of certain aspects in Gurov's types two and three. Cf. Anna's words "mne chotelos' čego-nibud' polučše; ved' est' že, – govorila ja sebe – drugaja žizn'." (I wanted something better. There surely must be a different kind of life, I said to myself.) with type 2: "... kotorye ljubili bez iskrennosti, s izlišnymi razgovorami, manerno, s isteriej, s takim vyraženiem, kak budto to byla ne ljubov', ne strast', a čto-to bolee znači-

tel'noe." (... who made love without sincerity, with unnecessary talk, affectedly, hysterically, with such an expression, as
though it were not love or passion, but something much more
significant.) Cf. also Gurov's evaluation of Anna's behaviour
(as represented by the narrator): "... možno bylo by podu-
mat', čto ona šutit ili igraet rol'." (... one might have thought
that she was joking or play-acting.) Reminiscent of type 3 are
Anna's words: "Chotelos' požit'! požit' i požit' ..." (I wanted
to live. To live, to live!) (Cf. type 3: "uprjamoe želanie vzjat',
vychvatit' u žizni bol'še, čem ona možet dat'." (an obstinate
desire to take, to snatch from life more than it could give.))

The comparison of this new affair with the old affairs is an
integral part of the whole story, not only implicitly present,
but also explicitly stated by Gurov or by the narrator (voicing
Gurov's opinions). What becomes increasingly important in
this respect, is the information which the authoritative narrator gives at the beginning of the story: about the bitter taste
the endings of Gurov's affairs always leave.

2.3 The scenes in Anna's hotel room are immediately followed by passages, which seem to lay a greater emphasis upon the
analogies between this love-affair and the enumerated three
possible types of affairs: the similarities now seem to be of
greater importance than the dissimilarities. To Gurov, Anna's
behaviour is incomprehensible, strange and burdensome. His
reaction to it creates the impression, that he considers whatever causes this may have, as unimportant, that he merely
wishes to conduct this affair according to the familiar pattern.
Anna's reaction seems to classify her as the first type of
woman: "dobrodušnye, veselye ot ljubvi" (good-natured
women, whom love had made gay); "On smotrel ej ... v ispugannye glaza, celoval ee, govoril ticho i laskovo ... i veselost'
vernulas' k nej; stali oba smejat'sja." (He gazed into her ...
frightened eyes, kissed her, spoke gently and affectionate to
her ... and her cheerfulness returned; both of them were soon
laughing.) The narrator depicts the subsequent development of
the affair by summarizing it as following an ever returning
pattern: "Ona ... zadavala vse odni i te že voprosy ... čto on

nedostatočno ee uvažaet;" (She asked the same questions ... that he did not respect her sufficiently;), "... často na skvere ... on vdrug privlekal ee k sebe i celoval strastno ..." (... again and again in the square, he would draw her to him and kiss her passionately ...) There is, as it were, a 'perpetuum mobile', in which Anna and her behaviour evoke the parallelisms with Gurov's previous affairs (and the, to Gurov so disconcerting, consequently evoked dissimilarities). As to Gurov, the 'perpetuum mobile' is characterized by words and deeds which evoke analogies with the previous affairs, i.e. the narrator tells us that Gurov tries to consider this affair as identical with the others: an exciting, but very temporary adventure. Thus, analogies and parallelisms alternate. This results in two intermittent and hence dispersive chains of oppositional motifs, that are scattered all over the story. At the same time the variations outside the integrational chain are continued; they, too, develop into a dispersive chain and become more and more strongly centered round the elements of reticence, lack of understanding.

The end of Chapter II deals with the parting. This parting differs greatly from the way Gurov's previous affairs usually ended. In the introductory passages we have been told about this by the narrator. There he outlines – with some display of authority – how troublesome and bitter the ending of his affairs is to Gurov. "Opyt mnogokratnyj, v samom dele, gor'kij opyt, naučil ego davno, čto vsjakoe sbliženie, kotoroe vnačale tak prijatno raznoobrazit žizn' i predstavljaetsja milym i legkim priključeniem, u porjadočnych ljudej, osobenno u moskvičej, tjaželych na pod''em, neizbežno vyrastaet v celuju zadaču, složnuju črezvyčajno, i položenie v konce koncov stanovitsja tjagostnym." (Long and indeed bitter experience had taught him that every new affair, which at first relieved the monotony of life so pleasantly, and appeared to be such a charming and light adventure, among decent people and especially among Muscovites, who are so irresolute and so hard to rouse, inevitably developed into an extremely complicated problem and finally the whole situation became rather cumbersome.)

Ending the affair with Anna is not difficult at all: she ends
it herself, when — as I have said before — her husband is unable to join her in Yalta, because he has fallen ill, and asks her
to come home. It even seems as if she reproaches herself for
leaving Gurov: "Gospod' s vami, ostavajtes'. Ne pominajte
lichom. My navsegda proščaemsja, èto tak nužno, potomu čto
ne sledovalo vovse vstretit'sja. Nu, gospod' s vami ..." etc.
(Good-bye. You're staying, aren't you? Don't think badly of
me, we are parting forever. Yes, it must be so, for we should
never have met. Well, good-bye ...) This is one more instance
of the striking difference with Gurov's other affairs, it comes
close to being antithetic. The counter-movement of the 'perpetuum mobile' (coming, of course, from Gurov and emphasizing
the analogous aspects) is never absent, however. The 'markers'
of this analogy are the semantic components, which classify
the relation as identical with all the others, which declare the
relationship to be 'fini', nothing but a memory' "I on dumal o
tom, čto vot v ego žizni bylo ešče odno pochoždenie ili
priključenie, i ono tože uže končilos', i ostalos' teper' vospominanie ..." (He told himself that this had been just one more
affair in his life, just one more adventure, and that it too, was
over, leaving nothing but a memory ...) Then some other
aspects of Gurov's thoughts are mentioned. Though there is no
indication of it in the actual text, the reader will suspect that
the described thoughts are stereotypes, that these are the
emotions he experiences every time an affair ends. Consequently, the description of them strengthens the analogy with
the old affairs. Gurov realizes the unhappiness he brings upon
his partners, he feels slightly sorry for this, he realizes the false
image his partners must have had of him: "On ... ispytyval
legkoe raskajanie; ved' èta molodaja ženščina ... ne byla s nim
sčastliva ... on kazalsja ej ne tem, čem byl na samom dele,
značit nevol'no obmanyval ee ..." (He felt a little penitent,
that the young woman ... had not been happy with him ... she
must have taken him to be quite different from what he really
was, which meant that he had involuntarily deceived her.)

2.4 In Chapter III the analogous relationship is further elaborated. The idea that time will eventually blur the vivid memories of the affair is expressed in a slightly forced way by means of conjectures about the future: "Projdet kakoj-nibud' mesjac, i Anna Sergeevna, kazalos' emu, pokroetsja v pamjati tumanom i tol'ko izredka budet snit'sja s trogatel'noj ulybkoj, kak snilis' drugie." (Another month, and nothing but a memory would remain of Anna Sergeyevna. He would remember her as through a haze and only occasionally dream of her wistful smile, as he had only occasionally dreamed of the others before her.) Then, however, a series of episodes follows, which forms an unmistakable antithesis with this. This time, the dissimilarity, which has now become antithetic, is not based upon Anna's attitude, but upon Gurov's. "Vospominanija razgoralis' vse sil'nee"; "zakryvši glaza, on videl ee kak živuju …"; "on slyšal ee dychanie, laskovyj šoroch ee odeždy." (His memories haunted him more and more persistently; closing his eyes he saw her as clearly as if she were before him …; he heard her breathing, the sweet rustle of her dress.) In between these antithetic elements, there are passages, that once more set forth the analogies with the earlier love affairs. A clear example is, for instance, the end of this passage: "uže tomilo sil'noe želanie podelit'sja s kem-nibud' svoimi vospominanijami. No doma nel'zja bylo govorit' o svoej ljubvi, a vne doma – ne s kem. Ne s žil'cami že i ne v banke. I o čem govorit'? Razve on ljubil togda? Razve bylo čto-nibud' krasivoe, poètičeskoe, ili poučitel'noe, ili prosto interesnoe v ego otnošenijach k Anne Sergeevne?" (he was beginning to be overcome by an overwhelming desire to share his memories with someone. But at home it was impossible to talk of his love, and outside his home there was no one he could talk to. Not the tenants who lived in his house, and certainly not his colleagues in the bank. And what was he to tell them? Had he been in love then? Had there been anything beautiful, poetic, edifying, or even anything interesting about his relations with Anna Sergeyevna?)

Further on in the story the elements that are antithetic to the earlier love affairs stand out more and more: Gurov does not manage to reduce the memory of Anna to a vague and faded picture of just another love affair; instead of this, he undertakes a journey to see her, thinks of ways to meet her again. At the same time he still regards his relationship with Anna as no different from his other adventures, he keeps emphasizing the analogies between them. At this moment, however, these analogies spring no more from his own thoughts and emotions, but from his conjectures about Anna's life and actions. He supposes that by now she will doubtlessly have started another affair. In a way he projects his former self upon Anna. Consequently, he now assumes the rôle of the cast-off partner: "(on) uže dumal s razdraženiem, čto Anna Sergeevna zabyla o nem i, byt možet, uže razvlekaetsja s drugim (... on) draznil sebja s dosadoju: Vot tebe i dama s sobačkoj ... Vot tebe i priključenie ... Vot i sidi tut." ((he) was already bitterly saying to himself that Anna Sergeyevna had forgotten him and had perhaps been having a good time with someone else (... he) taunted himself in vexation: A lady with a lapdog! Some adventure, I must say! Serves you right!) This is followed by certain text instances, which more emphatically than ever show the untruth of Gurov's original idea that the affair was a mere flirtation, a flirtation now over and done with.

The above mentioned projection of his former self upon Anna is now rejected as absurd. This is subtly and implicitly conveyed in the description of what Anna means to him. The phraseological expression of these antithetic motifs – in a few successive sentences – evokes a strong emotion: this effect is a token of the rush of emotion Gurov suddenly feels. In the first sentence the emotional effect is created by an object clause which reveals – almost hyperbolically – just how important Anna is to Gurov. In the second sentence the many appositions to the subject seem to be a mock inventory of Anna's looks, but the rest of the sentence clearly expresses the fascination she has for Gurov: cf. the object 'žizn'' (life), preceded by the significant modifier 'vsju' (whole), the following compound predicate, the third part of which is modified by the telling word 'edinstvennyj' (only): "... on ponjal jasno, čto dlja nego teper' na vsem svete net bliže, dorože i važnee čeloveka;

ona, zaterjavšajasja v provincial'noj tolpe, èta malen'kaja žen-ščina, ničem ne zamečatel'naja, s vul'garnoj lornetkoj v rukach, napolnjala teper' vsju ego žizn', byla ego gorem, radost'ju, edinstvennym sčast'em ..." (... he realized clearly that there was no one in the world nearer and dearer or more important to him than that little woman with the stupid lorgnette in her hand, who was in no way remarkable. That woman lost in a provincial crowd now filled his whole life, was his misfortune, his joy, and the only happiness that he wished for himself.) (About the syntactic triplicity and its function, here and elsewhere in *Dama s sobačkoj*, see Geir Kjetsaa:65.)

A short emotional passage that follows these sentences, describes a scene which has the character of a pursuit. This is a new and poignant element, that has an antithetic relationship with the vague memories and the not very deep feelings that are connected with the usual pattern of Gurov's adventures. This pursuit is depicted in an effective and very expressive phraseology. Kjetsaa mentions the 'bruchstuckartige Syntax' (i.e. the 'slitnaja konstrukcija' combined with the repetitions of to, po, etc.), which produces the almost breathtaking rhythm (67) (on the various types of repetitions in Čechov and their functions, see Matešić; Čudakov:97-8): "No vot ona vstala i bystro pošla k vychodu; on − za nej, i oba šli bestolkovo, po koridoram, po lestnicam, to podnimajas', to spuskajas' ..." etc. (She got up and walked rapidly towards one of the exits; he followed her, and both of them walked aimlessly along corridors and up and down stairs.) The semantic element 'end', 'finis' (of the affair) stands out in an exclamation, in which the former notion of its already being finished is rejected as impossible and unreal: "on vdrug vspomnil, kak togda večerom na stancii, provodiv Annu Sergeevnu, govoril sebe, čto vse končilos' i, oni uže nikogda ne uvidjatsja. No kak ešče daleko bylo do konca!" (he suddenly remembered how after seeing Anna Sergeyevna off he had told himself that evening at the station that all was over and that they would never meet again. But how far they still were from the end!) The exclamation (reported in free indirect speech) explicitly and emotionally expresses the discontinuance of the analogous relation-

ship. A very subtle aspect here is the element of stress connected with the antithesis: the realization that the affair will
end, is still there, however much it is repressed.

The relationship is continued as if there has never been a
final parting, but over it still hangs the shadow of an unhappy
ending (either because it will prove to be impossible to go on
with it, or because he or she will end it). Anna's words show
her sad presentiments of this: "Ja vse vremja tol'ko dumala o
vas. ... I mne chotelos' zabyt', zabyt', no začem vy priechali",
etc. (I've been thinking of you all the time. And yet I tried so
hard to forget you − why, oh why did you come?) The hopelessness of their relationship gives a tragic tinge to Gurov's
spontaneity, which differs very much from his earlier behaviour in Yalta. Then he only kissed Anna after having made sure
that nobody was looking at them, now he kisses her in the
theatre in full view of two schoolboys on the landing. Anna's
reaction expresses the sad knowledge, which will become
characteristic of the relationship: "Čto vy delaete, čto vy
delaete! My s vami obezumeli ... uezžajte sejčas ... umoljaju ...
Sjuda idut!" etc. (What are you doing? What are you doing?
We've both gone mad. You must go back this minute. I im-
plore you ... Somebody's coming!)

2.5 From then on the relationship with Anna Sergeevna ceases
to be antithetic to Gurov's previous affairs, it is once more the
parallelisms between them, that come to the fore: a (dispersive) chain of parallelisms which presents other similarities and
dissimilarities than the first. These new elements mark the
final phase in Gurov's psychological development, they effect
a different attitude towards both Anna and his earlier loves. It
is not until now, that he fully realizes that he has never really
loved a woman before and that therefore he has never made a
woman happy: "I ni odna iz nich ne byla s nim sčastliva.
Vremja šlo, on znakomilsja, schodilsja, rasstavalsja, no ni razu
ne ljubil; bylo vse, čto ugodno, no tol'ko ne ljubov'." (And not
one of them had ever been happy with him. Time had passed,
he had met women, made love to them, parted from them, but
not once had he been in love; there had been everything

between them, but no love.) He does not even bring happiness to Anna, not even after his realization that she is the woman he loves. This time, it is not the absence of love that causes the unhappiness, it is the fact that love is there. This new form of unhappiness is − indirectly − expressed by Anna, when she and Gurov have met again in the provincial town S.: "Ja nikogda ne byla sčastliva, ja teper' nesčastna, i nikogda, nikogda ne budu sčastliva, nikogda! Ne zastavljajte že menja stradat' ešče bol'še! Kljanus', ja priedu v Moskvu. A teper' rasstanemsja! Moj milyj, dobryj, dorogoj moj, rasstanemsja!" (I've never been happy, I'm unhappy now, and I shall never be happy, never! So please don't make me suffer still more. I swear I'll come to you in Moscow. But now we must part. Oh, my sweet, my darling, we must part!) This new unhappiness is connected with something that was characteristic of Gurov's previous affairs ànd of their relationship in Yalta: the need of concealment. At the time, this was the concealment of the affair as such, now it is their love that must be secret. In Gurov's past affairs, and in Yalta the need of concealment did not spring from love, but from the pretense of love: he always knew of his affairs that they would end, and secrecy was a necessary precaution to secure their eventual endings (with the minimum of emotional complications). Now the need of concealment is a most frustrating element in the relationship, it is incompatible with their love. Anna Sergeevna implicitly expresses the impossibility of a secret love-affair at their reunion: she confesses that she has constantly thought of Gurov, that her memories of him are more precious to her than her real existence; but she also asks him more than once: "Začem vy priechali? Začem?" (Why did you come? Why?) Later text-fragments widen the implications of this question: they come to reflect Anna's tragic awareness of the fact that the necessary secrecy will probably destroy their love.

At the end of the story their love and unhappiness are expressed twice, from two different narrative perspectives. The first time, they are expressed in the narrator's representation of Anna's state of mind: "Ona plakala ot volnenija, ot skorb-nogo soznanija, čto ich žizn' tak pečal'no složilas'; oni vidjatsja

tol'ko tajno, skryvajutsja ot ljudej, kak vory! Razve žizn' ich
ne razbita?" (She wept because she could not control her
emotions, because she was bitterly conscious of the fact that
their life was so sad: they could only meet in secret, they had
to hide from people, like thieves! Was not their life ruined?)
The narrator's observations again fall within Gurov's perspective. A rhythmically suggestive passage, which is, as it were, a
symbiosis of the narrator's, Anna's and Gurov's perspectives,
expresses these feelings for the second time: "Anna Sergeevna
i on ljubili drug druga, kak očen' blizkie, rodnye ljudi, kak
muž i žena, kak nežnye druz'ja; im kazalos', čto sama sud'ba
prednaznačila ich drug dlja druga, i bylo neponjatno, dlja čego
on ženat, a ona zamužem; i točno èto byli dve pereletnye
pticy, samec i samka, kotorych pojmali i zastavili žit' v ot-
del'nych kletkach. Oni prostili drug drugu to, čego stydilis' v
svoem prošlom, proščali vse v nastojaščem i čuvstvovali, čto èta
ich ljubov' izmenila ich oboich." (He and Anna Sergeyevna
loved each other as people do who are very dear and near, as
man and wife or close friends love each other; they could not
help feeling that fate itself had intended them for one another,
and they were unable to understand why he should have a wife
and she a husband; they were like two migrating birds, male
and female, who had been caught and forced to live in separate
cages. They had forgiven each other what they had been
ashamed of in the past, and forgave each other everything in
their present, and felt that this love of theirs had changed
them both.) The last sentence of this quotation introduces a
novel difference in the parallels between Gurov's other love-
relations and this one. It strongly sets off this love against all
the other affairs, including the one with Anna in Yalta. The
novel difference is to be found in Gurov's attitude towards
himself and his partner: he is now prepared to face the truth
of things, to acknowledge his partner's unhappiness, he no
longer seeks to justify himself with all manner of fallacies. The
next sentence expresses this difference explicitly: "Prežde, v
grustnye minuty on uspokaival sebja vsjakimi rassuždenijami,
... teper' že ... on čuvstvoval glubokoe sostradanie, chotelos'
byt' iskrennim, nežnym ..." (Before, when he felt depressed,

he had comforted himself by all sorts of arguments ... but now ... he felt profound compassion, he longed to be sincere, tender ...)

A characteristic difference with the past affairs, is the significance of its (possible) ending. In the past, when starting an affair Gurov always realized from the outset that it must eventually be cut off. This always was a bitter and long process, of which he refused to think at an affair's charming beginning. Now, the possible ending of the relationship is something inconceivable. Gurov is, to some extent, able to rationalize about it, Anna can't. Emotionally neither of them can face this possibility. The end of which they dream, is a way out of their present situation, out of the deceit, the secrecy it necessitates. Thus, for them 'end' means the beginning of a new life. In the background of their thoughts, however, there still is the other image of 'end', i.e. the disruption of the relationship. This image can be detected in earlier passages, in which it is especially Anna, who intimates the hopelessness of this love. In the final passages this insoluble problem is more than once explicitly indicated, from both their perspectives ("Kak osvobodit'sja ot ètich nevynosimych put?" (How were they to free themselves from these intolerable chains?)) and from Gurov's ("Kak? Kak? — sprašival on, chvataja sebja za golovu. Kak?" (How? How? he asked himself, clutching his head. How?)).

The whole point of the story is, in fact, centered in the ambiguity with which the word 'end' is echoed through it. Its last passage shows their desire to bring the end within reach, not the disrupting end, but the other: the extrication from the ties that impede a new beginning: "I kazalos', čto ešče nemnogo — i rešenie budet najdeno, i togda načnetsja novaja, prekrasnaja žizn'; i oboim bylo jasno, čto do konca ešče daleko-daleko, i čto samoe složnoe i trudnoe tol'ko ešče načinaetsja." (And it seemed to them that in just a little more time a solution would be found and a new beautiful life would begin; but both of them knew very well that the end was still a long, long way away and that the most complicated and difficult part was only just beginning.)

This final passage is the more poignant, because of the increasing expressiveness in the preceding fragments, which describe the love, the unhappiness, and Anna's and Gurov's position as social outcasts. Thus, Cechov draws the story to a close that is satisfactory to his artistic genius. About such a satisfactory ending, he himself said: "My instincts tell me that at the end of a story I must present the reader with a condensation of its whole impact, and therefore I must recall for however short a moment every person, who has figured in the story." (Letter to A. N. Pleščeev, September 30, 1889).

My addition to this statement of Čechov is this: the end of *Dama s sobačkoj* evokes such strong associations with the whole of the preceding story, because in it the story's prevailing chains of oppositions come to an intriguing conclusion. There are various chains of oppositions at the action level. The last of them, introducing new parallels between Gurov's old affairs and the relationship with Anna, is definitely the most important. It is the most important, because it is the last chain, because it shows the greatest expressiveness and because it disturbs the preceding balance of analogies and parallelisms. This last chain of parallelisms injects various preceding fragments with new, potential, semantic features, i.e. those fragments, that at first seemed to set forth the analogies between the affair in Yalta and the other affairs. After the reader has read the last phase in the development of the relationship with Anna, he may suspect that in Yalta Gurov was much more involved, than he cared to admit. The fragments that follow the Yalta episode, describe Gurov's futile endeavours to forget. These episodes together seem to actualize a semantic aspect, which may be described as an irrational, overwhelming experience of romance. (Kjetsaa argues that even in the first part of the story this is sometimes apparent in the phraseology: 64; it seems to be significant in this respect, that in the final version of the story some passages in Chapter I have been deleted. Cf. Papernyj:119.)

3. *The level of the characterization*

At the level of the characterization there are antithetical
oppositions (contrasts) between passages referring to Gurov's
wife and passages referring to Anna Sergeevna. There are
passages that set forth contrasts between Gurov and his wife,
and passages that bring out antitheses between Anna and her
husband. There is a (dispersive) chain of motifs that describe
Anna's inner and outer characterization (they are, of course,
partly identical with those that contrast Anna with Gurov's
wife). There is another such chain, describing Gurov – though
his personal traits are for the greater part hidden behind his
actions. I will discuss this aspect later on in greater detail, because – as I have said before – the dominant thematic level is
that of Gurov's characterization. All the other series are, of
course, subordinated to this dominant level, and their main
function is to set forth the process of Gurov's gradually growing insight into himself.

3.1 In the contrast between the two women, Gurov's wife
functions mainly to set forth Anna (both her general appearance and her psychology). The characteristic features of
Gurov's wife are only mentioned once (with the exception of
one sentence, which equals her in some respects with one type
of woman in Gurov's classification). The aspects that are connected with Anna, however, turn up repeatedly and do so in
many variations. These variations spring from differences in
the narrator's emotional and intellectual approach. Since the
narrator's perspective is nearly always based upon Gurov's, it
sometimes brings out the contrasts between Anna and his wife
very effectively. When Anna first appears in the story, she is
no more than one of the minor particulars of the sea-resort.
The narrator hides himself behind Gurov, who is presented in
the first paragraph as a representative of the 'boulevardiers'.
The first sentence is of the indefinite-personal type, a verbum
dicendi followed by a clause that tells of the appearance of a
new person on the boulevard, a lady with a lapdog. The second
sentence begins with the words "Dmitrij Dmitrič Gurov". It is

through his eyes that this lady is described as a young woman, small and fair-haired. All these attributes stand out in opposition with Gurov's wife. She seems to be almost twice as old as Gurov (in the course of the story Gurov appears to be almost twice as old as Anna) and she is a tall woman with black brows. This information about Gurov's wife is to be found in the very condensed description the narrator gives of Gurov's life and background. Though the narrator's perspective in this description is identical with Gurov's, he displays at times gaps in his knowledge, at times a certain reticence in connection with Gurov's opinions. This reticence is quite obvious, when he tells that Gurov was often unfaithful to his wife and that therefore 'perhaps' he always spoke ill of women, and would describe them as 'the lower breed'. The same paragraph contains more information about Gurov's wife, partly provided by the narrator, partly decidedly connected with Gurov's perspective. The narrator calls her 'erect, dignified, austere' and tells us she likes to describe herself as a 'thinking person'. He also tells us that Gurov secretly thinks her 'not particularly intelligent, narrow-minded and inelegant' and that he is 'afraid of her'.

More contrasts between Anna and Gurov's wife can be found in a passage describing Gurov's thoughts after his first meeting with Anna, and in later passages, that describe the scenes in Anna's room. In the former passage Gurov recalls Anna's youth, the angularity and diffidence she displayed in her conversation with him. He reflects that there is something pitiful in her appearance: "skol'ko ešče nesmelosti, uglovatosti bylo v ee smeche, v razgovore s neznakomym" (how much diffidence and angularity there was in her laughter and her conversation with a stranger) and "Čto-to v nej est' žalkoe vse-taki, – podumal on i stal zasypat'." (There's something pathetic about her all the same, he thought as he fell asleep.) In the descriptions of the scenes in Anna's room her 'nesmelost' ' and 'uglovatost' ' are more than once mentioned. These elements are always connected with her youth and naïveté (as they were the first time, in Gurov's thoughts). The perspective from which they are seen, is always Gurov's. He registers

her reactions, and his registrations are transmitted to the
reader via the narrator. The motifs of her behaviour and
actions thus come to sketch her emotions as well. This also
applies to Gurov: the actional motifs reveal his emotional reactions. Čiževskij's words "... the events are broken up and re-
shaped in people's psyches" (58) seem to be quite appropriate
here. Of great psychological relevance is the indirect characterization, which is to be found in passages where we are presented with the conversation between Gurov and Anna (especially
of the latter). Elements of Anna's speech in the hotel room for
a moment recall Gurov's wife. Cf. Anna's flow of words and
the 's izlišnimi razgovorami' of Gurov's wife, Anna's exclamations expressing her search for a different kind of life and the
words that are said about Gurov's wife: "to byla ne ljubov', ne
strast', a čto-to bolee značitel'noe" (it were not love or passion, but something much more significant.) The fact that
Anna's words make Gurov momentarily think she is play-
acting or joking, is reminiscent of what was said about love in
connection with Gurov's wife: "bez iskrennosti ... manerno"
(without sincerity ... affectedly). All these correspondences,
however, intensify the contrasts: Anna is not joking, she does
not play a part, her speech is that of a woman, who instinctive-
ly feels to be misunderstood. Gurov realizes her sincerity, but
at first he fails to grasp the tenure of her appeals to him. At
this stage of the story, Anna's diffidence and angularity come
to be more suggestive, and they are enlarged with elements of
fear and vulnerability. Think, for instance, of the sentence that
precedes Gurov's caresses and tender words with which he
ends her outburst: "On smotrel ej v nepodvižnye, ispugannye
glaza." (He gazed into her staring frightened eyes.) When
Gurov meets Anna again in the wretched provincial town of S.
her diffidence, angularity and her smallness are augmented
with the element 'nondescript': "ona, zaterjavšajasja v provincial'noj tolpe, èta malen'kaja ženščina, ničem ne zamečatel'naja ..." (who was in no way remarkable. That woman lost
in a provincial crowd ...) These seemingly negative aspects
suddenly become extremely important (subjectively and
emotionally) in the following change in Gurov's perspective,

and in the phrase that introduces that change: "dlja nego na vsem svete net bliže i dorože čeloveka" (there was no one in the world nearer and dearer or more important to him); and "napolnjala teper' vsju ego žizn' " (now filled his whole life) etc. As I have said in the section devoted to the action level, the description is almost hyperbolic.

3.2 In the same passage Anna's beauty is mentioned: "... on dumal o tom, kak ona choroša" (he thought how beautiful she was). Because this remark clashes so strongly with 'ničem ne zamečatel'naja' it acquires a very subjective significance. Anna's attractiveness (of which her youth is sometimes an integral part) is a repeatedly varied motif in the story. It turns up in paragraphs with a different thematic dominance and a different emotional and intellectual approach of the narrator (who always shares his perspective with Gurov, sometimes even leaves the comments to Gurov). Anna's beauty is first mentioned by the narrator in a sententious statement about an experience, shared by all human beings ("gluchoj šum morja ... govoril o pokoe, o večnom sne, kakoj ožidaet nas" (hollow roar of the sea ... spoke of rest, of eternal sleep awaiting us all, etc.). This statement exclusively represents the narrator's perspective. Then the narrator's voice mingles with Gurov's, and it is from their combined perspectives that we are told of Anna's youth and loveliness: "Sidja rjadom s molodoj ženščinoj, kotoraja na rassvete kazalas' takoj krasivoj, ... Gurov dumal o tom, kak v suščnosti ... vse prekrasno na ètom svete, vse, krome togo, čto my sami myslim i delaem ..." (Sitting beside a young woman, who looked so beautiful at the break of day ... Gurov reflected that, when you came to think of it, everything in the world was really beautiful, everything but our own thoughts and actions ...) They are mentioned in much greater detail later on in the story, but with a less absolute and with a strongly subjective connotation: the story describes the first phase of Gurov's amorous pursuit, and he "govoril Anne Sergeevne o tom, kak ona choroša, kak soblaznitel'na ..." (told Anna Sergeyevna that she was beautiful, that she was desirable ...) etc. Further on, the narrator reveals the exalted character of Gurov's new attitude towards Anna. When he discovers, that he cannot forget her, he begins to idealize her: "Zakryvši glaza, on videl ee, kak živuju, i ona kazalas' krasivee, molože, nežnee, čem byla." (Closing his eyes, he saw her as clearly as if she were before him, and she seemed to him lovelier, younger and tenderer than she had been.) The fourth mention of Anna's beauty is made by Gurov in direct speech, when he cannot restrain himself and says, when leaving the Medical club: "Esli b vy znali, s kakoj očarovatel'noj ženščinoj ja poznakomilsja v Jalte!" (If you knew what a fascinating woman I met in Yalta!) I have already quoted the fifth reference to it. In this passage, the increasing expressiveness seems to reach its climax, because of the intriguing co-occurrence of derision ("èta malen'kaja ženščina, ničem ne zamečatel'naja") and exaggeration ("na vsem svete net bliže, dorože i nežnee čeloveka"). A strongly subjective attitude seems to be apparent, too, in the words: "on dumal o tom, kak ona choroša. Dumal i mečtal".

There is, however, a sixth instance, in which Anna's beauty is even more emphatically connected with subjectivity and intimacy. This instance is to be found at the point of the story where the mutual love and affection between Anna and Gurov is unmistakable: "on počuvstvoval sostradanie k ètoj žizni, ešče takoj teploj i krasivoj, no, verojatno, uže blizkoj k tomu, čtoby načat' bleknut' i vjanut', kak ego žizn'." (he felt so sorry for this life, still so warm and beautiful, but probably soon to fade and wilt like his own.) Curious here, is the narrator's attitude. The description lacks the subjective quality that characterized the preceding passages, the expressiveness of the description is solely due to the narrator's emotional paraphrase. The immediately following sentence, however, re-establishes the subjective phraseology of the narrative mode: "Za čto ona ego ljubit tak?" (Why did she love him so?) etc.

3.3 The way in which Anna Sergeevna is characterized, allows us to infer different dispersive chains of variations, related to distinct semantic components (f.i. her beauty) or combinations of them (f.i. her beauty and her youth). Again and again these variations underline the implicit contrast with Gurov's wife. This contrast sets forth Anna's inner and outer individuality (Gurov's wife always represents the negative side). It also provides a potential explanation for Anna's irresistable attraction to Gurov. Another contrast is that between Anna and her husband. Though his officiousness and his snobbish demeanor are varied in only a few remote fragments, they decidedly clash with Anna's emotional craving for 'something better', for 'a different kind of life'. This contrast provides a potential explanation for the willingness with which Anna yields to Gurov's wishes in Yalta.

The husband-wife relation does not need many elaborated specifications in the story, because of the many literary connotations it evokes in the reader's mind. Think, for instance, of the relationship between Anna Karenina (emotional, lively, artistic) and Karenin (officious, impassive), which in itself offers a potential reason for Anna's liaison with Vronskij.

3.4 Gurov and his wife form another contrasting pair. It is from the combined perspectives of the narrator and Gurov, that we are told about this contrast in some remote text segments. She is a dominant woman, talkative, affected, non-artistic, he is dominated (afraid of her), taciturn, the very opposite of affected, artistic. These elements are only mentioned occasionally and indirectly. Gurov's artisticity appears for instance from these sentences: "po obrazovaniju filolog ... gotovilsja kogda-to pet' v častnoj opere" (he was a graduate in philology ... thought of singing in a private opera company), "vtajne sčital ee (ženu) nedalekoj, uzkoj, neizjaščnoj." (he secretly considered her not particularly intelligent, narrow-minded and inelegant.) These aspects are emphasized once more, when we are told that she doesn't write hard signs in her spelling and addresses her husband as Dimitrij instead of Dmitrij. This stresses not only her inartisticity, but also her affectedness. As I have said, the implicit contrasts between Gurov and his wife are a potential causality of his marital unfaithfulness in general, of his liaison with Anna in particular. The causal connection is almost directly expressed, since the rather unpleasant picture of Gurov's wife (given from his perspective) is immediately followed by "Izmenjat' ej on načal uže davno, izmenjal často" (He had been unfaithful to her for a long time, he was often unfaithful to her).

3.5 Between Anna and Gurov parallels can be drawn: motifs and clusters of motifs – occurring throughout the text – form a dispersive chain of parallelisms. The comparable features pertain to the fact, that both seek an adventure, that both are, to a greater or lesser extent, frustrated by their home-lives. Against this common background, the dissimilarities between them can clearly be observed: his experience, her timidity and angularity; his hunting for momentary pleasures, her desire for a better and different kind of life. In another fragment, Gurov's character seems to have an affinity with Anna's sense of guilt (and again with her desire for a better life). This is the fragment (which I have quoted above), where the narrator gives utterance to a more or less universal truth. He then connects this pronouncement with Gurov's thoughts and declares in rather general terms (using the personal pronoun 'we') that basically everything in the world is beautiful, except our thoughts and actions. To the reader, this statement will have a discordant quality, because Gurov does not react when Anna expresses her desire for a better life, a different kind of life. He fails to understand her aversion of the adultery, which this desire has led her to commit. Not only does he fail to understand this, it even looks as if he is deliberately making use of her emotional instability.

These conflicting elements, however, require additional, explanatory information. They are indeed complemented later on and, in a way, explained in the chains of motifs, related to Gurov's changing attitude towards Anna and towards all his former affairs. I have talked about this before, in connection with the interrelations between the constituents of the action level. Gurov comes to look with different eyes at the bitter and painful final stages of his past affairs. He comes to think less of himself, but gradually realizes, that he has always made his partners unhappy. He comes to realize, that now he does

not feel the need anymore to clear himself from guilt by thinking of all manner of justifications. There are not many fragments that directly express the changes in Gurov's mentality.
These changes are, as it were, the invisible incentive in the
sequence of the different types of oppositional chains.

It is, indeed, these chains, that reflect Gurov's mental
process, inherent to which are his changing evaluations of the
past and the present, both at the level of the action and that of
the social/geographical setting.

I will now briefly discuss the latter level.

4. *The social setting*

In the first chapter there is a slight indication of Gurov's position in his Moscow environment, apparently referring to a
male community. It is to be found in one of the already mentioned introductory passages. This passage is mainly concerned
with Gurov's characterization: "V obščestve mužčin emu bylo
skučno, ne po sebe, s nimi on byl nerazgovorčiv, choloden, no
kogda nachodilsja sredi ženščin ..." (He was bored and ill at
ease among men, with whom he was reticent and cold, but
when he was among women ...) etc. This information will
appear to have been deficient further on in the story. There it
proves to be incongruous with other facts: the necessary explanatory additions are given in the final phase of the story.

4.1 At the beginning of Chapter III the affair with Anna
seems to be ended, and Gurov has returned to Moscow. In the
first paragraph the town is described in a very positive way
(from Gurov's perspective). First a picture of Moscow itself is
given: the first frosts, the snow, the sleighs, the benignant lime
trees and birches, white with rime. All this is explicitly
opposed to the palms and cypresses of Yalta, to the mountains
and the sea, and implicitly to the heat and the dust etc. In the
second paragraph, this contrast is even more elaborated, half-
way the paragraph it is extended with social aspects. These
would have been additional positive aspects of Moscow, if the

narrator had not inserted some slight ironically-tinted comments. Apart from this disruption of Gurov's perspective, the repetition of the word 'uže' (translated as 'once more', 'once again') suggests a certain inauthenticity, hints at a mental effort to take up the old life again: "Malo-pomalu on okunulsja v Moskovskuju žizn', uže s žadnost'ju pročityval po tri gazety v den' i govoril, čto ne čitaet moskovskich gazet iz principa. Ego uže tjanulo v restorany, kluby, na zvanye obedy, jubilei, i uže emu bylo lestno, čto u nego byvajut izvestnye advokaty i artisty, i čto v doktorskom klube on igraet v karty s professorom. Uže on mog s"est' celuju porciju seljanki na skovorode ..." (Gradually he became immersed in Moscow life, eagerly reading three newspapers a day and declaring that he never read Moscow papers on principle. Once more he could not resist the attraction of restaurants, clubs, banquets, and anniversary celebrations, and once more he felt flattered that well-known lawyers and actors came to see him and that in the Medical Club he played cards with a professor as his partner. Once again he was capable of eating a whole portion of the Moscow speciality of sour cabbage and meat served in a frying-pan ...)

Further on in Chapter III, however, the whole contrast with Yalta is reversed. This happens in connection with Gurov's ineffectual attempts to forget the liaison with Anna: he constantly remembers the pier, the early mornings with the mist on the mountains. The vivid picture of Moscow disappears, and, what is more, its very positive social aspects of the second paragraph, are now presented in a negative way. This happens in connection with Gurov's futile attempt to rouse the interest of his partner at cards for his Yalta-encounter. The man answers, that Gurov had been quite right in saying that the sturgeon had gone off. The next paragraph may be seen as an antithetic opposition to the second paragraph of Chapter III, which gave a positive representation of social life in Moscow. We see a number of exclamations in free indirect speech, which voice Gurov's indignation about the barbarous, stupid life in Moscow. In a way, this can be seen as a relationship between text fragments, which is based upon a contradiction.

The antithesis (or contradiction) is weakened, however, by the ironic touch and the suggestion of inauthenticity and of mental effort in the preceding paragraph. The creditableness of the initial positive picture of Moscow has already been affected in that passage. In the next oppositional fragment the rose-tinted picture is completely distorted: "Kakie dikie nravy, kakie lica! Čto za bestolkovye noči, kakie neinteresnye, nezametnye dni! Neistovaja igra v karty, obžorstvo, p'janstvo, postojannye razgovory vse ob odnom. Nenužnye dela i razgovory vse ob odnom otchvatyvajut na svoju dolju lučšuju čast' vremeni, lučšie sily, i v konce koncov ostaetsja kakaja-to kucaja, beskrylaja žizn', kakaja-to čepucha, i ujti i bežat' nel'zja, točno sidiš' v sumasšedšem dome, ili v arrestantskich rotach!" (What savage manners! What faces! What stupid nights! What uninteresting, wasted days! Crazy gambling at cards, gluttony, drunkenness, endless talk about one and the same thing. Business that was of no use to anyone and talk about one and the same thing absorbed the greater part of one's time and energy, and what was left in the end was a sort of dock-tailed, barren life, a sort of nonsensical existence, and it was impossible to escape from it, just as though you were in a lunatic asylum or a convict chain-gang!)

The second part of this quotation has its echoes in certain utterances of both Gurov and Anna (in the narrator's representation of them). These utterances condemn the social environment in which they are emprisoned: the word 'prison' is quite appropriate for their situation. Thus, the antithetic opposition is extended over more than one fragment. It is noteworthy that this extension, this formation of a dispersive chain of oppositions of a negative Moscow vs. a positive Moscow, is based upon another important opposition: the antithesis between Gurov's life in Moscow and his life with Anna. I use the word 'noteworthy', because the extension has the consequence that the relationship with Anna is now not only opposed to Gurov's previous affairs, but also to his everyday life, to the private and social aspects of it: marriage, position, club.

The extended chain of oppositions becomes more and more refined by the addition of semantic components like 'sham', 'hollow', 'show' (referring to Gurov's life with his wife) vs. 'sincere', 'genuine', 'secrecy' (referring to the relationship with Anna). Let me quote a couple of sentences from a paragraph in the first half of Chapter IV: "U nego byli dve žizni: odna javnaja, ... polnaja uslovnoj pravdy i uslovnogo obmana ... i drugaja – protekavšaja tajno ... vse, čto bylo dlja nego važno, interesno, neobchodimo, v čem on byl iskrenen i ne obmany-val sebja, čto sostavljalo zerno ego žizni, proischodilo tajno ot drugich, vse že, čto bylo ego lož'ju, ego oboločkoj, v kotoruju on prjatalsja, čtoby skryt' pravdu, kak, naprimer, ego služba v banke, spory v klube, ego 'nizšaja rasa', choždenie s ženoj na jubilei, – vse èto bylo javno." (He led a double life: one for all who were interested to see, full of conventional truth and con-ventional deception ... and another which went on in secret ... everything that was important, interesting, essential, every-thing about which he was sincere and did not deceive himself, everything that made up the quintessence of his life, went on in secret, while everything that was a lie, everything that was merely the husk in which he hid himself to conceal the truth, like his work at the bank, for instance, his discussions at the club, his ideas of the lower breed, his going to anniversary functions with his wife – all that happened in the sight of all.) The opposition 'genuine life' vs. 'sham façade' is also present in Anna's speech, which is reproduced in free indirect speech. Here, the emphasis lies upon the fact that real and genuine values must be hidden, as if they were criminal: "Ona plakala ... ot skorbnogo soznanija, čto ich žizn' tak pečal'no složilas'; oni vidjatsja tol'ko tajno, skryvajutsja ot ljudej, kak vory! Razve žizn' ich ne razbita?" (She wept because she ... was bitterly conscious of the fact that their life was so sad: they could only meet in secret, they had to hide from people, like thieves! Was not their life ruined?)

4.2 Anna's environment – the provincial town S. – comes to the fore in Gurov's vision of it (which, again, conincides with the narrator's). In S. everything is grey. The different aspects of the town might be said to form a dispersive chain of varia-tions upon the theme 'grey'. The colour 'grey' becomes symbolic of the dull, dreary life in S. (cf. Kjetsaa:66). In Gurov's hotel "pol byl obtjanut serym soldatskim suknom" (the floor was covered with a fitted carpet of military grey cloth), "na stole černil'nica, seraja ot pyli" (an inkstand grey with dust on the table), "on sidel na posteli, pokrytoj deševym serym, točno bol'ničnym odejalom" (he sat on a bed covered by a cheap grey blanket, looking exactly like a hospital blanket). Anna's house is surrounded by a "zabor, seryj, dlinnyj, s gvozdjami. – Ot takogo zabora ubežiš', – dumal Gurov ..." (long grey fence studded with upturned nails. A fence like that would make anyone wish to run away – thought Gurov ... .) The local theatre, the audience, the orchestra are only briefly outlined. What happened in the opposition Moscow/negative and Moscow/positive happens again in these brief outlines. In the Moscow-opposition, a connection arose with another opposition: the suffocating influence of the social environment versus their love. The milieu of S. may be incorporated in that oppositional chain, but there are a few instances where Gurov's love for Anna forms a radiant contrast with the provincial banality. Cf. for instance: "I pod zvuki plochogo orkestra, drjannych obyvatel'skich skripok, on dumal o tom, kak ona choroša" (Listening to the bad orchestra and the wretched violins played by second-rate musicians, he thought how beautiful she was); cf. also the moment in the theatre when Gurov follows Anna to the exit: "O, gospodi! I k čemu èti ljudi, ètot orkestr ..." (Oh Lord, what are all these people, that orchestra, doing here?)

5. *Conclusions*

There are a number of oppositional chains in *Lady with Lapdog*: the antithesis Moscow-Yalta; the reversion in the positive and negative approach to these towns; the contradictory statements about the social life of Moscow; the variations of 'grey', connected with S.; the variations in Gurov's and Anna's Yalta-relationship; the subsequent chains of parallelisms and analogies (all resulting from the projection of characteristic features of the love-affair upon other, preceding motifs); the shifts from analogies to antitheses and vice versa (establishing either dominant similarities or dominant dissimilarities between the habitual pattern of Gurov's affairs and the post-Yalta situation); the ultimate discontinuance of this alternation in a chain of parallelisms, in which the differences between the old affairs and the post-Yalta relationship prevail; there are the actual realization, the extension, the refinement and the several phases in the exposure of the contrasts between Anna Sergeevna and Gurov's wife; the same stratagems establish a parallel relationship between Anna and Gurov, an antithetic relationship between her and her husband; apart from that, they set forth a chain of variations pertaining to Anna's personality. All these chains (of partly overlapping oppositions) are determined by the narrator's variable insight into his protagonists, by the narrator's variable rational and emotional approaches. Since his point of view almost constantly — there are a very few authoritative instances — coincides with Gurov's, the changes in it implicitly exhibit the latter's psychological development: this development actually dominates the story. It may be described as a gradual process of emotional and moral awakening (at first hardly acknowledged, then for a long time subject to uncertainties). This process is evident in Gurov's emotional metamorphosis with respect to Anna Sergeevna, in the change in his evaluations of his earlier love-affairs, in his changing attitude towards his social environment. In all this actional elements take the central place. The oppositions at the two other levels are provoked by them (most of all those at the level of the geographical-social setting, cf. the contradictory, inconsistent and contrastive descriptions of Moscow and Yalta). The opposition of a positive Moscow and a negative Yalta is established, when Gurov tries to label his liaison with Anna as just one more affair. The condemnation of Moscow follows as a result of the post-Yalta events. The Yalta and post-Yalta episodes also determine the oppositions that are connected with the inner and outer characterization of Anna Sergeevna: cf. the changing approach to her beauty, to her naïveté and her confusion. This also has its effects upon the contrasts between Anna Sergeevna and Gurov's wife: it gives a subtle finishing touch to them.

There are four successive (often alternating) chains of oppositions at the action level: parallelisms, analogies, antitheses and another chain of parallelisms. This last chain of motifs is the most important; the parallelisms and analogies in the first two chapters are the least important. From the events in these chapters we may infer Gurov's seemingly immobile disposition of mind. One aspect of this disposition is what he considers the 'bizarre' element in the relationship with Anna, i.e. her sense of guilt etc. (the first chain of parallelisms). A second aspect is Gurov's cold-heartedness, his unsympathizing approach to Anna's remorseful bewilderment, his treating her with the mechanical routine, which he obviously has acquired in his previous affairs (the chain of analogies). I have used the word 'immobile' as an apparent characteristic of Gurov's disposition of mind, because at this point of the story the reader will deduce its possible ending from this very characteristic: at the close of the second chapter he will expect the story to end with the ending of the affair, this ending being the result of the total lack of understanding between the two lovers. Anna does not realize that Gurov is only diverting himself, Gurov does not realize that Anna loves him. Surprisingly enough, the story continues. The alternating chains of analogies and antitheses now present the Yalta and post-Yalta incidents as just one more love-affair, now as a unique experience of love. There is a touch of irony in the sometimes abrupt alternation between analogous and antithetic text moments, i.e. between the notion of the affair with Anna being identical with the other affairs, and the notion of the singular, exceptional quality of the affair with Anna. All the same, it is these alternations that undermine Gurov's seemingly immobile standpoint in the first half of the story. As such they effect the transition to the last and most important chain of parallelisms. The dominance of this last chain is the result of two things: 1) the appreciative position which is taken by the narrator, 2) the fact that this chain leads to the final phase of the process of Gurov's psychological awakening, though there is no final outcome of the story's events. This, however, agrees with the narrative device of the use of an intriguing 'open' ending as the salient feature, the 'point' of the story.

The last chain shows Gurov's emotional and rational change-over: he acknowledges the fact that he loves, and inside him love awakens pity, sincerity and understanding. These new feelings, of course, have their effect upon Gurov's view of what happened after Yalta, but they also change his views of his pre-Yalta life and of the Yalta-episode itself. Various aspects of the Yalta-episode now appear to have a possible different interpretation: he may have been much more in-volved at Yalta, than he thought at the time. The descriptions of his loving caresses become overtures of later text-fragments, that describe his deep and sincere feelings for Anna. The former passages now appear to contain a sincere, though un-acknowledged, emotion. His original attitude towards the affair appears to have been presented uncompletely. What has been presented as truth, is revealed to be untrue: cf. Gurov's initial attitude towards the relationship with Anna, his initial opinions about Anna herself, his view of himself, of Moscow, of Yalta. In other words: potential semantic features are actualized in a regressive way. As a specific result of this regressive re-orientation, text fragments, which at first reading seemed to be slightly 'out of place', appear to be relevant to Gurov's belated emotional/rational awakening: think, for in-stance, of his generalization about the beauty of life and the contrast in it with human thought and actions. Thus the final and hierarchically superior chain begins to run through the whole story, it supplements deficient information, sets forth new implications and reveals the main thematic issue of the story: the process of Gurov's growing self-knowledge.

REFERENCES

Auzinger, Hélène
    1960   "Čechov und das Nicht-zu-Ende-sprechen", *Die Welt der Slaven* 5, 233-44.

Bachtin, Michail
    1963   *Problemy poètiki Dostoevskogo* (Moskva).
Barthes, Roland
    1966   "Introduction à l'analyse structurale des récits", *Communications* 8, 1-27.
Booth, Wayne C.
    1961   *The Rhetoric of Fiction* (Chicago-London).
Bremond, Claude
    1964   "Le message narratif", *Communications* 4, 4-32.
    1966   "La logique des possibles narratifs", *Communications* 8, 60-76.
Chizhevsky, Dmitri
    1967   "Chekhov in the Development of Russian Literature", in: Robert L. Jackson, ed., *Chekhov. A Collection of Critical Essays* (Englewood Cliffs, N.J.), 49-61. Abridged version of Chizhevsky's study published in: T. Eekman, ed., *Anton Čechov: 1860-1960. Some Essays* (Leiden, 1960).
Čudakov, Aleksandr P.
    1971   *Poètika Čechova* (Moskva).
Doležel, Lubomír
    1967   "The Typology of the Narrator: Point of View in Fiction", in: *To Honor Roman Jakobson* I (The Hague), 541-52.
    1972   "From motifemes to Motifs", *Poetics* 4, 55-90.
    1976a   "Narrative Modalities", *Journal of Literary Semantics*, vol. V/1, 5-14.
    1976b   "Narrative Semantics", *PTL. A Journal for Descriptive Poetics and Theory of Literature*, vol. I/1, 129-51.
    1976c   "*Die Hundeblume* or: Poetic Narrative", *PTL*, vol. I/3, 467-88.
Dorovatovskaja-Ljubimova, V. S.
    1928   "Idiot Dostoevskogo i ugolovnaja chronika ego vremeni", *Pečat' i revoljucija* 3, 31-53.
Dostoevskij, Fedor M.
    1928-1934 *Pis'ma I-III*. Pod red. i s prim. A. S. Dolinina (Moskva-Leningrad).
    1958   *The Brothers Karamazov*. Tr. by David Magarshack (Penguin Books Ltd, Middlesex, England; repr. 1967).
Eng, Jan van der
    1968   "Les récits de Belkin: Analogie des procédés de construction", in: Jan van der Eng, A. G. F. van Holk, Jan M. Meijer, *The Tales of Belkin by A. S. Puškin* (The Hague-Paris), 9-60.
    1973a   "Le procédé du suspense dans la première partie de *Crime et Châtiment*", *Russian Literature* 4, 72-86.
    1973b   "Priem: central'nyj faktor semantičeskogo postroenija povestvovatel'nogo teksta", in: Jan van der Eng and Mojmír

Grygar, *Structure of Texts and Semiotics of Culture* (The Hague-Paris), 29-58.

1977 (forthcoming) "Semantic Dynamics in Narrative Texts", to appear in: Dean Worth, ed., *Russian Poetics*.

Flaubert, Gustave
1963 *Extraits de la Correspondance* (Paris).

Forster, E. M.
1927 *Aspects of the Novel* (London; repr. 1958).

Ginzburg, Lidija
1973 "O strukture literaturnogo personaža", in: *Isskustvo slova. K 80-letiju D. Blagogo* (Moskva), 376-88.

Gorodetzky, Nadejda
1951 *Saint Tikhon Zadonsky. Inspirer of Dostoyevsky* (London).

Groot, A. W. de
1964 *Inleiding tot de algemene taalwetenschap* (Groningen; 2e, herziene druk).

Hrushovski, Benjamin
1974 "Principles of a Unified Theory of the Literary Text", in: Ziva Ben-Porat & Benjamin Hrushovski, *Papers on Poetics and Semiotics* 1 (Tel-Aviv; pre-publication paper), 13-23.

Kjetsaa, Geir
1971 "Tschechows Novellenkunst. Versuch einer Analyse der Erzählung *Die Dame mit dem Hündchen*", *Čechoslovenska Rusistika* 2, 60-68.

Lotman, Jurij M.
1964 *Lekcii po struktural'noj poètike* (Tartu).
1970 *Struktura chudožestvennogo teksta* (Moskva).

Matešić, Josip
1970 "Wiederholung als Stilmittel in der Erzählprosa Čechovs", *Die Welt der Slaven* 15.

Merleau-Ponty, Maurice
1948 *Sens et non-sens* (Paris).

Muir, Edwin
1928 *The Structure of the Novel* (London; 7th imp. 1957).

Nilsson, Nils Å.
1968 *Studies in Čechov's Narrative Technique "The Steppe" and "The Bishop"* (Uppsala).

Papernyj, Z.
1954 *A. P. Čechov. Očerk tvorčestva* (Moskva).

Pouillon, Jean
1946 *Temps et roman* (Paris).

Propp, Vladimir, Ja.
1928 *Morfologija skazki* (Moskva; Izd. 2e 1969).

Schmid, Wolf
1973 *Der Textaufbau in den Erzählungen Dostoevskijs* (München).

94   JAN VAN DER ENG

Šklovskij, Viktor
    1925   *Teorija prozy* (Moskva-Leningrad).
    1927   *Technika pisatel'skogo remesla* (Moskva-Leningrad).
Stanzel, Franz
    1955   *Die typischen Erzählsituationen im Roman* (Stuttgart).
Todorov, Tzvetan
    1966   "Les catégories du récit littéraire", *Communications* 8, 125-
            51.
Tomaševskij, Boris
    1928   *Teorija literatury. Poètika* (Moskva-Leningrad).
Tschiževskij, Dmitrij
    s.a.   *Dostojewskij und Nietzsche. Die Lehre von der ewigen
            Wiederkunft* (Bonn).
Tynjanov, Jurij
    1929   "O literaturnoj èvoljncii", in: *Archaisty i novatory* (Lenin-
            grad), 30-47; transl. by Ladislav Matejka and Krystnyna
            Pomorska, *Readings in Russian Poetics* (Cambridge, Mass.-
            London, 1971), 66-78.
Usmanov, L. D.
    1969   "Struktura povestvovanija u Čechova-belletrista", in: *Vo-
            prosy literatury i stilja. Trudy kafedry russkoj i zarubežnoj
            literatury Samarkandskogo instituta imeni S. Ajni* (Samar-
            kand), 3-22.
    1971   "Princip 'sžatosti' v poètike pozdnego Čechova-belletrista i
            russkij realizm konca xix veka", in: *Poètika i stilistika russkoj
            literatury*. Pamjati ak. V. V. Vinogradova (Leningrad),
            246-53.
Uspenskij, Boris A.
    1970   *Poètika kompozicii* (Moskva).
Vinogradov, Viktor
    1921   "Sjužet i kompozicija povesti Gogolja *Nos*", *Načala* 1, 82-
            105.
    1959   *O jazyke chudožestvennoj literatury* (Moskva).
Žirmunskij, Viktor
    1921   "Zadači poètiki", *Načala. Žurnal istorii literatury i istorii
            obščestvennosti* 1, 51-81.
Zola, Émile
    1880   *Le roman expérimental* (Paris).

ČECHOV'S WORD

JAN M. MEIJER

Čechov's Word

I

When we are about to make an utterance and when, as a result,
our stream of consciousness 'hits' the discrete words, it is only
rarely that the words we find will render adequately and completely what we want to express with them. We take into
account the situation we are in, we find we need the addition
of gestures and intonation, we may have to go back and find a
better word or sentence, and so on. When we come to write
our utterance down we will lack some of these possibilities and
will have to find different solutions. As a rule there will be a
certain tension between what we want to express and what we
do express. This is a direct result of our use of words. The
word has meaning. We use this meaning but do not exhaust it
in any single use of the word. If we want to restrict ourselves
to the simple or conjunct[1] meaning of the word, it requires
great care not to awaken any other, disjunct meaning of that
word, and vice versa. The word is always used in a context. It
is from this context that the conjunct meaning has to be made
up, and we probably create some kind of context even where
we see a word in isolation. The context, the thought or feeling
or fact we want to express, selects the required words and
checks them at the same time against those which have gone

before and those which are to follow. We do not quote ourselves, our selection has a creative element, only after the
selection do we know whether the word was good enough. We
want the words to follow completely the direction of our
thought, like iron particles follow the line of force of the
magnet. Words never do. They remain available to the language community for other uses also. They will always show a
minimum of resistance and will have the power to bring associations that give our thought a different direction. In the
progress of our thought processes this may appear in the form
of friction. In everyday communication such friction is rarely
noticed, but if we look closely, the limits between which we
use words are seen to be, on the one hand, the unimpeded
flow of consciousness, and, on the other, the word standing at
right angles to this flow and blocking it. Ordinarily this tension
goes unnoticed: a good listener needs only half a word, and we
can always correct ourselves[2].

When this tension is noticed it is experienced as a negative
phenomenon that we would rather get rid of. In fact, in
certain fields we do just that and make use of artificial or
symbolic languages, e.g., in traffic and in algebra. But there is
one field in which this tension is made into an asset: verbal art.
Here the tension, that is the underchargedness or overcharged-
ness of the word, is used to tighten the web of relationships
that form a complete and independent utterance.

Every writer and every literary movement has its own way
with words. This way may be more or less conscious. Not
every artist will seek expressly 'the new word' as Raskol'nikov
put it, but a writer and a literary movement of any importance
can be distinguished by the way he or it uses words. This is
true even if the new element that distinguishes him or it from
what has gone before does not emphasize words in the first
place, but, for example, new themes. In time these changes
will be reflected in the use of words.

It is, therefore, a legitimate approach to characterize a
writer by the way he uses his medium. In this paper we will try
to do so with respect to Čechov. What we shall be aiming at is
to consider the word in a larger context, in the stories, and

finally in his oeuvre as a whole. It constitutes a preliminary survey that will need much further study and elaboration. Perhaps at some future stage statistical methods will have to be used, but we do not reach that stage here. Our approach differs from the study of Čechov's style[3] in that we do not study the expressive possibilities of words and groups as such, but the way the word functions in the text. It has something to do with what Vinogradov calls the aesthetics of the word[4] and it may have some bearing on problems of artistic speech.[5] It combines aspects of stylistics and semantics. Our approach is literary rather than linguistic.

The word in the literary context carries meaning and it does this in a certain way. The conjunct meaning, usually the first meaning in a lexical entry and that which comes to mind first, is used, to quote Reichling "when all shades of meaning are related to the thing we are speaking of", for example, in the sentence: this house is built of stone. We speak of disjunct meaning, according to Reichling, when only one or a few shades of meaning are used.

The word can to some extent be circumscribed by the combinations it can enter into with other words. These combinations are conditioned by the class the word belongs to (verb, noun, etc.) and by its meaning. The combinational possibilities we call valencies. In this paper we distinguish between vertical and horizontal valencies.

In normal speech we make the combination of words in our utterances as unmarked as possible, i.e., we will adapt as much as possible to the situation and use our words as instruments, invisible by themselves, of our thoughts. We must have a special reason for acting differently. If we 'mark' the combination this hampers the progress of what we are saying, often because we include more in such a combination than in an unmarked combination.[6] In literature we are concerned with finite texts with a considerable degree of organization. In such texts in particular the combinations into which the words enter extend beyond their immediate contacts. Such texts can be considered as a horizontal line of a given length. We call all valencies horiziontal that are activated by contacts in this plane exceeding those of a directly syntactical nature.

Two things should be noted. Naturally many words refer to things either inside or outside the story and these references could be considered vertical on the horizontal line of progress. But they all refer to the world of the story and they do not necessarily have the same referent in this world as they have outside it. These references then, are not to a differently organized plane. Secondly, the pull and push on and at a word can be analyzed into a horizontal and a vertical vector. With horizontal valencies this vertical vector is by definition never equal to zero: there will always be some friction. But the horizontal vector will be larger than the vertical one.

Some combinations into which words enter create valencies that refer to a plane that is different from the story and that has a structure of its own. Such references are vertical in regard to the progress of the story. We will call them vertical valencies. Parodies and stylizations belong to this category.

Within the horizontal plane of the story we can, of course, distinguish several planes, for example, that of the author and that of the characters (direct speech). This fact also influences the combinations into which the word can enter. It should be remembered, in this connection, that every statement we make is made from a certain perspective which is not, as a rule, expressed in that sentence itself. The narrative perspective differs clearly, as a rule, from that of the character. But they may intermingle. Formally speaking a story is a relay race between author and character; but the author may accompany the next runner for a while. Or he may be content with the coach's rôle.

We will have to pay attention to the phonic aspects of the word. In many cases they will not be marked. There must be special reasons for the phonic aspect to influence the meaning of the word. These reasons can be emotional, e.g., when we repeat a word in order to overcome an emotional block; we find these aspects also in onomatopoea. In some cases the word appears as noise, e.g., when we do not catch its meaning. This does happen in Čechov's works. The opposite also occurs: a sound or a combination of sounds that do not have a meaning of their own may be imbued with meaning by the context.

The definitions given here are first and foremost pragmatic. We have tried not to depart from accepted usage, but the wider validity of these concepts will have to be analyzed further.

II

The early 'eighties witnessed the end of the age of the great Russian novel and the beginning of Čechov's literary work. In 1880-81 Dostoevskij's *Brat'ja Karamazovy* was published and in the latter year he died. This is also the period of Tolstoj's crisis. In 1883 Turgenev dies; his last novel dayes from 1878. In 1880 Čechov published his first story.

This event was of course not on a level with the earlier events. The moment of Čechov's entry into 'real' literature was still some years off and even then he never felt that he was on a par with the other authors mentioned. Yet this series of events is more than a mere coincidence. It signifies the end of a period in Russian literature and the beginning of a new one. The period of the novel ends, that of the short story begins. This is a change within the general current of realism. It is a striking fact that Russian realism both begins and ends with the short story. Even if we leave out the transitional figures of Lermontov and Gogol' we can say that Russian realism begins with Puškin's Belkin. But if we want to restrict ourselves to the great writers mentioned the same still holds. All three made the transition from the shorter to the longer form. Turgenev was the first and the oldest, he made the transition with Rudin. The genesis of the novel shows that this transition to the longer form was, in Turgenev's case, directly connected with his efforts to render 'the body and pressure of time.'[7] In Dostoevskij we observe a similar phenomenon. His confrontation with the times also required the longer form, preceded and announced by the "Notes from the Underground". In Tolstoj's case the picture is less clear but remains essentially the same. His prolonged efforts to arrive at a longer form resulted in a historical novel. But in *War and Peace* the confrontation with the times is no less real for being 'hidden' in history. It comes out clearly enough, for one thing, in the epilogue on history.

This is, then, a more than personal phenomenon in which 'the body and pressure of time' counted for much. In the period of the great novel ideas and ideologies exercised a certain pressure on literature. The air was saturated with them. From a literary point of view they require careful handling. The 'natural' expression of an idea is the treatise or a text in the exhortatory mode. Handling ideas through characters presents added difficulties. The idea may be reduced to a means of characterization, or it may overshadow the hero. There are instances of both of these tendencies. Dostoevskij's *Brat'ja Karamazovy* presents 'ideas with legs', whereas Turgenev often manifests the opposite tendency. Bachtin considered Dostoevskij's way of handling ideas his unique contribution to literature.[8] He could indeed absorb more of them in his novels than any other writer.

These writers did not themselves create the urge of ideas. They found it already in existence and their effective way of 'harnessing' ideas in their works gave an added dimension to Russian literature. They made their own contribution to the climate of opinion and their critics discussed their ideas in isolation rather than with respect to their artistic realization; but the climate was not of their making. This climate itself also changed around 1880. Ideas 'went their own way' in a more directly political context. (It was not so much that they found better possibilities outside literature, but that the separation was a fact, and people were subjected to by ideas in more 'direct' ways than through literature.) After the 'going to the people' in the 'seventies and the great trials that followed it, after the murder of Alexander II, a painful period or reorientation set in in which not only the ideas themselves changed but also the attitude to them. Overstating the case a bit one might say that ideas became too 'pronounced' to be effective in literature. There occurred a kind of shake-out and the tension which had held the world of literature and the world of ideas together snapped.

We will leave open the question whether or not the process depicted here is a general one, as Lukacs thinks.[9] If it is, then it must be agreed that in Russia it occurred in a very pronounced form.

The transition from the shorter to the longer form had been made by a number of writers consecutively and by each in his own way. This transition to the short form as the representative of a period of literature brought with it a changing of the guard. The last short stories of Turgenev and Dostoevskij did not signal a goodbye to the novel. Tolstoj, the survivor, for the time being bade farewell to literature altogether, irrespective of form. Among the secondary figures that survived none made a significant transition to the shorter form. Further, it cannot be said that the public lost interest in the novels which had been written. Evidently the form could no longer be galvanized. The thrust of ideas, directed outward and upward, was becoming a downward pressure, almost a burden on literature. In his famous letter to Strachov, Tolstoj had said that ideas in the novel, when removed from their context, lost enormously in value.[10]

If ideas could no longer be brought to a state of tension in literature, this did not mean that ideas and their bearers, the intellectuals, disappeared from literature; what happened was that the link between then became less direct. Either the literary character still spoke of ideas but did not live up to them. In which case, they built a small world with big words, and the word became inadequate. Or ideas proceeded to take over: character and author might use roughly the same language, but the character would recede behind the idea, and the work of literature became a work a thèse.[10a] There was no inherent reason why the first situation could not result in good literature. But in order to attain this, it was necessary for a different kind of word to be found.

This was the literary situation when Čechov began writing. Prose still dominated, but the longer form which had emerged in confrontation with the times had lost much of its organizing power. The word had become instrumental. In order to function again it had to be 'de-instrumentalized'.

III

Čechov was not the only writer responsible for making the shorter form the representative form of the period, but he was the most form-conscious and the best. And there is one more reason why he was such a clear herald of the transition. While 'literature' moved from the longer to the shorter form, Čechov moved from the shortest to the shorter form. His earlier work is an essential stage in this development, even if he himself was not to claim the name of literature for most of his earlier productions.[11] His very first pieces show a different attitude to words as compared to that which was dominant in later realism. They also reveal a parodistic approach to some literary traditions.

Parody as a signal of literary change is by no means un uncommon phenomenon. *The Tales of Belkin* come to mind as an example. In Čechov's circumstances the parodistic approach was natural for another reason as well. Every literary current has its humoristic fringes. But they belong to and are conditioned by the main current. Thus Čechov's parodies were different from those of the *Iskra* of the 'sixties, and its humour in turn was different from Mjatlev's; this was not a humoristic tradition on its own outside the main current of literature, but a comparable reaction to different stages of this current.

At this earliest stage in his writing Čechov was more subject to than a subject of literature. His first products are significant, not so much for their inherent value as as a pointer to the literary modes available and the choice he made from them. His first hero approaches his learned neighbour concerning the latter's 'umstvennye idei' in the way a provincial man approaches a man from the capital, and *inter alia* invites this learned neighbour to occupy himself with literature ("Pis'mo u učenomu sosedu"). The title of his second piece is relevant in this respect: *Čto čašče vsego vstrečaetsja v roma- nach, povestjach i t.p.?* (What is most often found in novels, stories, and so on). The *1001 passions, or, the terrible night, a novel in one part, with an epilogue*, dedicated to Victor Hugo, is another example. Here parody is laid on so thickly that the author finds it necessary to add an epilogue, which closes with the words: "none of this has ever happened, goodnight", thus making the work a parody of a parody. Another piece makes fun of an aspiring littérateur's pursuits (*Moj jubilej*).

In another story again, *Za Jabločki* (1880) Eugène Sue is mentioned as an indication of how long the description of the hero would really have to be "nužno prosidet' nad pisaniem po krajnej mere stol'ko, skol'ko prosidel Evgenij Sju nad svoim tolstym i dlinnym 'Večnym židom". The beginning of this story is emphatically humoristic: "Between the Pontos Euxeinos and Solovki, under the corresponding degrees of latitude and longitude, the landowner Trifon Semenovič has for a long time now been living off his black earth". The author does not give his surname. There follows an elaborate bit of business about his failure to give it which is taken up again at the end of the story. About one third of the tale is taken up by a characterization of the hero and his milieu. This is somewhat unusual. It shows a degree of social criticism which links this production with Čechov's first real story, *Papaša* (1880). In both stories there is a good deal of direct speech. Both have an 'I' author who is not essential to the stories but who tends to appear when a moral has to be drawn.

Čechov's very first stories strike the reader through their use of words and through their literary references rather than through the form in which they are cast. The form is, in fact, rather hesitant and derivative, conditioned as it was by the papers for which he wrote: we find, for example, a letter, an examination paper, an enumeration, notes from a diary. The stories themselves are short to very short. His first try at a somewhat longer form (*Petrov den'*, 1881) is a failure. The most complete is *Sud* (1881) which is a situation rather than a story proper. (It has an ending that is not unworthy of the later Čechov who did indeed have a hand in it. Pondering its inclusion in his collected works he revised and finally discarded it.) A grown-up son is whipped because he is suspected of taking money from his father. When the money is finally found in the latter's jacket pocket there is no violent reversal of the story.

The element of 'literature' is quite noticeable in the earliest stories. There are references to the young littérateur who is not accepted by the periodicals (*Pered svad'boj*, 1880 and *Petrov den'* 1881), there are references to the longer French novels (Sue, Hugo, Zola), but not to Russian ones. There are, though, obvious reminiscences, of Saltykov (*Papaša*, *Za Jabločki*) and Gogol'. This is a matter of literary availability, however, rather than of conscious choice. The clear element of parody in Čechov's earliest stories is not directed towards the great realists. Overstating a bit one might say that there is a kind of taboo on the great names of Russian literature. The names which are mentioned refer to an earlier French generation of writers.

The attitude towards the word is a mixed one. The words that are marked are so through vertical valencies. There is much punning on names. Words have extra references of a literary character. Both marked and unmarked words serve the theme, and rarely or never shape it; they are as yet largely instrumental. The word performs on its own rather than through syntax. It is not without importance that the sober use of words with their horizontal valencencies that characterizes the later Čechov was not there at the beginning but was something which was attained gradually by much effort.

The shortest form, then, was the dominant one in the early Čechov. The notable exception presented by *Švedskaja Spička* owed its length to the genre it parodied. The shortest form was represented by the anecdote, as we have seen, but also by what could perhaps be called the *feuilleton*. This is the report of a stylized spectator who states what he has seen in the city or in public places. Examples are *Žalobnaja Kniga*, and *V Moskve na trubnoj ploščadi*. This genre was a second generation descendent of the *fiziologia*[12]. In this genre the observation is disconnected from the event forming the centre of the anecdote. Whereas the anecdote has a structure of its own, in the 'feuilleton' the things observed are arranged by the narrator. What organizes them is the point of view, the angle, a new look at things or a look at new things, as in *V Moskve na trubnoj ploščadi*, or the presentation, as in *Žalobnaja Kniga*. In the first case they often start or finish with some general observation that establishes or formulates the point of view.

There is a variant of this genre in which the event described, although not exactly an anecdote, yet organizes the presentation to some extent. The *fabula* is, consequently, weak, but there is a strong emotional impact which while remaining unexpressed helps to organize the stories. There is a strong element of *skaz*. *Ustricy* and *Unter Prišibeev* are examples of this. The author is almost absent. These stories are more tightly organized than the 'feuilletons' proper. In the case of *Ustricy* this is achieved through the I-form; in the case of *Unter Prišibeev* all is in direct speech, – or was, until Čechov added a final commentary in 1900.

Anecdote and 'feuilleton' were the two dominant forms of Čechonte's oeuvre. In order to check these first observations we shall take a look at a slightly later story taken from among those that Čechov himself selected for his collected works. It is *Smert činovnika* (*The Death of a Civil Servant*) of 1883.

The story is simple. A man sitting in the theatre sneezes and then realizes that in the process he sprinkled the man sitting in front of him. This man turns out to be superior to him in rank, namely a civil general. He apologizes and the general nonchalantly accepts the apology, concentrated as he is on the play. The hero thinks he did not apologize enough and goes to the general's office three times but is never given the chance to come to the end of his apology. He gets on the other man's nerves and is told to leave. The hero goes home and dies. "Pridja mašinal'no domoj, ne snimaja vicmundira, on leg na divan i ... pomer."

The cognitive structure of this story can be rendered by the sentence: This is how a certain civil servant died: he did this, and this and this, and died. The aesthetic structure is a classical climax, a repetition of an action between the same participants with a sudden release at the end. The aesthetic structure 'keeps open' the cognitive one until the very last word, when the death announced by the title occurs. This end is at the same time the release of the climax which carries the aesthetic structure. It thereby receives a very strong emphasis. But somehow the ending is less energetic than we are made to expect by the beginning of the story. This promises a comic story: "One fine evening a no less fine *eksekutor*, Ivan Dmitrič Červjakov was sitting in the second row of the stalls and was looking through his binoculars at the 'Bells of Corneville'. He was looking and he felt himself at the summit of bliss."

The traditional initial words: "V odin prekrasnyj večer", stressed by the repetition: "ne menee prekrasnyj" have decidedly literary valencies. One that is even more direct is added to these: "No vdrug ... V rasskazach ..." etc. This, plus the name of Červjakov – punning on worms – create the expectation that the approach is not entirely serious. The subsequent sentences only strengthen this expectation. The one element that does not fit in with this picture is the title – the first thing that strikes the reader. There is a contradiction between the title and the introductory paragraph. Together they create uncertainty as to what to expect, but at the end of the first paragraph the humorous impression predominates. There we find another name played upon, Brizžalov – besprinkling. It is taken up by the very next sentence: "Ja ego obryzgal." (I besprinkled him.)

The exchange between the central characters is rendered in direct speech, which is also used to render their thoughts. Up to the first exchange the author's paragraphs are humorous, but after that they become neutral, unmarked. Červajakov's thoughts and feelings are described not by marking words, but by syntactical means, mainly through inversion: "gljadel on, no už blaženstva bol'še ne čuvstvoval; ego načalo pomučivat' bezpokojstvo; pis'ma generalu on ne napisal". They are absent in the purely descriptive passages.

There is a clear element of stylization in Červjakov's direct speech, with its repetitions and variations on the excuse he is never going to finish. But this is conditioned by the theme and the composition. The auctorial sentences are self-contained and neutral. The sentences shape and organize the paragraphs but they do not extend their rôle beyond that. There is no stylistic pressure from one paragraph to the next, little from one sentence to another. The dynamics of the story is established, not by stylistic means, but exclusively through the composition. The style follows, but does not lead the accelerations and retardations of the anecdote's development.

This is reflected in the use of words: in the descriptive passages they are least striking. Where Červjakov's emotions are described there is a fair amount of repetition. This is also true, naturally enough, of Červjakov's direct speech, which is full of clichés, socially stylized, but not otherwise striking by its vocabulary. As we move back towards the beginning of the story we find more repetition in the auctorial sentences, and the pun-names. But these repetitions do not bring out new valencies in the repeated words, these repetitions are compositional. What extra valencies there are are vertical. Like the style, the word follows, it does not 'resist' the flow of the story as a way of imparting new energy.

The story is an anecdote, it is almost a realized metaphor: the hero was frightened to death. The end of the story meets the formal requirement of a sudden reverse, but much of the energy seems to have been somehow absorbed before the final word.

For the climax of the story to function it is necessary that the repetition be acted out and not merely related. Direct speech is a necessity for the direct exchanges, it is less so for the thoughts rendered. In fact, direct speech is more or less thematized here: Červjakov is not going to speak to the general any more, he is going to write him a letter. It is in the rendering of the thoughts and feelings of his characters that Čechov was to develop markedly. But for that to happen the narrator had to become mobile. What we have here is a fixed narrative position. This is in itself a gain as compared to the earlier stories. The I-narrator has disappeared. But the narrator is still close to the reader. This is reflected in the time structure. An anecdote that happened in the past is related to the reader who is at one time addressed in the present "čichnul, kak vidite". Reader and narrator are in the same milieu and time layer, the story in a different one. This fact, too, influences the use of words. The similarity of perspective of author and reader limits the possibilities of extra meanings. There is mutual understanding before the story begins.

A piece like *The Death of a Civil Servant* did not pretend to be literature in any sense which might claim to approach the great novels. The latter were fundamental facts of literary life, but beyond the horizon of Čechov's literary activity, one must assume. His letters written during these years were silent about them. To himself Čechov was, at best, a littérateur. There is no reason to distrust what he wrote to Grigorovič in 1886: "If I do have a talent that I must honour, then I must confess before the purity of your heart that I did not honour it up to now".[13] The artistic world at first sight seems quite separate from his own world as an intellectual. They each have their own development, and that in the one field is not automatically reflected in the other. It was easier in a way for Čechov to keep his intellectual preoccupations out of his early stories than to bring them in. A certain tension developed between the two in the mid-eighties. Grigorovič's letter helped to bring out this tension and contributed to its resolution. For this to come about something in the stories had to change.

The question arises whether this had to be a change of genre, or whether the earlier genres left open possibilities for development. In the case of the 'feuilleton' such development would have been difficult if it was not to become a mannerism. If this form is extended the cognitive structure takes even more precedence and the aesthetic structure is overstretched. The anecdote seems a little better placed in this respect, in that the final tension offers several different ways of exploitation, but this form is not amenable to much lengthening. However, a certain combination would seem possible of the *Ustricy* and *Unter Prišibeev* type of 'feuilleton' with the anecdote. This could be done in several ways. Either through a combination, or through giving the background and exposition a feuilleton-like form, against which the anecdote stands out. This had already been done occasionally in very early stories, e.g., in *Za Jabločki*, or through the 'emotion absorbing' character of Čechov's anecdote-endings.[14] This latter seems to be the case in *Tolstij i Tonkij* and in *Tragik* (both of 1883). In both of these stories we notice the repetition of the same element on different emotional planes, but neither of these stories is noticeably longer than the average. Another possibility, perhaps, would be to introduce characterization in an anecdote. Characterization in general requires a longer form than the anecdote: in fact it is held by many to be impossible in a short story, but to some extent a short story can be considered as a combination of anecdote and character. For this combination to succeed, however, the closeness between reader and author that was proper to the Čechonte stories would have to be broken up and the social distance between author and hero would have to be reduced. Both requirements could be met by turning to the world in which Čechov the intellectual had matured, which is more or less what did happen. The author-figure of the Čechonte stories had become highly stylized by the mid-eighties and this figure too, did not offer many ways of development. In such circumstances a relatively small signal – Grigorovič's letter – could be sufficient to effect or to herald the change. And when it came the old forms were not completely discarded. What could be kept was kept.

Grigorovič's letter was itself in part a reaction to Čechov's moving out of the genres he had been using and perfecting. In his answer to Grigorovič Čechov wrote: "The first thing to stimulate my self-criticism was a very kind and as far as I understand sincere letter from Suvorin. I planned to write something worthwhile, but yet I did not really believe in my own literary worthwhileness".[15] He at once followed Grigorovič's request to add his own name to Čechonte's in a collection of stories that was in the press. But during 1886 and part of 1887 Čechov and Čechonte[16] appeared both. The difference was not only that Čechov wrote in the Novoe Vremja, and Čechonte elsewhere, but it was also one of genre. Čechonte kept to the anecdote, but, no longer a prisoner of it, loosened up this form as much as possible. Thus *Vyigryšnyj bilet* of 1887 is, in structure, still an anecdote in which, as it were, not only the author, but also the characters exploit the final tension. In addition, the characters begin to open up. They are still placed before the reader by an author close to him, but the characters are looking at each other.

This change of place by the author makes the vertical valencies less useful. Both the social stylization and the literary allusion can function only if author and reader are close: both are understandings between author and reader at the expense, or without the knowledge, of the characters. Čechonte's social stylizations come to be replaced by Čechov's social characterizations. These are more objective and do not need a previous understanding between reader and author. In *Vyigryšnyj bilet* the social characterization is rather general (through the mentioning of the salary earned which shows that the hero is moving up the social ladder). The author's descriptive paragraphs are objective in the rendering of actions but begin to 'borrow' from characters in the description of their thoughts and feelings. There is more than one subject, more than one sentient centre. To the extent that the author's and character's utterances inter-penetrate, the field of possible horizontal valencies is widened.

But this was a process of some duration. 1886 and 1887 are transitional years. We have stories like *Košmar* and *V sude* which can without trouble be considered as 'accusing literature' (*Obličitel'naja literatura*). The authorial stance is rather immobile. The author addresses the reader over the heads of his characters, which reminds one of Čechonte. The stories themselves are highly thematized and there is no inter-penetration between the author's and the character's level. *Panichida*, the first Čechov story[17] is a different matter. What we have here is the barest outline of an anecdote, reminiscent of Puškin's *Stancionnyj smotritel'*. The story concentrates on what in earlier stories was the exploitation of the anecdote. The bare outline of an anecdote serves only to furnish a perspective to the description. The author has left the reader and immersed himself to a large extent in the character. In some paragraphs, for example the final one, the two inter-penetrate to a large extent. The authorial word becomes audible in the character's and vice versa. There is more of the later Čechov in this story than in *V sude* and *Košmar*.

Next we have case histories of illnesses, like *Tif* and *Žitejskie nevzgody*. They, too, can be considered as a search for a different perspective. The form chosen, of a memory by an I-author, seems to stress this point.

The processes under way are, in the first place, an inter-penetration of anecdote and feuilleton and, in the second an interpretation of author's and character's planes. The latter process set in later than the former. These processes entailed a different use of words.

Enemies (*Vragi*) (1887) shows the inter-penetration of the old and the new Čechov. It has two structural kernels; one is a story with a structure comparable to that of *Košmar*, and the other is an anecdote on the ancient theme of the deceived husband. The emotions caused by the death of the doctor's son are absorbed by the arrival of Abogin. The paragraph devoted to this in which the transition is made is one of Čechov's finest. The flow of emotion is only held up by Abogin's arrival, to burst forth in a different direction at the conclusion of the anecdote. The 'strong' ending of the anec-dote, which is unusual for Čechonte, flows over into the ending of the story. The anecdote is thus contained within it. Despite the thematic double focus the story has a fundamental unity. This is achieved in part by the author's position. The author hovers over the story, as it were, and auctorial sen-tences have a lightness of tone which seems incompatible with what they express. Čechov manages this by combining in one sentence or passage an observation of the non-expression, or incomplete or inadequate expression, of an emotion with an auctorial statement of the force of such expressions. These statements are made from within a world that both author and characters share. This combination makes the statements somehow interdependent, they become each other's context. As a result, a wide field for horizontal valencies is opened up: "Kirillov i ego žena molčali, ne plakali, kak budto, krome tjažesti poteri, soznavali i ves' lirizm svoego položenija. (...) Golos Abogina drožal ot volnenija; v etoj drože i v tone bylo gorazodo bol'še ubeditel'nosti, čem v slovach, (...) Voobšče fraza (...) dejstvuet tol'ko na ravnodušnych." They have a clear thematical function, to the extent that the non-correspond-ence between the two characters in this story has been made into a theme. It sounds throughout: not only in the above examples but also in the description of Abogin's arrival, when the doctor does not really see him, and in their altercation in Abogin's house right through to the end. In this connection the auctorial statements play an important rôle and are very much in evidence. Later, when the main structural elements become (more) adapted, horizontal valencies take over part of this rôle and the author's voice becomes less pronounced. At the time of this story the process was only just beginning.

The auctorial statements retard the story. The dynamics of the anecdote enclosed within it are exploited to the full: only when the story has almost come to a standstill is the next 'instalment' of the anecdote given. Its ending is exploited in the negative. But as the authorical statements are also an expression of the theme, the events and their dynamics become less important.

The style reflects this situation. There is a very little over-flow from one paragraph to the next. Even then sentences within the paragraph resemble a number of parallel brush strokes rather than an organized continuous line. After Abogin has repeated his request, which is rendered in direct speech, there follows a long descriptive passage covering five paragraphs. This passage does not contain a reaction to Abogin's request. The first paragraph begins as follows: "Nastupilo molčanie. Kirillov povernulsja spinoj k Aboginu, postojal i medlenno vyšel iz perednej v zalu". All the sentences that follow are descriptive and of the same type. They are, however, longer. Those describing the doctor's emotions have modal adverbs or adverbial clauses: "Sudja po ego nevernoj, maši-nal'noj pochodke (...) sumerki i tišina zaly, povidimomu, usilili ego ošalelost' ". They function quite well, rhythmically as well as otherwise. One wonders, on second thoughts, what purpose these modal adverbs play. If the author can state of the doctor that he "prinadležal k čisle natur, kotorye vo vremja duševnoj boli čuvstvujut potrebnost' v dviženie", he can also state directly that "sumerki i tišina zaly usilili ego ošalelost' ". Why does he not do so?

This is an extension of the device we considered before,

which consists of an observation on the lack of expression by a character plus an authorial observation on the expressive force of such a phenomenon. This combination of events, and the variable perspective on them implied in the mobile author, shift the events to the background of the story. This is one way of linking the two stories. We are in an area of the story, evidently, where style and theme can exchange rôles at any given moment.[18] The change of perspective entails the possibility of a change in motivation and widens the field of possible motivations.

The use of anecdote entailed a fixed and close relationship between reader and author. Now that the anecdote is no longer being used, not only does the author's position change, but the time structure changes as well. The author's observations are given not only in the present tense, but also in the future and past tenses. This temporal mobility in turn results in a spatial mobility. Sometimes author and character are quite close: speaking of Abogin, the author mentions his "sytosti, zdorov'ja i aplomba, kakim dyšala vsja ego figura". Very shortly afterwards he says of the doctor: "tol'ko mel'kom uvidel on (...) da (...) zametil čučelo volka, takogo že solidnogo i sytogo, kak sam Abogin". The author and the doctor are almost indistinguishable here. There is an occasional exclamation mark in the author's description ("Skol'ko živogo dviženija čuvstvovalos' v izgibach ee tela i v rukach!" 5.23). In another case such an observation is followed by a present tense, the only one in a descriptive paragraph in the past tense. For a moment the author moves closer to the character ("... vmeste s etim mal'čikom uchodilo navsegda v večnost' i ich pravo imet' detej. Doktoru 44 goda, on uže sed i vygljadit starikom; ego poblekšej bol'noj žene 35 let. Andrej byl ne tol'ko ..." ibid.). As a result of these processes — the joining of author's and character's observations, the mobility of the author and the extended time-perspective — the sentences acquire under- and overtones; this question of tone may become as important as the theme, i.e., the connection between sentences may be made either through the same theme or by way of the same tone. *Vragi* shows the importance of thematic connections:

the final paragraph is very clearly dependent on tone for the effect, precisely because its meaning is so clear. If it had been toneless it would have been merely banal.

The mobility of the author, and the combination of which we spoke, imply that there is no clear difference between the author's and the character's 'voice' (= tone plus vocabulary). The function of direct speech is compositional here and does not aid characterization.

Vragi was a first attempt; it did not set the pattern right away. In the second half of 1887 we observe a resurrection of Čechonte, in stories like *Zinočka*, *Otec*, *Sirena*, and to a lesser extent *V sarae*. In these stories the differentiation of voices is an important factor. One of the means that can be used to achieve this end is *skaz*. The latter is what we find in *Zinočka*.

Zinočka has a narrator who does not differ much, socially speaking, from the Čechov heroes of this period, but whose voice is much clearer than the latter's. Words like *fiziomordija* remind one of Čechonte. The development it represents, however, becomes clear if we compare it to *Zloj mal'čik*, written four years earlier and thematically similar. The author-narrator has been replaced by a character-narrator who relates memories and whose presence is therefore much more motivated than the earlier author's. The anecdotal structure has been opened up, the memory gives a different perspective, there is more 'mood' in the narrator's voice.

A further stage of the phase opened by *Vragi* is *Knjaginja*. It has no trace of an anecdote, nor is it a feuilleton. The mixture of feuilleton and anecdote has, as it were, been homogenized. Plot is minimal. In *Knjaginja* it consists of a meeting set apart by stressing the similarity between arrival and departure. We find the same in *Svjatoj noč'ju* and in *Pečeneg*.

In *Knjaginja* the author is less in evidence than in *Vragi*. The homogenization has been achieved. An approximate description of the process would be to say that on each separate paragraph 'tone' and 'plot' entered into a complete fusion and that the connection between one paragraph and the next can go either way: theme can select tone and vice versa. Čechov's treatment of these paragraphs can be compared to the poet's treatment of words. We must distinguish of course between auctorial passages and direct speech. The thematic function of the character's way of speaking influences the sentence structure and sometimes makes such sentences striking or elliptical, when taken separately. In the auctorial passages this is much rarer and departures from the normal structure register strongly.

With the creation of these stories Čechov's word is beginning to come into its own. At first it had been purely instrumental. Valencies were vertical, i.e., to speech organized outside the work in which it was used. This phase coincided with the fixed author position. Next comes the juxtaposition of author and character, when the author observes and comments on what remains unexpressed. The word is more closely affected, paragraphs and sentences are becoming autonomous, but not, as yet, the word. But the context is much more closely knit than before. There is a twofold connection between sentences and paragraphs, (a) through direct meaning, positively, and (b) through tone, which for the time being operates negatively: the tone must not be destroyed. This implies two things: horizontal valencies become stronger, and there is a certain exploitation of the inadequacy of the word.

We have said before that Čechonte was unable to reflect the intellectual development of Čechov the man. The new Čechov could be expected to be more responsive in this respect. As it turns out, he was, but this does not imply that the new form would reflect or absorb the entire spectrum of Čechov the intellectual. The structural autonomy of an art form implies a certain amount of resistance to intellectual pressures. There is a two-way relationship between 'form', or 'genre', and 'ideology'; they can either hamper or stimulate each other, and the 'initiative' can come from either side, i.e., earlier artistic realizations can play a rôle in selecting what part of life will find expression. A further stage in Čechov's development is represented by *Ward 6 (Palata No. 6)* (1892). This story shows features of earlier stories as well. To begin with, it can be considered as a case-history of an illness. This kind of narrative

can be found in each stage of Čechov's oeuvre. The plot structure of these stories seems to be somewhat tighter than that of
other stories belonging to the same phase. Secondly, after a
phase in which feuilleton and anecdote seemed to have lost
their identity and to have been homogenized into the typical
Čechov story we have, in *Palata No. 6*, a story in which these
elements can be clearly distinguished again. Formally, it has
something in common even with an early story such as *Za
jabločki*. Lastly, after having taken leave of the I-narrator, we
again meet with him at the beginning of this story.

In general, features belonging to an earlier phase of a
writer's development are not taboo in a later one; but they
may have a different function in a later phase. This is true in
the case we are dealing with, both as regards the division into
feuilleton and anecdote and as regards the I-narrator. The
story is divided into chapters. The first eight or so give the
background. They are narrated in the imperfective and relate
events that are typical or routine, with one or two bits of
suspense. From Chapter IX onwards, against this background
the story develops that leads to the deceitful induction of the
doctor into the mental ward and to his death. It is handled in
the perfective mode. The end of the story meets the requirement that the anecdote have a turning point, a *Wendepunkt*. It
is against this background of routine that the plot stands out
so clearly: the reader can see the importance and the impact of
even small changes.

The I-narrator does not appear often or emphatically, and
he disappears altogether after Chapter V. His presence in itself
is not more essential than in the earliest stories, but here he is
not the moralizer. His presence, however, highlights the
mobility of the narrator. From a plane close to the reader in
the beginning of the story he moves to a plane near the main
character and sometimes indistinguishable from him. This
happens even before the story proper begins. An example
taken at random is furnished by the beginning of Chapter VII.
Its purely descriptive character is in line with this part of the
story. But a slight deviation from it is the word *it seems*
(*kažetsja*) in the second sentence. To whom does it seem? The

answer can be that this is simply an adverbial construction. But this will not do for the second *kažetsja* in the same sentence. The notion that nothing exists besides this book and the lamp with its green shade is already largely the doctor's[19]. The perspectives of character and narrator coincide here to a large extent. The next sentence is clearly the narrator's. Then follows a rendering in direct speech of the doctor's thoughts, this develops gradually into *Erlebte Rede*[20]. We have the latter certainly in the beginning of the next paragraph, which contains passages in which the two perspectives again seem to cover each other. Such passages can be found in other chapters, too, e.g., Chapter XIII. The words, in such passages, share in this double perspective. As the area of double perspective expands, this begins to affect the semantics of the individual word. At this stage the author moves freely, he varies the distance between himself and the characters. As he moves towards the character or away from him the density of the word varies. The word in a double perspective is less dense, less fixed in its lexical meaning. One can look through the words, from narrator to character and back. Neither is blurred by it.

In a later stage this double perspective leads to a certain autonomy of the separate scene in relation to the plot. With a mobile author, such as we have here, and with a clear distinction existing between plot and background this is not yet possible. This mobility leaves open all possibilities of rendering, from straight description to direct speech. After having been addressed directly at the beginning of the story, the reader is out of the author's sight. He looks in on the world, it is open to him on all sides.

The double perspective is much more in evidence in a slightly earlier story *Gusev* (1890). This is much more homogeneous than *Palata No. 6*. There are other differences also. Here we have some vertical valencies, for example in Gusev's speech. But their function is not the same as in the earlier stories, such as *The Death of a Civil Servant* (*Smert' činovnika*). There, it was mainly social typification, here it indicates a different and lesser degree of articulateness on the part of the hero as compared with another character; such valencies are absent from the parts dealing with Pavel Ivanych. A less articulate hero can express himself less clearly — the narrator has to do more for him, so to speak. This tends to widen the area of double perspective. In this way, things can now be presented by Čechov, which with other writers require a reflecting medium. Or, looking at it the other way round, non-intellectual heroes are opened up by this means. Such is what we find in *Gusev* and *Spat' chočetsja*, while the inner life of articulate heroes is to a much larger extent rendered by verbs of thinking, feeling, and observing. Confirmation of this can be found, on the one hand, in the story immediately preceding *Gusev*, namely *Vory*, written in the same year; this also has vertical valencies, references to the modes of speech belonging to definite social strata, and a larger proportion of double perspective. On the other hand we also find it substantiated in *Neighbours* (*Sosedi*) which immediately precedes *Palata No. 6*. Here, too, the narrator's mobility is far greater: there is more and more articulation, direct speech and thought, and a smaller area presented in double perspective; but nevertheless, as in *Palata No. 6*, these areas are an essential element in the story.

Earlier on, in speaking of thematic and tonal connection in Čechov's stories, we noted that these features had much in common with the double perspective. Another way of stating the case is this: a paragraph or even a sentence constitutes a cluster of valencies; from this cluster one valency is selected to which the next sentence or paragraph will react. Both this device and the double perspective widen the field of thematic connections, or rather, seem to blur the boundaries between thematic and 'atmospheric' connections and connotations. The distinction between plot and background may thereby be blurred. The double perspective thus assumes clearly a structural rôle. The story can move on either through plot or through atmospheric selection. This is what happens in the last stage. As an example one might take *In the Ravine* (*V ovrage*). It is a story with a real plot, but there is no going back on earlier achievements. The story is also developed through thematical clusters. One would suppose that the existence of plot lines would exclude any progress by means of atmospheric selection, but somehow the two do manage to combine. A tension between the two is created through the extension of the thematic clusters into virtually self-contained scenes[21]. These scenes are much more eventful than they are in earlier stories. As a rule the inner world of the characters is not described (Lipa being an exception), but revealed or suggested in other ways, e.g., by drawing attention to an action or a characteristic more than once. The connections between the scenes are made either along plot-lines or through selection by tone or atmosphere. This would seem to indicate that the plot is dominant and the structure of the story traditional. But the separate clusters cannot be analyzed into elements of plot: from that point of view there remains much unstructured, or superfluous, material. The valencies of the separate clusters either carry over to the next paragraph, in the form of suggestions or innuendo, or remain open to be taken up later, i.e., the horizontal valencies reach out, their connecting lines become larger. This is different from suspense in the traditional sense, which is part of the plot and which is also used occasionally in *In the Ravine* e.g., in regard to Anisim.

In some cases the valencies connecting one paragraph and the next almost hide the plot. There is a faint suggestion now and then of two parallel stories, with the plot going on in the background, making the separate scenes diaphanous. This is, however, not a structural fact but results from Čechov's use of words. That is to say it is not a result of the interaction of plot and separate scene, but exists at the level of the word, between the direct and the contextual meaning of the words, between the field of meaning and the thrust of meaning. This widens the field of tension between plot and cluster. It enables the author to drain emotional scenes of nearly all emotion, as is the case when Lipa's son is murdered or to merely suggest events central to the plot, like Anisim's crimes.

The time structure of the story seems at first sight to be traditional: it is the three-tiered framework of a story told *ex post*: imperfective praeteritum for the background, perfective praeteritum for the story proper, and present for the final situation which lasts into the present. But the separate scenes

show a tendency towards a similar three-tiered build-up.
A point in case is the first paragraph of Chapter III. If there
were only the plot it would have been sufficient to say that
the ladies had new dresses made for the occasion. Instead we
have a small story in itself. We learn that two seamstresses
lived in the village of Šikalovo. This is the only time in the
story that we hear of these women. They lived there (ipf.).
They were given the order ("Im byli zakazany") — the
perfective action that sets the story going. They used to come
to the house often for measuring and drinking tea (ipf.). The
results are mentioned (pf.), and their being paid in goods they
had no use for. They leave and "vyjdja iz sela v pole, seli na
bugorok i stali plakat' ". The final words suggest a different
Aktionsart. What will happen to them further we do not
know. We would for a moment like to know. The cognitive
impulse is not taken up directly, the story recedes into the
background, the expectations raised by it in part blend with
the atmosphere of the house, in part we are used to give the
overall story a tiny push forward, and some of the valencies
are taken up later. This is the case, for example, when the
motif of the two women alone in the field is later taken up
through Lipa and her mother, which show, incidentally, the
close connection between horizontal valency and motif. Thus
it is possible in Čechov's work to detect a spectrum of meaning
that runs from theme, through motif, valency, word, and
sound to noise.

The author is omniscient, but he does not have a fixed point
of view. In the descriptive passages the distance to what is
described varies. Normally it is marked, but from time to time
the author moves close to the characters, for example, in
describing Elizarov: "ego davno uže znali starym, takim že vot
toščim i dlinnym, i davno uže ego zvali kostylem". A sentence
in which this happens is more organized, rhythmically and
stylistically, than those around it. With "byt' možet", the
beginning of the next sentence, the distance is resumed. There
are more examples of this phenomenon "(...) i v eto že vremja
na dvore baby veličali, vse v odin golos, — i byla kakaja-to
užasnaja, dikaja smes' zvukov, ot kotoroj kružilas' golova"

(whose?). We find something similar in the description of the *duchovenstvo*. It is said of the "volostnoj pisar' " and of the "volostnoj staršina" that they had signed no papers and had helped nobody without cheating. There is a slight tension here between the figure of speech and the information imparted. The distance is varied by *Kazalos'*, and again it is not stated to whom it seemed. In a stylistically reticent milieu such small variations stand out. This applies in particular to the description of sounds.

The passage on the marriage banquet serves as well as any to illustrate Čechov's style. The passage we have in mind begins with: "Varvara chodila vokrug stola" and closes with: "Vse eto končilos' pozdno". In the very first sentence the author varies the distance: "... utomlennaja, rasterjannaja i, vidimo, byla dovol'na". We have come across this device in our discussion of *Vragi*. Next we have "nesobstvenno-prjamaja reč": "nikto ne osudit teper' ". This refers back to *dovol'na* and to earlier instances in which such fears on her part were suggested, and refers forward to the cry: "nasosalis' našej krovi, irody". The word *osudit* exploits more valencies than it would if there were only the plot to reckon with and no scenes that were almost self-contained. The sentence which is brought to a close by "osudit teper' " is one such scene; so is the next one, but to a lesser degree. The exclamation with which the next sentence ends functions both through its meaning and as sound. It gives expression to the deepening sense of injustice, this time as felt by one who suffers from it, after actions have been depicted and with the fresh memory of the author's observation on the *volost'* officials.

The next small paragraph again constitutes a tiny scene. The connection with the preceding paragraph is the usual one of time sequence; it also takes up the sound motif of the preceding paragraph. The description of Chrymin dancing is followed by: "i eto vsech smešilo". The choice of this, out of possible other commentaries or its omission, which structurally would have been equally possible, highlights the changed attitude towards the word characteristic of the later Čechov. Precisely because the alternative between plot line and tiny scene offers

itself so often, the words which are chosen are particularly
telling. The very presence of such alternatives seems to argue
against the use of similes and other tropes. There is, in fact, a
certain dearth of images in Čechov's prose. When they do
occur, they stand out, and acquire special emphasis. We have
the bird simile in *Knjaginja*. We have the snake simile in this
passage. First we read that in some respects Aksin'ja was
snake-like. Only after that is it stated that she looked the way
an adder in the young rye looks at a passer-by in spring, with
its head outstretched and held high. The point is not developed further, it is kept hanging in the air, as it were, but is
repeated later, first in Chapter V, where she is twice referred
to in an animal context,[22] and afterwards in Chapter VI, in so
many words ("kak zmeja iz molodoj rzi' "), combined with a
reference to Aksin'ja's naive smile. The sentence that follows
the simile: "Chryminy derzalis' s nej vol'no", takes up only
one, secondary valency of the preceding statement; it is not
the visible part of the comparison, but an associative one, of
unrealiability and viciousness. Only after this is the contact
between the younger Chrymin and Aksin'ja made by the
author, and her husband's rôle in it commented upon. In the
sentence concerning the husband's words denoting sounds are
prominent. They create a valency that is taken up later
("Gluchoj ... tak gromko ... kazalos', streljal iz pistoleta").
This introduces us to a directly presented scene ("No vot i sam
starik") the reaction to which on the part of the crows is
absorbed by a word denoting sound: "gul odobrenija". The
author's commentary has a touch of sound concentration towards the end, in its orientation on *i* and *o*: "... prost*i*li emu
vs*ë* − *i* ego b*o*gatstv*o* i *o*bi*d*y". Something similar can be said
of the sentence that announces the end of the feast: "Vs*e* et*o*
kon*či*lo*s'* p*o*zdn*o*, v*o* vtor*o*m času n*o*či".

The description of the wedding feast is a Breughel painting
stripped of its mirth, in the sense that the multitude of
separate little scenes almost crowds out the line of the plot.
There are two passages in which the author comments directly
on the injustice, one on the *volost'* officials and the one just
mentioned. They show a certain similarity stylistically: in both

sentences the element of repetition is strong. Such auctorial judgements cannot be said to belong to the plot, nor are they a motif in the sense that we use the term here. However, the theme of injustice, of *obmanut'* and *obida* is very strong in the story. It is a dynamic element even if the logical term of retribution is not, or only partly, arrived at. Thus the scene with the volost' officials 'selects' the later scene of the *urjadnik* when he finally takes note of irregularities committed. The other case mentioned is connected with the earlier exclamation: "nasosalis' našej krovi, irody, net ne vas pogibeli". It would seem that if a motif reaches a certain degree of density the result is an auctorial statement. In any case, such statements are more the result than the cause of the series of motifs. These statements occupy an intermediate position between motif and plot.

The axis of the separate scenes is perpendicular to the plot line. They do not help the plot forward, but rather halt it for a while. As self-contained scenes they have a 'plot' that has no direct thematical link with the main plot. Looked at from another angle, the plot itself in this way opens up, or moves through much more of the world than it would by itself. Nevertheless, while this is true, it leaves out of consideration the interconnection of motifs. The motif: They, too, were a force, they, too, held seniority over someone ("i oni sila, i oni starše kogo − to,") is connected with Kostyl's habits, with the weakness of Lipa and her mother, and with Aksin'ja's becoming an important force ("bol'šaja sila"). There is the theme of the talk between Varvara and Anisim, on God and conscience. As it happens, this thematic conversation is much more homogeneous than is usual with Čechov; in that respect the final conversation between Kostyl' and the guard is more true to type. Such *dialogues des sourds* hardly ever constitute a single motif. The creation of motifs through horizontal valencies establishes 'lines of force' between points on the plot line. This in turn enables the plot to recede into the background from time to time. The plot, then, moves slowly forward through nearly autonomous scenes. Each of these is directly connected to the plot, but a number of them have connections with other scenes not through the plot but by the activating of other valencies. The compositional rôle of this inter-linking will become clear if we realize that the plot in itself is lacking in symmetry. We cannot complain that nothing happens: two crimes occur. But their plot potential is hardly used. The first crime, Anisim's, does generate some plot, it sets into motion causal chains that lead to discovery and retribution. Indirectly it occasions Aksin'ja's crime. But the plot nowhere thickens. Aksin'ja's crime is not punished, it is even confounded by her chasing Lipa from the house. How then is the final equilibrium of the story achieved? It is here that the motifs play their rôle. In the first place, Aksin'ja's crime is set apart by silence: "posle etogo poslyšalsja krík (...) I na dvore vdrug stalo ticho. Aksin'ja prošla v dom molča". The event is made to sink in. This also gives a twist to the theme in the direction of an opposition between sound and silence. It is echoed at the end of the story when, on the appearance of Cybukin, "stalo vdrug ticho-ticho".

In the second place, in terms of plot Aksin'ja and Lipa are antagonists. This antagonism is not fought out either: "... Lipa ušla". But in this respect, too, the final scene establishes the equilibrium. The story as such seems finished by Chapter VIII. After an introductory chapter we are given the story itself in Chapters II-VIII, and an epilogue in Chapter IX which begins with the words, "v nastojaščee vremja" and in the present tense. But about half way through this chapter the author slips back into the past tense and relates the events of one particular day. The epilogue is not complete, evidently, without a meeting between the uncorrupted and the corrupted loser. This final scene, with its silence, in which Lipa gives the old man something to eat – he does not eat in the house from which he is being driven by Aksin'ja –, and in which Lipa and her mother bow to him and go away, crossing themselves, compensates entirely for the lack of equilibrium in the plot. This is the rationale of the slipping back into story from the epilogue. Structurally speaking the plot issues into a final scene, as autonomous with regard to it as any in which the plot and motif change places, as it were, giving a change of perspective that superficially reminds one of a *Wendepunkt-Novelle*.

A story of this kind can be considered as the final and most nature result of the mixture of the ingredients 'anecdote' and 'feuilleton'.[23] Such a mixture could not be successfully achieved until not only the paragraph and the sentence, but even the word itself became the field of tension between different shades of meaning. With Čechov the word attained an autonomy within the context that was not found in earlier prose and only rarely among later writers. With him the word can function directly, as carrier of a theme, express a motif, operate through valencies, assert its sound aspect or function as noise. Its contribution to the dynamics of the story is in direct relationship to the function which is dominant at the moment. In other words, the 'axis' of the word may be entirely directed by the flow of the story, it may be entirely 'in line' but it can also deviate from it to a greater or lesser degree. The *dialogue des sourds* is the clearest example of this. It shows that this greater freedom acquired by the word may also entail scepticism as to its 'real' meaning.[24]

IV

Two further developments seem possible from this point. On the one hand the plot valencies may be entirely absorbed by the other valencies. The result is then lyricism. Something like this is what we find in *Archierej*, where Čechov might be said to have paved the way for poetry. On the other hand a new parallelism between plot and scene can be achieved in which each seems constantly to be transformed into the other. This is what happens in his later theatre work.

It is perhaps stretching things somewhat to speak of a possible influence of the plays on the short stories. As soon as Čechonte became Čechov he began to write plays. The above hypothesis (like its possible opposite) suggests a difference in time that does not exist. Yet there is some justification for raising the possibility. Čechov's last two plays are the most

Čechovian; they are the clearest and fullest realization of Čechov the playwright. Moreover, after 1900 Čechov wrote more plays than stories. This justifies our taking a look at the last two stories to see whether any devices have been used which were not in the earlier stories and which could possibly derive from the plays.

In Čechov's later theatre work there is no fundamental change with respect to the stories of the preceding years. The words in the plays show as many horizontal valencies as they do in the stories. There are as many *dialogues des sourds*. They show a wide range of forms, from Čebutykin's distracted answers to the literal *dialogue des sourds* between Andrej and Ferapont. The separate scenes are as autonomous in the plays as they are in the stories. The motifs, too, may join to form series suggesting lines of development for the plot. Thus, in *The Three Sisters* the words "konečno, vzdor!" in relation to the departure for Moscow, appears later to be thematical. The same applies to Solenyj's saying, at the beginning, that he may one day shoot Tuzenbach ("ili ja vspylju i vsažu vam pulju v lob"). At a more thematic level, the same thing happens. Veršinin arrives from Moscow. It appears he has known the father of the three sisters there. He comes to their town as a battery commander, – the same position their father held in Moscow. So Veršinin appears for a moment in the perspective of their father.

As an example of an autonomous scene we could take the third scene of Act 2. Here we find Maša and Veršinin in the middle of a talk. Maša has evidently said that the military are the most decent people in town. The main themes of her first clause are those of habit and of interesting people. These connect the scene with the preceding one between Andrej and Ferapont, with which there is no direct thematic tie. In his reply Veršinin expresses his wish for tea. He is to repeat it twice and by the time the tea finally comes he has been called away: there is trouble again with his wife. This is, as it were, a comment on his talk with Maša in which this theme is sounded, in terms almost identical to what Irina has said of him before. Veršinin declares his love. Maša replies she has to laugh when he talks like that, although she feels ill at ease ("mne strašno"). She asks him not to say it again. "A vpročem, govorite, mne vse ravno." Both "mne vse ravno" and "mne strašno" will be taken up again. The repetition at once, of "vse ravno" gives this expression a horizontal valency. All the motifs mentioned so far are realized through word groups rather than through separate words. Nevertheless in most of these groups one word stands out (*vzdor, ravno, strašno*). At the other end of the spectrum there is a noise in the hearth that becomes meaningful in the context (*primeta*). We find in this scene almost all the stages of the treatment of motifs, with the directly thematic as the weakest. In other scenes we do occasionally find thematic discussions, for example between Irina and Tuzenbach. As in the stories (cf. *V ovrage*) this occurs only when the theme has considerable significance.

If there are no notable differences between stories and pieces with regard to the autonomy of scenes and to the dialogues there is an essential difference in that direct speech and auctorial text have changed places. But this does not mean that the latter is less significant. It is well-known how important the stage directions are in Čechov's work and what minute attention he paid to their realization on the stage. This concern even extended to the quality and pitch of the thunder to be produced.[25] But essentially we still have a thin plot line, realized through near-autonomous scenes. Now that direct speech has moved to the foreground, however, its context has to be seen and heard. One important means to this end is the physical division of the scene into foreground and background. What happens in the background may serve either as comment on or as setting for what is said in the foreground. For example in the first act, every time one of the sisters in the foreground expresses the wish to go to Moscow, the background acts in a way that can be considered as a derisive comment on that wish: (1) chotelos' na rodinu často -x- čorta s dva; (2) (Ol'ga) Da! Skoree v Moskvu! -x- (Čebutykin i Tuzenbach smejutsja); (3) (Ol'ga:) Maša budet priezžat v Moskvu na vse leto, každyj god -x- (Maša:) (ticho nasvistyvaet pesnju).

Neither in his stories, however, nor in *The Three Sisters* and the *Cherry Orchard*, do these ever become independent planes with a structure and continuity of their own, which can relate only as planes. They can and do mingle or separate at any time. There is no play in which both foreground and background are continually present or in action. This division is only one means out of several for making clear and visible the connections between the conjunct and disjunct meanings of the word. What we obtain in this way is indeed the see-through word.[26]

We have mentioned sounds. These play a highly important rôle in the plays, ranging from directly referential (a shot) to a kind of summing-up, like the breaking string. An extreme case is the replacement of words by sounds in the dialogue. While there are some comparable instances in the stories, it is a much more frequent phenomenon in the later plays. Because of the direct impact of the spoken word the effect is much more telling in the theatre. Our above examples concerning the departure for Moscow and the noise in the hearth are in this category. So is Solenyj's *Cip-cip-cip*. A very clear example is the *tram tam tam* exchange between Veršinin and Maša.

In such cases, the last one in particular, the contextual valencies of the other words take over and fill the sounds with meaning. It is in this context that we have to look for that meaning. The *tram tam tam* scene reminds one of the famous exchange between Kitty and Levin in *Anna Karenina*. The latter is however essentially different in that the initial letters in this scene refer expressly to words. The rendering of Maša's and Veršinin's words can only be approximate. Her's can be rendered by something like: "just talk on and on, I love to hear you go on like this, whatever you say". The reply is something like this: "it is wonderful to at least exchange sounds with you on the same wavelength, as second best to talking love". The exchange follows upon a line from Čajkovskij's *Evgenij Onegin* sung by Veršinin. A realization seems possible, therefore, in which the exchange is partly sung. This would perhaps add to the meaning without essentially changing it. The second exchange is a kind of verification and confirmation of their attitude (the third time it has become simply a signal).

This interpretation has to take into account the fact that the *tram-tam-tam* exchange is in the affirmative and not in the form of a question, as it was in an earlier version[27]; also the fact that it is terminated by Fedotik entering the room. Thus its meaning is entirely contextual. But the most important material for the interpretation of this passage is still the objective meaning of Veršinin's entire talk. It remains a fact that the very expressive exchange it leads to has no objective meaning of its own. But it also is a fact that such a passage can only be achieved by means of Čechov's words, i.e., in a context where the contextual valencies of the word can be so exploited. One of the functions of *tram-tam-tam* is also to make us see through the words of its context. It is a function that in other scenes is rendered by the two planes. It is probably essential that the *tram-tam-tam* occurs in a scene that does not have these two planes. In general, it will be clear that as the surface text becomes less directly meaningful the context has to be organized better. There are some instances in which the sound of the words brings out extra meanings. Thus: *ja dovolen, ja dovolen, ja dovolen — nadoelo, nadoelo, nadoelo*, and to a lesser extent: *amo amas amat*.

One step further and we have arrived at sounds without any meaning of their own. These are frequent in the plays: instruments playing in the background, people humming on the stage, *šum v pečke*, thunder. In the stories such sounds did occur, as heard by a character. Their further development had to wait for the plays. In the plays the sounds could be made instead of described, and the character was no longer a necessary intermediary. The function of the sounds can be several. The humming of a character can reflect his well-being, while the sounds at the end of the *Cherry Orchard* sum up the theme of the play.

It is perhaps in this way that the plays in turn influenced the stories. There are no *tram tam tam* effects in either *Nevesta* or in *Archierej*, but there are many sounds. There is the breaking string in *Nevesta* and there is the *tok-tok-tok* of the watchman. The sounds in *Archierej* are less direct, but more pervasive: it is what the *Archierej* hears that activates his memory. Rhythm and sound repetitions play a structural rôle.

Memory has an important part to play in these last stories. Its most important function is to unite the two planes, in time and in space. It effects a telescoping of what in the plays were separate planes. In earlier stories memory was connected with a separate narrator (for example *Doč' Al'biona, Veročka, Moja žizn'*).[28] Now it brings the two planes into each other's direct perspective, making both the past and the present diaphanous. The omniscient author becomes almost invisible and is extremely mobile. The word as a direct referent, as a carrier of meaning and the word as a carrier of tones and atmosphere have in these last two stories completely interpenetrated.[29]

Historically speaking Čechov cleared the way for the symbolists. It is understandable that they claimed him as their own, as did Belyj.[30] Čechov, according to Belyj, made reality diaphanous and showed what was behind it. This was enough to make him a symbolist without his knowing it. The claim cannot be sustained in its entirety. While it is possible to agree with Belyj that Čechov did make reality diaphanous he did not attribute more reality or more meaning to what was behind it than to that reality itself. What was behind it was not more essential than what was in it. Belyj was not the only one who interpreted him in this way. In his production of the plays Meyerhold showed the same tendency.[31] Čechov's handling of words made him a predecessor of the futurists also. Majakovskij vindicated him as such. In his article *Two Čechovs*[32] of 1914 he even went so far as to say that all Čechov's works were solutions of problems exclusively concerned with words.

To sum up our finding briefly: Čechov started his literary career at a time when the literary medium was losing its autonomy and expressive force and was becoming subservient and instrumental to ideology. His earliest stories remained outside the main current of literature, at its humoristic fringe. In these stories the element of 'literature' was strong. He created them in words that had no distinction within this genre, except through the economy of their use. If he marked them it was through vertical valencies. There was a full understanding between reader and author, who were on a different plane from the narrated world. Anecdote and *feuilleton* were the kernels of his narration.

In the next phase anecdote and *feuilleton* begin to inter-penetrate, the author moves towards the character and away from the reader. Horizontal valencies become more important and vertical ones become less important. A first step in this direction is the juxtaposition of an observation on a charac-ter's inadequacy of expression and an authorial comment on the expressive force of this inadequacy.

After this the author's and characters' planes of speech begin to inter-penetrate. *Erlebte Rede* becomes an important, but not the only manifestation of this interpretation. The word enters into a double perspective that strengthens its horizontal valencies. This in turn makes possible a twofold connection be-tween the sentences and paragraphs, either thematically, or through associative selection. This can lead to a situation in which a plot realizes itself through near-autonomous scenes. In these finally the word attains a degree of autonomy within the smaller unit comparable to that of the scene with respect to the plot. Some of these developments were further refined on the stage. In his very last stories the inter-penetration of plot and scene gives them a strong lyrical character. The difference be-tween marked and unmarked words virtually disappears. It is neutralized by the strengthening of the horizontal valencies. Schematically speaking Čechov's artistry began with the story as a whole and gradually worked inward until the individual word could release its full energy. In the final phase it could realize it-self in five ways: thematically, through motifs, through valen-cies, as sound, and as noise.

Čechov made possible the transition from the great realists to the symbolists. As we have seen this was realized by those who came after him. What he did was to set the word free. Too much in bondage to ideology when he started writing, directly subservient and instrument of express meanings, the prose word under Čechov's hands explored its limits and opened up new views. It made the world in which he lived both visible and transparent.

(Amsterdam-Utrecht 1973)

NOTES

[1]   A. Reichling, *Verzamelde studies over hedendaagse problemen der taalwetenschap*[4], Zwolle 1966, pp. 43-44.

[2]   There are other factors at play also, among them: the inertia of the speaking process, inner censorship (Freudianisms), etc.

[3]   The literature on the subject is extensive. See in particular A. P. Čudakov, "Ob evoljucii stilja Čechova", in: *Slavjanskaja filologija* vypusk V, Moscow, Izd-vo MGU 1963, pp. 310-331; id., *Poetika Čechova*, M. 1971; N. A. Koževnikova, "Ob osobennostjach stilja Čechova (nesobstvenno-prjamaja rec')", in: *Vestnik MGU* 1963.2.51-62; and the articles by H. Hamburger, the latest being: "The Function of the Time Component in Čechov's Na podvode", in: *Dutch Contributions to the Seventh International Congress of Slavists*, The Hague 1973, pp. 237-270; the others are mentioned there, p. 237, n. 2.

[4]   V. V. Vinogradov, *Stilistika. Teorija poetičeskoj reči, Poetika*, M. 1963, pp. 62, 204.

[5]   Cf. Vinogradov, *o.c.*, p. 130. We prefer the term artistic to: poetic, the fundamental distinction being that between artistic and non-artistic, functional speech. The distinction between poetic speech in the narrow sense and prose speech is less important and much harder to make.

[6]   In such cases there is friction between words somewhere in the statement. Its progress is hampered. With words this means the suggestion of more than one possible combination: there is a 'fork' of meaning. We have to realize why we chose the one we did, and not the other.

[7]   "Predislovie k romanam" (1880), in: I. S. Turgenev, *PSSiP v dvadcati vos'mi tomach, Sočinenija*, t. XII, M.-L. 1966, pp. 303, 501. Cf. Jan M. Meijer, "Some notes on Dostoevskij and Russian Realism", in: *Russian Literature* 1973.4.5-17.

[8]   M. Bachtin, *Problemy poetiki Dostoevskogo*[2], M. 1963.

[9]   Georg Lukács, *Russische Literatur – Russische Revolution*, Rowholt, n.p. 1969, p. 296.

[10]   L. N. Tolstoj, *PSS*, serija 3-ja, pis'ma, t. 62, Pis'ma 1873-1879, M. 1953, pp. 268-9.

[10a] This does not mean, of course, that Dostoevskij, or Tolstoj themselves succumbed to this tendency. They were artists first and foremost and their greatness consists, *inter alia*, in resisting this tendency. It means that this tendency is inherent in later realism in Russia and that lesser talents succumbed to it or, at least, could not sufficiently resist it.

I am grateful to my first critical readers, Messrs W. Scmid and E. Amsinga, who pointed out to me the possibility of such an inference.

[11]   As appears from the following table he did not think a single story of the period 1880-1882 worthy of a place in his collected works. For the years 1883-1885 it was less than half. From 1886 the proportion

changes. (The data are made up from the 12-volume Ogonek edition of 1950.)

year	accepted	rejected	year	accepted	rejected	year	accepted	rejected
1880	–	8	1888	9	1	1896	2	–
1881	–	3	1889	2	–	1897	4	–
1882	–	24	1890	2	–	1898	6	1
1883	20	61	1891	2	–	1899	4	–
1884	21	29	1892	7	4	1900	1	–
1885	38	49	1893	2	–	1901	–	–
1886	55	44	1894	7	–	1902	1	–
1887	50	13	1895	6	–	1903	1	–

[12] On the fiziologija, cf. A. G. Cejtlin, *Stanovlenie realizma v russkoj literature*, M. 1965. The term feuilleton has been used with different meanings. See, for example, the entry s.v. fel'eton in: *Kratkaja literaturnaja enciklopedija* (M. 1962, t. 7), and in: *Bol'šaja enciklopedija* (Spb. 1900-1909, t. XII). It does not appear among the sub-titles Čechov often gave his stories, especially in the Čechonte period, perhaps because at that time it designated rather the part of the paper in which his stories were placed than these stories themselves. A term he frequently used was *scenka*.

[13] Letter of March 28, 1886, *PSSiP* t. XIII, M. 1948, p. 191.

[14] P. Bicilli, *Anton P. Čechov*, München 1966, p. 113, considers the 'Nullösung' as a characteristic of the humorous anecdote as such. One should, we think, distinguish between explosive and 'implosive' endings. In stories like *Sosedi* he sees a different and more complex treatment of anecdotical matter: instead of the Nullösung we find a phenomenon one might describe as the decay of human relationships. These two phenomena do not seem to be of the same order, the former being a formal, and the latter a thematical characteristic.

[15] Letter of March 28, 1886, *l.c.*, p. 192.

[16] From here on, when speaking of the Čechonte period, we have in mind the period up to 1886-7, that is, not only those stories in which this pseudonym was used, but the period he used pseudonyms (besides Čechonte, often Čelovek bez selezinki and brat moego brata). Occasionally he had signed a story Čechov before, e.g., *V more* and *Švedskaja spička* of 1883, and *Gordyj čelovek* of 1884.

[17] It is striking that both the first and the last (but one) Čechov story are located in church and that in both these stories the memory of the main character is an important structural element.

[18] This choice presents itself in principle to every writer at almost any point of the story. A comparative study seems possible that would start from the most general outline of the fabula and that would inquire into the division of narrative 'matter' over stylistic and thematic devices. Čechov seems particular in this respect in that the transitions between theme and style are so fluent and so visible. Cf. Bicilli, *o.c.*, p. 99. In

the same category falls the fact, often commented upon, that Čechov often describes nature indirectly, through the prism of a character. (See, e.g., Vinogradov, *o.c.*, p. 56-7). For the descriptions as a whole the connection between word and referent becomes indirect and thereby longer. This also has a spatial aspect. But it does not apply to the separate words making up the description. Perhaps under the influence of Trigorin this fact has been overstressed. The moon he commented on can appear directly also, see for example *Pečeneg*: "kak raz nad dvorom plyla po nebu polnaja luna i pri lunnom svete dom i sarai kazalis' belee čem dnem." (IX, 127).

What has been called Čechov's *nedogovorennost'* (cf. Hélène Auzinger, "Čechov und das Nicht-zu-Ende-sprechen", in: *Die Welt der Slaven* (1960), 5, 233-244) refers to essentially the same phenomenon. One can maintain the position that each literary current and each writer choose their own zones of expression and of the ineffable. Čechov's nedogovorennost', impressionism, or what terms one chooses, strikes the reader by its contrast to the great writers that preceded him.

[19] P. Bicilli, *o.c.*, p. 61, stresses the frequency and the importance of this verb in Čechov's stories throughout the years. A statistical inquiry would probably show a higher frequency in the early, and middle 'nineties. Cf. also L. D. Usmanov, "Princip 'Sžatosti' v poetike pozdnego Čechova-belletrista i russkij realizm konca XIX veka", in: *Poetika i stilistika russkoj literatury, Pamjati akademika Viktora Vladimiroviča Vinogradova*, L. 1971, pp. 246-253.

[20] Cf. L. A. Sokolova, *Nesobstvenno-avtorskaja (nesobstvenno-prjamaja) reč' kak stilističeskaja kategorija*, Tomsk 1968. In her minimum definition she calls it "a way of narration that includes both the author's and the character's plane" (sposob izloženija, zakljucajuščijsja v sovmeščenii sub"ektivnych planov avtora i geroja). At the end of the book she gives a fuller definition: one of the three ways of rendering the content of a literary work which consists in the combination of the planes of author and character in an equilibrium between the including and excluding means of speech and which participates in the division of functions between the voices of author and characters (*o.c.*, pp. 10, 276).

Against this inclusive definition cf. Wolf Schmid, *Die Textaufbau in den Erzählungen Dostoevskij's*, München 1973, in particular pp. 55-6. We use the term in the wider sense, because the double perspective in which the word functions is the fundamental fact from the point of view of this article. Cf. also N. A. Koževnikova, "Ob osobennostjach stilja Čechova. nesobstvenno-prjamaja reč' ", in: *Vestnik MGU* 1963.2.51-62. The article has a number of interesting observations. It postulates a direct link between the disappearance of the I-narrator and the strengthening of the character's voice. This is true to some extent for the period 1886-7. In the longer perspective the omniscient narrator succeeded the I-narrator.

See also L. D. Usmanov, "Iz nabljudenij nad stilem pozdnego Čechova", in: *Vestnik LGU* 1966.2.95-88.

[21] This is akin to what Nilsson terms bloc technique. In his penetrating study of some aspects of Čechov's narrative technique (N. A. Nilsson, "Studies in Čechov's Narrative Technique. "The Steppe" and "The Bishop", *Stockholm Slavic Studies* 2, Acta Universitatis Stockholmiensis, Stockholm 1968) he describes it as "placing small complete scenes next to each other without any comments. There is still a clear chronological scheme and logical development from one scene to another, but the reader should never feel that there is a narrator guiding him, anxious to explain everything" (p. 63), and "scene is added to scene (...) but there are no clear transitions, no comments" (p. 70). In our opinion it is not so much the absence of comment that is essential, but the choice between thematical and atmospheric connections that is important in this respect.

[22] On repetition cf. Josip Matešić, "Wiederholung als Stilmittel in der Erzählprosa Čechovs", in: *Die Welt der Slawen* (1970), XV, 1.17-25.

[23] It is for this reason that we have taken this story as an example. It does not mean that the possibilities this story illustrates necessarily occur in other stories of this period also. Rather the reverse – a story like *Dama s sobačkoj*, written only a few months earlier, has many features of previous phases: an I-narrator puts in a fleeting appearance, there is less stress on separate scenes, the connection through plot lines dominate over the 'atmospheric' ones.

[24] In a number of respects we differ from Čudakov's views as they have been laid down in an article (A. P. Čudakov, "Ob evoljucii stilja Čechova" in: *Slavjanskaja filologija*, vyp. V, izd-vo MGU 1963, pp. 310-331). For the mature Čechov he distinguishes two periods (1887-1894-1904). In the first the subjective plane of the hero dominates, in the second period the narrator has more rights and the events can be presented through the prism of more than one hero. The difference between the periods is not in the language means used, but in the structure of the stories and in the functions of the language means that are used. In this second period the narrative remains within the narrator's field and the hero's phraseology constitutes only a slight modulation of this plane. For Čudakov, finding out the style of a writer is equivalent to finding out the 'narrative system' of that writer. The notion of system, in our view, should be used with care in regard to historical developments: precisely as a style becomes a system, i.e., highly predictable, it loses its effectiveness and will have to be discarded.

Čudakov's theses are further developed in his book (*Poetika Čechova*, M. 1971). At the end of the first period, i.e., towards 1887 the closed spheres of narrator and character inter-penetrate, and an objective phase sets in in which "the word is as belonging to the character as it evidently is foreign to the narrator's style" (p. 51). The objective stories are of two kinds: one in which the evaluation implied in the hero's word is close to the narrator's position, and one in which they differ. In the third period "the voice of the narrator occupies the central place in the story. The narrative (...) does not include the character's speech in its full scope, but transformed. The half-direct speech is partly crowded out by indirect speech" (p. 90). While in the first period "the narrator acts as the final valuating instance, he passes judgement in the name of the author", in the third "the narrator is only somehow close to the author but does not pass final judgement in his name" (p. 101). Čechov fuses the descriptive and the narrative elements of a story (p. 135). The world is presented through a sentient centre (konkretnoe vosprinimajuščee soznanie, p.136).

The section of the book from which we quote is the most valuable. We cannot follow him when he develops the 'slučajnostnyj princip' in Čechov rendering of the world, and in the way he distinguishes author and narrator. Finally we do not agree with the statement that "The notion of the ineffable lies at the root of Čechov's poetics of the beyond" (p. 273). But the reader of this careful, if not thoroughly organized book may find arguments against our positions that we could well have overlooked.

[25] K. S. Stanislavskij, *Sobr. soč. v vos'mi tomach*, t. 1, M. 1954, pp. 223, 237, 439.

[26] We have avoided the term podtekst here: it has been used so widely that the concept has lost its clarity. For a short survey, see the entry by V. Chalizev in: *Kratkaja literaturnaja enciklopedija* (vol. V, M. 1968) and the literature mentioned there; also T. I. Sil'man. "Podtekst kak lingvističeskoe javlenie", in: *Naučnye doklady vysšej školy, filolgičeskie nauki*, 1969, 1.84-90. See also N. Berkovskij. "Čechov. Ot rasskazov i povestej k dramaturgii", in: *Russkaja literatura* 1965.4., in particular p. 37.

[27] *Literaturnoe nasledstvo*, vol. 68. "Čechov", M. 1960, p. 58.

[28] For Čechov the writer memory was always an important element, almost a required filter. Cf. his letter to F. Batjuškov of 15.XII.1897 (*PSSiP* vol. 17, p. 193): "I can only write from merory and I never wrote directly from nature. A theme has to pass through my memory so that remains only that which is important or typical". This is an entirely different question from that what rôle memory plays in the characters, but it may help to explain the fact why memory was an important ingredient in the later stories. Cf. n. 17.

[29] The process was a difficult one, in particular for *Nevesta* – at least we are better documented on this one. The gestation of this story was a long one. The juxtaposition of scenes reminds one more of the theatre pieces than of *V ovrage*. The reduction process which led to the final text took away some of the more theatre-like scenes. Cf. V. Gol'diner, V. Chalizev, "Rabota Čechova nad rasskazom 'Nevesta' ", in: *Voprosy literatury* 1961 9.167-183. Cf. also Thomas G. Winner, "Theme and Structure in

Čechov's 'The Betrothed' ", in: *Indiana Slavic Studies* III, The Hague 1963, pp. 163-172.
[30] A. Belyj, *Arabeski*, M. 1911, p; 391-408. Even in 1901 an anonymous reviewer to *The Three Sisters* used the term to characterize aspects of it: Čudakov, *Poetika Čechova o.c.*, p. 211.
[31] See *Literaturnoe nasledstvo*, vol. 68, *o.c.*, pp. 431-2, 447-8.
[32] V. Majakovskij, "Dva Čechova", in: V. V. Majaovskij, *Sobranie sočinenij v vos'mi tomach*, t. 1, M. 1968, pp. 341-348.

BIBLIOGRAPHY

Auzinger, Hélène
    1960   "Čechov und das Nicht-zu-Ende-sprechen", *Die Welt der Slaven* 5, 233-44.
Bachtin, M.
    1963   *Problemy poetiki Dostoevskogo*[2] (Moskva).
Belyj, A.
    1911   *Arabeski* (Moskva).
Berkovskij, N.
    1965   "Čechov. Ot rasskazov i povestej k dramaturgii", *Russkaja literatura* 4.
Bicilli, P.
    1966   *Anton P. Čechov* (München).
Čechov, A. P.
    1944-50 *Polnce sobranie sočinenij i pisem*, 20 vols (Moskva).
    1950   *Sobranie sočinenij*, 12 vols (biblioteka ogonek) (Moskva).
Cejtlin, A. G.
    1965   *Stanovlenie realizma v russkoj literature* (Moskva).
Čudakov, A. P.
    1963   "Ob evoljucii stilja Čechova, *Slavjanskaja filologija* vyp. V, Moskva, Izd-vo *MGU*, pp. 310-331.
    1971   *Poetika Čechova* (Moskva).
Gol'diner, V. and V. Chalizev
    1961   "Rabota Čechova nad rasskazom 'Nevesta' ", *Voprosy literatury* 9, 167-83.
Hamburger, H.
    1973   "The Function of the Time Component in Čechov's Na Podvode", *Dutch Contributions to the Seventh International Congress of Slavists* (The Hague), pp. 237-70.
Koževnikova, N. A.
    1963   "Ob osobennostjach stilja Čechova (nesobstvenno-prjamaja reč')", *Vestnik MGU* 2, 51-62.

Literaturnoe nasledstvo
  1960   vol. 68 (Moskva).
Lukács, G.
  1969   *Russische Literatur – russische Revolution*, Rohwolt, n.p.
Majakovskij, V. V.
  1968   *Sobranie sočinenij v vos'mi tomach*, t. 1 (Moskva).
Matešić, J.
  1970   "Wiederholung als Stilmittel in der Erzählprosa Čechovs",
            Die Welt der Slaven (XV) 1, 17-25.
Meijer, J. M.
  1973   "Some Notes on Dostoevskij and Russian Realism", *Russian
            Literature* 4, 5-17.
Nilsson, N. A.
  1968   *Studies in Čechov's Narrative Technique "The Steppe" and
            "The Bishop"* (Stockholm).
*Poetika i stilistika russkoj literatury Pamjati akademika Viktora Vladimi-
roviča Vinogradova*
  1971   Leningrad.
Reichling, A.
  1966   *Verzamelde studies over hedendaagse problemen der taal-
            wetenschap*[4] (Zwolle).
Schmid, W.
  1973   *Die Textaufbau in den Erzählungen Dostoevskij's* (München).
Sil'man, T. I.
  1969   "Podtekst kak lingvističeskoe javlenie", *Naučnye doklady
            vysšej školy, filologičeskie nauki* 1, 84-90.
Sokolova, L. A.
  1968   *Nesobstvenno-avtorskaja (nesobstvenno-prjamaja) reč' kak
            stilističeskaja kategorija* (Tomsk).
Stanislavskij, K. S.
  1954   *Sobranie sočinenij v vos'mi tomach*, t. 1 (Moskva).
Tolstoj, L. N.
  1953   *Polnoe sobranie sočinenij*, serija 3-ja, pis'ma, t. 62 (Moskva).
Turgenev, I. S.
  1966   *PSSiP v dvadcati vos'mi tomach, sočinenija*, t. XII (Moskva-
            Leningrad).
Usmanov, L. D.
  1966   "Iz nabljudenij nad stilem pozdnego Čechova", *Vestnik LGU*
            2, 95-98.
  1971   "Princip 'sžatosti' v poetike pozdnego Čechova-belletrista i
            russkij realizm konca XIX veka", *Poetika i stilistika russkoj
            literatury, Pamjati akademika Viktora Vladimiroviča Vino-
            gradova* (Leningrad), pp. 246-53.
Vinogradov, V. V.
  1963   *Stilistika. Teorija poetičeskoj reči. Poetika* (Moskva).

Winner, Th. G.
  1963   "Theme and Structure in Čechov's 'The Betrothed' ", *In-
           diana Slavic Studies* III (The Hague), pp. 163-72.

and Studies, no. ... the Regional
data base, item ... Wellington, pp. ...

EIN BEITRAG ZUR DESKRIPTIVEN DRAMATISCHEN POETIK

HERTA SCHMID

Ein Beitrag zur deskriptiven
dramatischen Poetik

I. PRINZIPIEN DES DRAMATISCHEN TEXT- UND BEDEUTUNGS-AUFBAUS

Das Ziel dieser Studie ist, ein Begriffsinventar zu entwickeln, das eine strukturale Analyse des dramatischen Textes ermöglicht.

Die strukturale Analyse orientiert sich an den beiden Strukturdimensionen eines literarischen Textes, der vertikalen und der horizontalen Dimension. Die vertikale Dimension erfaßt die drei grundlegenden Schichten des literarischen Werks, nämlich die Ausdrucks-, die Bedeutungsschicht sowie die Schicht der dargestellten Welt. Diese drei Schichten sind simultan gegeben, da die jeweils 'höher' gelagerte Schicht die Funktion der 'zuunterst' liegenden Schicht ist. In der horizontalen Dimension dagegen wird die Aufeinanderfolge der Teile in jeder einzelnen Strukturschicht, woraus sich sukzessiv das Strukturganze als ein Sinnganzes entwickelt, erfaßt. Bei der Untersuchung der horizontalen Dimension stellt sich das Problem der Textsegmentierung. In der vorliegenden Studie wird der Versuch gemacht, solche Textsegmente zu definieren, die Teile im Sinne von einander gleichberechtigten Bedeutungseinheiten des Strukturganzen, welches der gesamte Text repräsentiert, darstellen.

1. *Der Aufbau des dramatischen Textes*

Die Ausdrucksseite des dramatischen Werks zeichnet sich durch einen gattungsspezifischen Textaufbau aus: im dramatischen Text laufen obligatorisch zwei heterogene *Textbänder*[1] simultan nebeneinander her. Diese beiden Textbänder werden durch die sog. Anmerkungen und durch die direkten Reden der Personen konstituiert. Sie sind heterogen, insofern sie auf unterschiedliche Subjektarten zurückgehen. Die direkten Reden müssen primär den dargestellten Personen zugeschrieben werden, während die Anmerkungen auf ein Subjekt außerhalb der dargestellten Welt, das im folgenden als *Autorsubjekt* bezeichnet werden soll, zurückgehen. Zu diesen beiden Subjektarten, den *Personensubjekten* und dem Autorsubjekt, muß aber noch eine weitere Instanz hinzugedacht werden: diejenige Instanz, die sich der direkten Reden der Personen und der Anmerkungen in ihrer gegenseitigen Koppelung bedient, um eine einzige, den einheitlichen Sinn des gesamten Dramas konstituierende Äußerung zu tun. Wir wollen diese Instanz als den *abstrakten Autor* bezeichnen. Die Unterscheidung dieser drei Subjektarten ist nötig, um die Leistungen der verschiedenen im dramatischen Text implizierten Sinnebenen zu differenzieren.

Zunächst soll das gegenseitige Verhältnis der beiden heterogenen dramatischen Äußerungsbänder untersucht werden. Die Anmerkungen sind den direkten Reden strukturell übergeordnet, da die Anmerkungen erst die Personen als die Träger der direkten Reden existentiell fundieren. Vom Gesichtspunkt der Anmerkungen aus sind die direkten Reden nur Konkretisationen des Attributs 'sprechende' Personen. Als solche sind die Personen das Korrelat der Darstellungsfunktion der Anmerkungen. Neben dem Attribut des Sprechens können die Anmerkungen die Personen auch mit Attributen des Soaussehens und des gestischen oder mimischen Verhaltens ausstatten. Darüber hinaus stellen sie auch andere Gegenständlichkeiten als die Personen, nämlich die äußere Situation mit deren räumlichen und zeitlichen Bestimmungen dar. Alle Darstellungsleistungen der Anmerkungen bleiben jedoch ein schematischer Vorentwurf der entsprechenden Gegenständlichkeiten, obwohl, je nach dem Stil des Werks, die Gegenstände im Raum oder auch das Aussehen und das sichtbare Verhalten der Personen sehr detailliert bestimmt sein können. Die Schematik ergibt sich daraus, daß die Rolle, die Funktion aller durch die Anmerkungen vorentworfenen Gegenständlichkeiten erst durch die direkten Reden eindeutig festgelegt wird.

Dieser Vorrang der direkten Reden in der eigentlichen Sinnkonstitution des dramatischen Textes kann erst später belegt werden. Die direkten Reden machen den Anmerkungen aber trotz ihrer strukturellen Abhängigkeit eine wesentliche Funktion in der Textbildung, nämlich die *Kontextprogression*, streitig. Unter der Kontextprogression soll die fortlaufende Entfaltung des Kontextes, der eine Sinneinheit darstellt, in der linearen Abfolge der Texteinheiten verstanden werden. Diese Funktion beanspruchen die direkten Reden insofern, als sie unmittelbar aufeinander folgen und formal und eventuell auch sinngemäß aneinander anknüpfen. Denn die direkten Reden der im Drama dargestellten Personen sind keine voneinander isolierten Äußerungen, sondern *Wechselreden*[2], die sich gegenseitig bedingen. Im Gegensatz dazu bilden die Anmerkungen keinen fortlaufenden Kontext, sondern werden punktuell eingesetzt. Je nach dem Typ der Anmerkungen geschieht dies auf zweierlei Weise. Die Anmerkungen, die Akte oder Szenen einführen, entwerfen die äußere Situation des kommenden Abschnitts, die für die folgenden Reden einen *Rahmen* abgeben, der durch sie ausgefüllt und konkretisiert wird. Die Anmerkungen hingegen, die die direkten Reden durch das Nennen des Namens der Person einführen, erfüllen nur die formalen Voraussetzungen für das Zustandekommen der Rede an dieser Stelle. Die Anmerkungen, denen eine Rahmenfunktion für die Szenen- oder Akteinheiten zukommt, überschreiten den fortlaufenden Kontext, der sich aus den direkten Reden und den bloß benennenden Anmerkungen zusammensetzt. Demgegenüber bleiben die bloß benennenden Anmerkungen insofern außerhalb der Kontextbewegung, als sich zwischen ihnen keine direkten Sinnbeziehungen ergeben, sondern jede dieser Anmerkungen ausschließlich dem von ihr entworfenen Gegenstand, Sachverhalt oder der sprechenden Person zugeordnet ist. Wenn

gesagt wurde, daß der dramatische Text durch zwei simultan
laufende Textbänder konstituiert werde, so gilt die Bestimmung der Simultanität nur für die Anmerkungen des zweiten
Typs. Denn nur diese sind den von ihnen entworfenen Gegenständen und Sachverhalten, insbesondere dem Verhalten des
Sprechens der Personen, direkt zugeordnet. Die Akte oder
Szenen entwerfenden Anmerkungen hingegen nehmen den in
ihren Rahmen eingefaßten Kontext vorweg. Doch auch die
bloß benennenden Anmerkungen können ihr Simultanitäts-
verhältnis zu den Gegenständlichkeiten zu einem Verhältnis
der Vorwegnahme des einen durch das andere modifizieren.
Eine solche Modifikation des Verhältnisses zwischen den
beiden Äußerungsbändern des dramatischen Textes hängt von
der Veränderung ihrer Funktionen bei der Konsituierung des
Gesamtsinns des Textes ab. Diese Funktionen und ihre möglichen Veränderungen sollen nun näher betrachtet werden.

2. Die Bedeutungskonstitution des dramatischen Textes

Den beiden den dramatischen Text bildenden Äußerungsbändern obliegt die Funktion der Darstellung ein und derselben Gegenständlichkeit. Diese Gegenständlichkeit ist im
Drama die *aktuelle, hier und jetzt gegebene Situation*. Das
Subjekt der Darstellung ist der abstrakte Autor, die beiden
heterogenen Äußerungsbänder sind die Mittel dieses abstrakten
Autors, um die aktuelle Situation darzustellen. Die Leistung
der beiden Textbänder bei ihrer gemeinsamen Aufgabe ist
unterschiedlich nach Maßgabe ihrer unterschiedlichen bedeu-
tungskonstituierenden Fähigkeit, und sie ist variabel in Abhängigkeit von der veränderlichen inneren Strukturierung der
aktuellen Situation.

Die wesentlichen Komponenten der aktuellen Situation sind
auf der einen Seite die äußere, objektive Situation und auf der
anderen Seite die Personen, die in dieser objektiven, vorgegebenen Situation subjektive Wahrnehmungszentren darstellen. Zu
den die äußere Situation konstituierenden Gegenständen gehören neben Dingen und Prozessen auch solche Objekte, die

nur durch die Reden von Personen vergegenwärtigt werden.
Darüber hinaus wird die aktuelle, hier und jetzt gegenwärtige
Situation perspektivisch verlängert auf das zuvor Gewesene
und das zukünftig Seiende. Zu dem Gesamtkomplex des in der
objektiven Situation Vorgegebenen und Angetroffenen gehört
für eine Person schließlich auch die andere Person oder andere
Personen. Die andere Person jedoch unterscheidet sich von den
übrigen die äußere Situation ausmachenden Gegenständen dadurch, daß sie ebenfalls ein subjektives Wahrnehmungszentrum
innerhalb der äußeren Situation darstellt. Die äußere Situation
fungiert für alle in ihr anwesenden Personen als ein gemein-
sames Wahrnehmungsfeld, innerhalb dessen sie sich nach Maßgabe ihres Standorts und ihrer inneren, subjektiven Voraussetzungen orientieren. Zwischen den Personen ergibt sich auf der
Basis dessen, daß jede von ihnen bei der andern mit einem solchen subjektiven Wahrnehmungszentrum rechnen muß, eine
besondere Beziehung, die die Voraussetzung für die Kommunikation ist. Den Begriff des subjektiven Wahrnehmungszen-
trums muß man auf folgende Weise interpretieren: zu ihm gehört nicht nur das im Hier und Jetzt von einem bestimmten
Punkt aus die aktuelle Situation wahrnehmende Bewußtsein,
sondern dieses Bewußtsein mit allen seinen vorgegebenen, die
aktuelle Wahrnehmung bedingenden Inhalten hat eine eigene
Geschichte, die durch die Gesamtheit all seiner Erfahrungen
ausgemacht wird, und eine Zukunftsperspektive, die durch
seine Erwartungen bestimmt wird. Diese die 'perspektivischen
Verlängerungen' der Wahrnehmungszentren der Personen ausmachenden Daten wollen wir die *innere Situation* der Personen
nennen. Jede Person muß bei der anderen mit einer solchen
inneren Situation rechnen und ihr eigenes Kommunikations-
verhalten an dieser orientieren.

Zwischen äußerer Situation und Person besteht eine spezifi-
sche, die Gesamtstruktur der aktuellen Situation im Drama be-
stimmende Beziehung: die äußere Situation, nun aufgefaßt im
globalen, auch die andere Person mit einbeziehenden Sinn, ist
der Person vorgegeben als ein Objekt, dem gegenüber sie sich
verhält, mit dem sie sich auseinandersetzt. Dieses Verhalten
kann auf zweierlei Weise beschaffen sein: die Person kann

gegenüber der äußeren Situation aktiv sein, wenn sie diese zum
Gegenstand ihrer Einwirkung macht, oder sie kann ihr gegenüber passiv sein, wenn sie selbst Objekt einer an ihr aus der
äußeren Situation ergehenden Einwirkung ist. Das Verhältnis
zwischen äußerer Situation und Person ist demnach struktu-
riert als ein *Aktions-Reaktionsverhältnis*, wobei jeder Pol
Träger der Aktion wie auch der Reaktion sein kann. Wesentlich für die individuelle Gestaltung der dargestellten aktuellen
Situation in einem Drama ist nun, ob die Person der aktive
oder passive Pol in diesem Spannungsverhältnis ist und welche
der Komponenten der äußeren Situation Träger des Aktions-,
resp. des Reaktionspols ist.

Grundsätzlich können Träger des Gegenpols in dem Aktions-Reaktionsverhältnis zwischen äußerer Situation und
Person eine andere Person, resp. ein Kollektiv, Vorgänge und
Ereignisse der gegenständlichen Situation oder auch Objekte in
dieser Situation und in der Rede aufgeworfene Gegenstände
sein. Dabei ist folgendes zu bedenken. Wenn die Aktions-Reaktionsspannung nicht auf der Personenebene verläuft, so ist der
Träger des Gegenpols kein selbständiges Subjekt. Wie macht
dann der abstrakte Autor seinem Adressaten, dem Leser, klar,
daß es sich bei dem Redethema, dem Gegenstand oder dem
Ereignis in der äußeren Situation um den Träger der Aktion
oder Reaktion handelt? Um die genannten Gegenständlichkeiten zu entwerfen, kann er sich der Anmerkungen oder der
direkten Reden der Personen bedienen. Ihre eigentliche Funktion und damit ihre Bedeutung und ihr Rang im gesamten Aufbau des dargestellten Situationskomplexes ergibt sich aber erst
aus dem Verhalten der mit ihnen konfrontierten Person, und
hier vor allem aus deren direkter Rede. Insofern bleiben alle
Anmerkungen, selbst wenn die von ihnen entworfenen Gegenstände Träger eines der Spannungspole sind, auf die bedeu-
tungspräzisierende Tätigkeit der direkten Reden angewiesen.
Erst durch die Bewertung in den direkten Reden der Personen
kann der abstrakte Autor dem Leser die Verteilung der Rolle
eines Aktions- oder Reaktionsträgers an die Komponenten der
äußeren Situation eindeutig klarmachen.

Zu bedenken ist aber auch noch, daß sich mit der Gegenwart mehrerer Subjekte in der dargestellten aktuellen Situation eine Verkomplizierung in den gegenseitigen Beziehungen aller Situationskomponenten über die Aktions-Reaktionsspannung hinaus ergibt. Denn zwischen zwei oder mehr Personen in derselben aktuellen Situation besteht eine offene *Kommunikationsspannung*, die im Leser, dem eine solche Situation dargestellt wird, die Erwartung auslöst, daß sie durch eine gegenseitige Zuwendung der Personen zueinander in der Rede eingelöst wird[3]. Die Aufnahme des Redekontaktes zwischen den dargestellten Personen bedeutet ein Erfüllen der von der objektiven Situation aus – zu der ja auch die andere Person gehört – an die in ihr sich befindenden Personen ergehenden Anforderung, sich mit der Situation auseinanderzusetzen. Doch braucht dieses Moment der Situationserfüllung nicht mit dem durch die Aktions-Reaktionsspannung bestimmten Verhalten der Person zusammenzufallen. Man muß daher bei den direkten Reden der Personen verschiedenartige Motivationsfaktoren unterscheiden: die Motivation, die sich aus der Aktions-Reaktionsspannung ergibt und die die *Hauptmotivation* der Rede ausmacht, und diejenige Motivation, die sich aus der Kommunikationsspannung zu dem oder den Partnern in derselben Situation ergibt und die im Verhältnis zu der Hauptmotivation eine nur sekundäre, *mitmotivierende Funktion* erfüllt. Erst wenn die Haupt- und mitmotivierenden Faktoren einer direkten Rede erkannt sind, entschlüsselt sich der volle Sinn dieser Rede.

Im Zusammenhang mit der Unterscheidung zwischen der Haupt- und der Mitmotivation der direkten Reden im Drama muß auch die Frage gestellt werden, wann man diese direkten Reden als *Dialog* bewerten kann. Soll man das formale Merkmal der Gliederung der direkten Reden in Wechselreden zum Kriterium des Dialogs machen, oder sollte man die Aktions-Reaktionsspannung, aus der heraus die direkten Reden erfolgen, darüber entscheiden lassen, ob es sich um einen Dialog oder um monologische Rede handelt? Der sicherste Weg zur Entscheidung dieser Fragen scheint mir der über die Rolle der direkten Reden in der aktuellen Situation zu sein.

Die Form der Wechselrede ist nur möglich, wenn zwei oder

mehr Personen in der aktuellen Situation vereint sind. Die von
Person zu Person überwechselnden Repliken scheinen dann an-
zuzeigen, daß die Personen einander wahrnehmen und sich in
ihrem Gesamtverhalten in der Situation aneinander orientieren, einander berücksichtigen. Dieses gegenseitige Sichwahr-
nehmen kann entweder eine mitmotivierende Funktion für das
Verhalten der Personen haben, wenn die Aktions-Reaktionsspannung außerhalb der zwischenpersonalen Beziehungen verläuft, oder sie kann auch die Hauptmotivation ausmachen,
wenn die verschiedenen Personensubjekte Träger der gegensätzlichen Spannungspole sind. In beiden Fällen kommt es zu
einer semantischen Verkomplizierung der einzelnen geäußerten
Repliken: in die Replik jeder Person geht nicht nur die Summe
aller von dieser Person zuvor geäußerten Repliken in der Rolle
des sinnbestimmenden Kontextes ein, sondern auch die Gesamtheit aller Repliken des oder der Partner. Jede Replik einer
Person ist also zweifach bedingt, durch den eigenen Kontext
der Person, den diese Replik an der Stelle, an der sie im Text
auftritt, resümiert und weiterträgt, und durch alle voraufgegangenen fremden Kontexte, die sie ebenfalls resümiert und –
oppositionell – weiterführt[4]. Vom Gesichtspunkt des sprechenden Subjekts aus zeigt sich diese doppelte Kontextver-
knüpfung innerhalb der Wechselrede in einer doppelten Motivation der von ihm für die Replik gewählten Redegegenstände
und deren Benennungen: die getroffene Wahl ist nicht nur
Resultat der eigenen Beziehung des Sprechers zum Gegenstand
der Rede und zu dem oder den Partnern, sondern auch der Beziehung, die der oder die Partner zu dem Gegenstand und zu
dem Sprecher hegen und soweit sie dem Sprecher bewußt ge-
worden sind.

In dem genannten Fall ist die Form der Wechselrede Anzeichen dafür, daß die sprechenden Personen dem aus der objektiven Situation in Gestalt der mitdargestellten übrigen Personen an sie ergehenden Verhaltensdruck nachgeben; sie lösen
die Kommunikationsspannung, die durch die Situation vorgegeben ist, ein. Will man dann dieses Sprechen als Dialog bezeichnen, so ist sein dialogischer Charakter durch das in der aktuellen Situation existierende kommunikative Beziehungsnetz

begründet. Die Reden realisieren einen Dialog, der in der aktuellen Situation offen angelegt ist. Die aufeinander folgenden Repliken verschiedener Sprecher bedingen sich dabei gegenseitig nach dem Muster von *Replik und Gegenreplik*, wobei ein Minimum an gegensätzlicher Beziehung zwischen den Repliken verschiedener Personen immer schon dadurch bedingt ist, daß jede Person ein individuelles Wahrnehmungszentrum innerhalb der gemeinsamen aktuellen Situation darstellt[5]. Doch läßt sich auch der Fall denken, daß sich die Personen dem Kommunikationsdruck der objektiven Situation nicht beugen. Die Personen nehmen dann einander gleichsam nicht wahr oder sehen auch bewußt einer von der Gegenwart des andern ab, und die von ihnen geäußerten Reden führen nur einen Kontext, den der sprechenden Person, fort und werden nur einseitig durch die Beziehung des Sprechers zum Gegenstand der Rede motiviert. Obwohl hier die Repliken das Aussehen einer Wechselrede haben, indem die Replik der einen Person formal als *Folgereplik* an die Replik der andern anschließt, handelt es sich nicht um Gegenrepliken, da sie einander bedeutungsmäßig nicht durchdringen. Wechselreden dieser Art müßte man ihrem semantischen Charakter nach als monologisch bezeichnen. Auf dem Hintergrund der auf eine Kommunikation hin angelegten Situation jedoch muß man sie als nicht erfüllten oder verweigerten Dialog bewerten. Aufschluß über den dialogischen oder monologischen Charakter der Wechselreden von Personen in einer dialogischen Situation gibt die *intentionale Einstellung* der Sprecher im Akt der Rede: stellt sich der Sprecher auf den oder die andern während seines Sprechens ein, orientiert er die Wahl des Redegegenstands und des Wortausdrucks an der Position des oder der andern, so wird die Wechselrede zum Dialog, sieht dagegen der Sprecher bei seiner Äußerung von der Gegenwart aller übrigen Personen ab, so ähnelt die Wechselrede nur formal einem Dialog, ihrem Bedeutungsaufbau nach entstehen Monologe.

Die bisherigen Erörterungen zum Dialog gingen von der offen dialogischen Situation und der Erscheinung der Wechselrede aus. Wie ist aber die Rede einer Person ohne Kommunikationspartner in der aktuellen Situation zu bewerten? Und ist tatsächlich jede Rede einer Person, die sich nicht intentional auf die Situationspartner einstellt, auch monologisch? Die Erscheinung des Dialogs einer Person mit sich selbst kommt hier ins Spiel, und ein solcher Dialog kann in Abwesenheit wie auch in Anwesenheit anderer Personen geführt werden.

Beim Dialog einer Person mit sich selbst übernimmt ein Sprecher zwei gegensätzliche Standpunkte, die er im Hin und Wider der Wechselrede zur Entfaltung bringt. Die resultierenden Reden erfüllen in formaler wie auch in bedeutungsmäßiger Hinsicht die Kriterien der dialogischen Rede, da hier die Wechselrepliken der beiden Sprechinstanzen zwei voneinander abhängige, gegensätzliche Kontexte aufbauen. Auch die dialogspezifische intentionale Einstellung wird in diesem Fall realisiert, indem die eine dargestellte Person abwechselnd die beiden von ihr imaginierten gegensätzlichen Wertungspositionen übernimmt und jeweils aus der einen Position gegen die andere anspricht. Der Unterschied zu dem oben untersuchten Fall liegt allein darin, daß hier die aktuelle Situation nicht von vornherein dialogisch angelegt ist, sondern daß sie erst durch die Sprechakte der in ihr dargestellten Person dialogisiert wird. Sind zwei oder mehr Personen in der aktuellen Situation vereint und führt eine Person dennoch einen Dialog mit sich allein, so mißachtet sie die an sie ergehenden objektiven Kommunikationsanforderungen ebenso wie eine monologisch sprechende Person in einer solchen Situation, doch baut sie eine zweite, subjektive dialogische Situation auf, die sich eigene Beziehungen zu der aktuellen objektiven Situation schaffen kann.

In welchem Verhältnis steht nun die Aktions-Reaktionsstrukturierung der dargestellten aktuellen Situation im Drama zum Problem des monologischen oder dialogischen Charakters der direkten Reden? Sollte tatsächlich, wie es nun den Anschein hat, die nur mitmotivierende Beziehung zwischen den Personen in der aktuellen Situation über den dialogischen oder monologischen Aufbau der Reden dieser Personen entscheiden?

Um diese Fragen zu beantworten, müssen wir noch einmal die in der aktuellen dargestellten Situation implizierten Subjektarten betrachten, denn ein Dialog kommt nach der bisherigen Definition dann zustande, wenn sich zwei oder mehr Subjekte im Akt ihrer Rede aneinander orientieren und sich aufeinander einstellen. Vorrangig ist hier das Subjekt der dargestellten Person(en), das sich einer objektiven Situation konfrontiert sieht, mit der es sich auseinanderzusetzen hat. Als Subjekt konstituiert sich die Person durch ihre Akte, zu denen auch die Redeakte gehören, selbst, obwohl die sprechend sich verhaltende und damit subjektbegabte Person durch die Anmerkungen des Autorsubjekts vorentworfen ist. Als darstellende Instanz bleibt das Autorsubjekt außerhalb des Bewußtseinsbereichs der dargestellten sprechenden Person, desgleichen der abstrakte Autor, der noch 'hinter' dem Autorsubjekt stehend zu denken ist. Wenn nun die Aktions-Reaktionsspannung, in die das dargestellte Subjekt eingelassen ist, auf der Gegenseite nicht durch ein ebenfalls dargestelltes anderes Subjekt getragen wird, steht dem Subjekt der Person kein gleichberechtigtes Subjekt als Partner gegenüber. Da sich die Person jedoch agierend oder reagierend auf die äußere Situation (in Gestalt eines Ereignisses, eines Gegenstandes) einstellt und entweder auf ihre eigene Einwirkung auf diese Situation eine Rückwirkung erwartet oder selbst auf eine an ihr ergangene Einwirkung reagiert, findet durch das dargestellte Subjekt eine sekundäre Subjektverleihung an die äußere Situation statt, zumindest in dem Sinne, daß das aktive Subjekt sich von seinem 'Partner' eine mehr oder weniger vorhersehbare Rückwirkung seines eigenen Verhaltens erwartet. Diese sekundäre Subjektivierung der äußeren Situation hat zur Folge, daß die Redeakte der dargestellten Person, die aus diesem Spannungsverhältnis heraus erfolgen, ebenfalls dialogisiert werden, obwohl sich in ihnen, da nur eine Seite 'spricht', auch nur ein Personenkontext entwickelt. Der subjektivierte Gegenpol konstituiert sich hier nicht wie bei der dialogischen Wechselrede durch Repliken selbst, sondern wird durch die Autoranmerkungen oder durch die Darstellungsfunktion der direkten Reden der Person entworden. Die seine Gegenposition markierenden Werte müssen aus den Repliken der einzigen sprechenden Instanz abgeleitet werden. Auf Grund dieser sekundären Subjektverleihung kön-

nen auch Reden einer Person in Abwesenheit personenhafter
Situationspartner, die normalerweise als Monolog eingestuft
werden, zur Kategorie der dialogischen Reden gezählt werden.
Unter dem Gesichtspunkt einer so interpretierten Aktions-
Reaktionsgliederung der aktuellen Situation im Drama muß
man nun noch einmal das Problem der Rolle der direkten Reden
und das Problem des dialogischen Charakters dieser Reden angehen. Im Gegensatz zu der offenen Dialogizität, die in der
Kommunikationsspannung zwischen zwei oder mehr dargestellten Personen enthalten ist, ist die Dialogizität des Aktions-
Reaktionsverhältnisses zwischen Person und äußerer Situation
(von anderen dargestellten Personen als Komponenten dieser
Situation muß in diesem Zusammenhang abgesehen werden)
nur latent. Sie wird erst durch die Subjektivierung der äußeren
Situation in den direkten Reden hervorgebracht. Erst durch
die Reden wird auch bestimmt, welche Komponente der aktuellen äußeren Situation Träger des Gegenpols in diesem für das
Drama grundlegenden Spannungsverhältnis ist. Die Person hat
jedoch nicht die Möglichkeit, aus diesem Spannungsverhältnis
zur vorgegebenen Situation herauszutreten, wie sie dies bei der
Kommunikationsspannung tun kann, wenn sie die Aufnahme
eines Sprechkontaktes mit dem Situationspartner verweigert.
Alle ihre Verhaltensweisen, auch ihr Schweigen, wird aus
diesem Grundverhältnis heraus bewertet, in das sie dadurch gestellt ist, daß sie selbst eine Komponente der vom abstrakten
Autor dargestellten aktuellen Situation bildet. Zur Realisierung der dramenspezifischen Grundstruktur ist somit die Darstellung einer Person in der aktuellen Situation völlig ausrei-
chend[6]. Die Darstellung zweier oder mehrerer Personen bringt
eine zusätzliche Kommunikationsspannung ein, die das Beziehungsnetz der direkten Reden um die mitmotivierenden
zwischenpersonalen Beziehungen erweitert und damit den Bedeutungsaufbau dieser Reden und des gesamten Textaufbaus
verkompliziert. Wenn allerdings die Aktions-Reaktionsspannung mit der Kommunikationsspannung zusammenfällt, kehrt
sich das Verhältnis von haupt- und mitmotivierenden Faktoren
der direkten Reden um: die zwischenpersonale Beziehung wird
nun zum Träger der Hauptmotivation, und die Beziehung der

Personen zu den übrigen Komponenten der aktuellen äußeren Situation übernimmt die mitmotivierende Funktion, indem sie stärker oder schwächer in den Gang der Reden eingreift.

Zusammenfassend läßt sich sagen, daß Darstellungsgegenstand des abstrakten Autors im Drama die aktuelle, hier und jetzt gegebene Situation ist, mit der sich eine Person aktiv oder reaktiv auseinandersetzen muß. Mittel der Darstellung sind einerseits die Anmerkungen des Autorsubjekts, die vornehmlich die objektive äußere Situation vorentwerfen und in ihren Einzelbestandteilen ergänzend präzisieren und die in ihr sich befindliche(n) Person(en) als sprechende existentiell fundieren, anderseits aber die direkten Reden der Person(en) selbst. Diesen direkten Reden kommt nun ein spezifisches bedeutungskonstituierendes Gewicht in verschiedenerlei Hinsicht zu. Auf der Ebene des Dargestellten bilden sie eine wesentliche und unumgängliche Komponente des Gesamtverhaltens der Person innerhalb und gegenüber der objektiven Situation, unumgänglich insofern, als sich das Drama etwa von der Pantomime gerade durch das Sprechen der in ihm dargestellten Person(en) unterscheidet. Durch die Einbindung in die Aktions-Reaktionsspannung zwischen Person und Situation erfahren die direkten Reden eine innere Polarisierung und Dialogisierung, so daß die im Drama vorfindliche direkte Rede, die immer zugleich als situationsgebundene (weil auf die aktuelle Situation bezogene) Rede bewertet werden muß, gleichzeitig stets auch Merkmale der Dialogizität aufweist. Diese Dialogizität kann ihren direkten Ausdruck in einer dialoghaften Wechselrede finden, wenn die der Person vorgegebene Situation eine oder mehr andere Personen enthält und wenn die Aktions-Reaktionsspannung zwischen diesen Personen verläuft, oder wenn die Mitberücksichtigung der anwesenden Person(en) eine das Sprechverhalten der Person spürbar beeinflussende Rolle spielt. Die Dialogizität der direkten Rede hängt aber nicht von dem Vorhandensein und dem Berücksichtigen oder Mitberücksichtigen anderer Personen in der aktuellen Situation ab. In ihrer Relation schließlich zu den Anmerkungen des Autorsubjekts erhalten die direkten Reden ein Übergewicht dadurch, daß sie erst eindeutig bestimmen, welche Komponenten der äußeren Situation Träger des Gegenpols der Aktions-Reaktionsspannung für die sprechende Person ist und wie die Beziehung zwischen den Anmerkungen und den direkten Reden selbst gestaltet ist: ob sie zueinander in einem Verhältnis der Gleichzeitigkeit stehen, oder ob sich zwischen ihnen ein Folgeverhältnis nach dem Muster von Aktion und Reaktion ergibt, wenn nämlich die Grundspannung der dargestellten aktuellen Situation zwischen Person und äußerer, gegenständlicher Situation verläuft. Die möglichen Verlagerungen dieser dramenkonstitutiven Grundspannung und die aus ihnen sich ergebenden Folgen für die Gesamtstruktur des Dramas sollen nun untersucht werden.

3. *Die Konstruktionsdominante des dramatischen Textes*

Die Träger der Aktion, resp. der Reaktion sind einander nicht gleichberechtigt hinsichtlich ihrer Wirkung auf die gesamte Konstruktion des dramatischen Textes. Vielmehr kommt der Aktionskomponente eine vorrangige Rolle zu, insofern sie alle übrigen Komponenten der dargestellten Situation hierarchisiert, die dramatische Textkonstruktion typisiert und die Strukturbildung für das gesamte Werk in der vertikalen und horizontalen Dimension dominiert. Die Aktionskomponente wird damit zur *Konstruktionsdominanten* des dramatischen Textes.

   Da Aktionsträger nicht nur eine Person, sondern auch die äußere gegenständliche Situation sein kann, soll der Begriff der Aktion möglichst formal definiert werden, nämlich als aktive Beziehung zwischen zwei Komponenten der im Drama dargestellten aktuellen Situation, wobei ein Pol in der Aufnahme der Beziehung initiativ ist. Einer der beiden Pole dieser Beziehung ist dabei immer eine Person, die entweder eine an ihr ergehende Aktionsinitiative aus der vorgegebenen Situation erleidet oder die selbst eine Aktionsinitiative gegenüber der Situation ergreift. Die aktive Beziehung kann den Charakter einer am Gegenpol orientierten Handlung haben, wenn etwa eine Person auf eine andere oder auf die äußere Situation zielbewußt einwirken will, um eine Veränderung des gegebenen

Situationsstandes in einer von ihr vorbedachten Richtung zu erzielen; sie kann aber auch den Charakter eines bloßen Angehens oder Betreffens für den Gegenpol haben, wenn z.B. ein Vorgang in der äußeren Situation eine Person berührt, das Ziel, resp. der Endpunkt dieses Vorgangs aber nicht an der betroffenen Person orientiert ist. Die Reaktion zu der so definierten Aktion ist dann das Sich-Verhalten des Gegenpols gegenüber der an ihm ergangenen Beziehungsinitiative. Dieses Sich-Verhalten kann seinerseits aktiv sein, wenn es in eine Gegenaktion umschlägt, oder passiv, wenn es ein bloßes Erdulden der empfangenen Initiative bleibt. Die Vorrangigkeit der Aktion vor der Reaktion ergibt sich daraus, daß die Reaktion immer durch die Aktion bedingt ist, sei sie nun selbst aktiv oder passiv. Diese Bedingtheit drückt sich einerseits in der qualitativen Beschaffenheit der Reaktion aus, die immer die Spuren der ergangenen Aktion an sich trägt, und anderseits auch in dem Stellenwert der Reaktion: die Reaktion bedarf der Initiierung durch die Aktion, die Aktion soll daher in ihrer Beziehung zur Reaktion als der *initiierende Faktor* bezeichnet werden.

Der initiierende Faktor bestimmt nicht nur den Reaktionsfaktor und weist allen übrigen Komponenten der aktuellen dargestellten Situation ihre Rolle zu, sondern er entscheidet auch *dauernd* über die Fortentwicklung der gesamten Situation durch die einzelnen Ausgleichsphasen im gegenseitigen Verhältnis der Aktions-Reaktionspole hindurch. Er bestimmt damit auch die horizontale Strukturierung der Schicht der dargestellten Welt im Drama. Auf diese Funktion der Konstruktionsdominanten soll im weiteren noch einmal zurückgegriffen werden. Von der ständigen, den Gesamtverlauf des Dramas beeinflussenden und bestimmenden Wirkung des initiierenden Faktors muß man den einzelnen *Redeimpuls* unterscheiden, der *momentan* den Redeakt der Person auslösen kann und von wechselnden Komponenten der äußeren oder inneren Situation der Personen ausgehen kann.

Auf welche Weise vermag nun der initiierende Faktor der dargestellten Situation die Textkonstruktion zu typisieren? Dies geschieht über die Weise, wie sich die direkte Rede als die maßgebliche bedeutungskonstituierende Komponente im dra-

matischen Textaufbau zum initiierenden Faktor verhält. Hier-
für sind verschiedene Typen denkbar, die gleichzeitig verschiedene Typen der dramatischen Struktur darstellen[7].

Für die Einzeltypen der direkten Rede lassen sich zunächst
zwei Hauptgruppen feststellen, deren unterscheidendes Merkmal die Weise der Ausnutzung bzw. Nichtausnutzung der Kommunikationsspannung in der dargestellten Situation ist. So
kann einmal die Aktions-Reaktionsspannung zwischen den in
derselben Situation vereinten Personen verlaufen. Eine Person
verfolgt gegenüber der andern ein Ziel, zu dessen Durchsetzung
sie die Redeakte als ein Mittel benutzt. Dieses Ziel, das von
dem Interesse der aktiven Person an dem Situationspartner
und ihrem eigenen, durch die innere Situation bestimmten
Interesse determiniert wird, ist der eigentliche den gesamten
Verlauf der Wechelrede zwischen den Personen lenkende initiierende Faktor. Aktion und Reaktion werden hier von der
Spannung zwischen den Personen getragen, und die Wechselreden sind der direkte Ausdruck dieser Spannung. Ein Zu-
sammenfallen zwischen der Aktions-Reaktionsspannung und
der Kommunikationsspannung liegt auch dann vor, wenn keine
der Personen gegenüber der oder den andern ein bestimmtes
Ziel verfolgt, sondern wenn der Hauptzweck der Redeakte die
Kontaktaufnahme und das Aufrechterhalten dieses Redekontaktes ist. Bei einem solchen Sprechverhalten stehen die formalen Sprechbeziehungen im Vordergrund, der initiierende
Faktor, der den Sprechkontakt immer wieder in Gang bringt
und weiterführt, kann bei einer Person liegen, aber auch von
Person zu Person überwechseln. Eine wichtige Rolle erhalten
hier die einzelnen Sprechimpulse, die aus der äußeren gegenständlichen Situation, aber auch aus dem von der inneren Situation jeder einzelnen Person bestimmten Assoziationsbereich
kommen können. Etwas anders liegt der Fall, wenn ein bestimmtes Thema der Rede im Vordergrund steht. Die Personen
bemühen sich dann, in ihren Sprechakten die ihrer Meinung
nach richtige Bewertung des Themas oder auch verschiedenartige Seiten dieses Themas gegen die von den Partnern aufgeworfene Bewertung oder die von ihnen herausgestellten Seiten
zu entwickeln. Zum initiierenden Faktor wird hier das Rede-

thema selbst, wenn die Absicht der Überzeugung oder Überredung des andern zu der eigenen Meinung bei den Personen hinter der Absicht der sachadäquaten Entfaltung und Bewertung zurücktritt. Eine Person kann dann auch aus der Kommunikationsspannung mit dem Partner heraustreten und den Redegegenstand in vor sich selbst vertretenen gegensätzlichen Bedeutungspositionen dialogisch entfalten. Ihre Rede ist dann zwar in sich dialogisiert, erscheint aber gegenüber einem eventuell anwesenden Situationspartner als verweigerter Dialog oder als Monolog. Typen, die auf einem Nichtausnutzen der Kommunikationsspannung basieren, sind dort gegeben, wo die Aktions-Reaktionsspannung zwischen der Person und der äußeren, gegenständlichen Situation verläuft. Der initiierende Faktor kann hier einmal bei der äußeren Situation liegen, wenn in ihr Prozesse ablaufen oder Ereignisse eintreten, die die Person betreffen und zur Reaktion herausfordern. Die Reaktion in der Rede ist dann durch die Art der ergangenen Aktion ebenso wie durch die mit der inneren Situation der Person gegebenen Reaktionsbedingungen bestimmt; eine eventuelle Kontaktaufnahme zu einem Situationspartner hat keinen entscheidenden Einfluß auf den Verlauf der Aktions-Reaktionsschritte zwischen der Person und der äußeren Situation. Der initiierende Faktor kann aber auch bei der Person liegen. Ziel des Verhaltens und der Reden der Person ist dann die aktive Einwirkung auf die äußere Situation, wobei die Hinwendung an einen Situationspartner Mittel zum Durchsetzen dieses Ziels sein kann. Dabei ist denkbar, daß die Person auch den Reaktionspart mit ihren Reden gestaltet, wenn sie die mögliche oder unterstellte Wirkung ihrer Aktion auf die äußere Situation in ihren Redeprozeß aufnimmt. Die äußere, objektiv gegebene Situation kann dann Reizmomente liefern, die die Person zu Stützmomenten für ihre Interpretation der Reaktion der Situation macht. Die Kommunikationsspannung spielt in beiden Fällen eine sekundäre Rolle.

Die Verschiebung der Achse der Aktions-Reaktionsspannung auf unterschiedliche Träger innerhalb der äußeren Situation hat Folgen für die Kontextgestaltung. Zum einen wirkt sie sich auf die Weise aus, wie die direkten Reden der Personen

sich zueinander verhalten, und zum andern modifiziert sie das
Verhältnis zwischen den beiden Textbändern des dramatischen
Textes. Im letzteren Fall treten dann Spannungen zwischen
den verschiedenen am Zustandekommen des dramatischen
Textes beteiligten Subjektarten auf.

In den Fällen, wo die Kommunikationsspannung zwischen
den Personen mit der Aktions-Reaktionsspannung identisch ist
oder wo ein Redethema in den Redeakten einer oder mehrerer
Personen dialogisch entfaltet wird, sind die aufeinander folgenden Repliken tatsächlich auch Gegenrepliken in dem Sinne,
daß die eine die folgende als Reaktion nicht nur stellenmäßig,
sondern auch inhaltlich bedingt. Die Kontextprogression ver-
bleibt auf der Ebene der direkten Reden der Personen, die Anmerkungen haben hier Zuliefererfunktion, d.h. sie benennen
die äußeren Situationsumstände und Gegenständlichkeiten, auf
die die Personen in ihrem Dialog je nach Bedürfnis zurückgrei-
fen können, um ihre momentanen Kommunikationsabsichten
zu realisieren. Insbesondere können die durch die Anmerkungen benannten Objekte augenblickliche Sprechimpulse für die
direkten Reden stellen. Wenn jedoch die Kommunikationsspannung nicht mit der Aktions-Reaktionsspannung zusammenfällt, sondern eine nur sekundäre Rolle bei der Entfaltung
des Aktions-Reaktionsspiels zwischen Person und äußerer,
gegenständlicher Situation erfüllt, so verändert sich das Verhältnis zwischen den beiden textkonstitutiven Äußerungsbändern wesentlich. Die in den Autoranmerkungen benannten
Situationselemente treten zu den Repliken in ein Folgeverhältnis, wobei entweder die benennende Anmerkung die nachfolgende Replik als eine Reaktion der Person auf die benannte
Sache bedingt, oder die Replik geht als Aktion der benennenden Anmerkung voraus, wobei aber der tatsächliche Reaktionscharakter der benennenden Anmerkung erst durch die subjektive Interpretation der Person in deren Repliken gegeben ist,
da die äußere Situation nicht wie die Person subjektbegabt ist.
Die aufeinander folgenden Repliken verschiedener Personen
sind hier nicht eine durch die andere inhaltlich motiviert, sondern sie stehen in einem bloß formalen Folgeverhältnis zueinander, das durch eine mehr oder weniger stärkere Mitmotivie-

rung der einzelnen Repliken modifiziert sein kann in Abhängigkeit von der Intensität, mit der sich die einzelnen Personen neben ihrer Ausrichtung auf die äußere Situation auch noch aneinander orientieren.

Spannung zwischen verschiedenen Subjektarten treten bei dem situationsgesteuerten Ablauf der direkten Reden nun insofern auf, als die Kontextprogression nicht mehr unmittelbar zwischen den von den Personen geäußerten Repliken verläuft, sondern zwischen den Repliken der Personensubjekte einerseits und den Anmerkungen des Autorsubjekts anderseits. Die Anmerkung kann hier auch durch die Replik einer Person ersetzt werden, wenn diese einen Gegenstand der aktuellen Situation oder auch ein die innere Situation einer andern Person berührendes Thema benennt, ohne eine Einwirkung auf die darauf reagierende Person intendiert zu haben, so daß die geäußerte Replik für die reagierende Person den Charakter einer in der vorgegebenen Situation vorgefundenen 'Sache' erhält. Die Spannung macht sich dann darin geltend, daß nicht mehr die sprechenden Personen allein die Zusammensetzung und Aufeinanderfolge der Aktions-Reaktionsteile, aus denen der gesamte dramatische Kontext sukzessiv entsteht, bestimmen. Und für den Leser gibt die Aufeinanderfolge der Repliken verschiedener Personen auf dem Textband der Personenreden keinen sicheren Hinweis mehr, wo er die Aktions-Reaktionsschnitte des dramatischen Kontextes anzulegen hat.

Bei der Erörterung der Weise, wie das Autorsubjekt in die Abfolge der Personenrepliken direkt eingreift, muß eine generelle Anmerkung zur Rolle des abstrakten Autors bei der Bestimmung der Abfolge der einzelnen Kontexteinheiten gemacht werden. Sobald mehr als eine sprechende Person in der aktuellen Situation dargestellt wird, tritt der abstrakte Autor als die Instanz auf, die alle von den verschiedenen Sprechern im Verlauf des Dramas geäußerten Reden zu einer umfassenden Sinneinheit koordiniert, die nur dem Leser, nicht aber den sprechenden Personen selbst zugänglich ist. Diese Sinnkoordinierungsfunktion tritt dann um so stärker hervor, je weniger die Personen sich aneinander orientieren und ihre Sprechakte wechselseitig motivieren. Die tatsächliche Aufeinanderfolge der Repliken der verschiedenen Sprecher bedarf, wenn sich die Personen nicht selbst darum kümmern, welche Rede einer andern Person der ihrigen vorausgegangen ist und welche sich an sie anschließt, einer besonderen Motivation, die sich aus dem Sinn des Gesamtkontextes, in den alle geäußerten Repliken eingehen, ergibt. Prinzipiell muß zu der hier versuchten Untersuchung des Charakters und der Rolle der direkten Reden im Textaufbau des Dramas auch noch folgendes in Erwägung gezogen werden: sobald in einem Drama mehrere sprechende Personen in derselben aktuellen Situation dargestellt werden, ergibt sich auch die Möglichkeit, daß verschiedenartige Typen von Wechselreden gleichzeitig in dieser Situation realisiert werden, die dann wiederum in besondere gegenseitige Beziehungen eingelassen werden müssen. Ein solcher Fall liegt z.B. vor, wenn der Situationsraum (bei der Bühnendarstellung der Bühnenraum) in verschiedene Ebenen (Vordergrunds- und Hintergrundsgeschehen) eingeteilt ist, auf denen Wechselreden mehrerer Personengruppen stattfinden. Jede dieser Wechselreden kann dann je eigene Beziehungen zu der aktuellen Situation eingehen, und gleichzeitig bestehen zwischen ihnen Beziehungen, die den Wahrnehmungshorizont der sprechenden Personen überschreiten können.

Daraus wird deutlich, daß sowohl die Anmerkungen als auch die direkten Reden der Personen in ihrer wechselseitigen, vielgestaltigen Koordinierungsmöglichkeit nur textliche Mittel in der Hand des abstrakten Autors sind, um einen komplizierten, dramenspezifischen Bedeutungsprozeß in Gang zu setzen, dessen Resultat die dargestellte, von einer immanenten Aktions-Reaktionsspannung gekennzeichnete aktuelle Situation ist. Das Bewußtsein des Lesers von dieser letztlichen bedeutungsschaffenden Instanz hinter den scheinbar autonom sprechenden Personen ist jedoch je nach der Beschaffenheit der Konstruktionsdominanten des dramatischen Textes in unterschiedlichem Maß gefordert.

4. Die Segmentierung des dramatischen Textes

Die gesuchten Segmente sollen einerseits einander gleichberechtigte Teile eines Ganzen sein, das durch den gesamten dramatischen Text getragen wird, anderseits sollen diese Teile durch Schnitte im fortlaufenden dramatischen Text feststellbar sein. Nun stellt sich die Frage, welches ist das Ganze, in bezug auf das diese Teile als untergeordnete, einander aber gleichberechtigte Sinneinheiten definiert werden können und, wie sind die erzielten Textabschnitte in sich aufgebaut? Bevor die zweite Frage beantwortet werden kann, soll die Bezugsgröße der gesuchten Teileinheiten, deren Eigenbeschaffenheit und Relationen zu anderen Bezugsgrößen derselben Ebene untersucht werden.

Das Ganze der gesuchten Sinneinheiten ist die im Drama dargestellte Welt, die hier eine aktuelle, durch die Koordinaten des Hier und Jetzt bestimmte Situation ist. Diese dargestellte Situation wird nun aber, bei der Suche nach sukzessiv aufeinander folgenden Textsegmenten, die zugleich Sinneinheiten darstellen sollen, nicht mehr, wie bei der Analyse der inneren Zusammensetzung dieser Situation, statisch betrachtet, sondern als ein dynamisch sich entfaltendes Sinnganzes. Dynamisch ist die Situation durch das gespannte Verhältnis zwischen Person und äußerer Situation, das in den einzelnen Aktions-Reaktionszügen wechselseitig zum Ausgleich gebracht wird. Die Phasen im gegenseitigen Verhältnis von Aktion und Reaktion sind dann die gesuchten Teile zu dem Ganzen, das von dem Gesamtverlauf der Aktions-Reaktionsspannung bestimmt wird. Dieses aus einzelnen Phasen sich entwickelnde Ganze kann eine schwächer oder stärker ausgeprägte innere Entwicklungsdynamik haben in Abhängigkeit von den Trägern der beiden Spannungspole von Aktion und Reaktion. Dementsprechend stärker oder schwächer ist die Markierung des Anfangs und des Endes als des Entwicklungsziels des ablaufenden Spannungsausgleichs spürbar. Und auch die innere Dynamik des Teils dieses Ganzen, nämlich der Entwicklungsphase im gegenseitigen Verhältnis von Aktion und Reaktion, ist stärker oder schwächer.

Für die Art der Entwicklungsdynamik der dargestellten Situation ist primär der initiierende Faktor, also der Träger des Aktionspols, verantwortlich, da er die Reaktion bedingt. Der initiierende Faktor bringt wie jeder andere Faktor der Gesamtsituation ein immanentes Gesetz der Anordnung der diesen Faktor konstituierenden Elemente mit, und dieses Gesetz teilt sich der Gesamtsituation als dominierendes Gesetz ihrer Entwicklungsdynamik mit. Für einen Handlungsprozeß, sei es die zielgerichtete Einwirkung einer Person auf die andere oder der Person auf die äußere gegenständliche Situation, ist dabei eine zeitlich-kausale Verkettung der einzelnen Phasen des Ausgleichs von Aktion und Reaktion anzusetzen, für einen in der äußeren Situation ablaufenden Prozeß, der die Person angeht, eine ebenfalls zeitlich-kausale Verkettung, für einen den Sprechvorgang dominierenden Redegegenstand dagegen eine eher logische Entfaltung des gesamten Redegegenstands aus den einzelnen Redeteilen und für einen dominierenden formalen Redeprozeß eine vorrangig assoziative Verknüpfung der einzelnen Redeteile zu einem nur locker gefügten Ganzen der Reden. Je stärker sich dabei das sich allmählich konstituierende Ganze als Ganzes zu profilieren vermag und je deutlicher es seinen Teilen eine Anfang-Mitte-Schluß-Strukturierung aufzuprägen vermag, desto spürbarer tritt seine immanente Entwicklungsdynamik hervor. Diese immanente Dynamik trifft auf den Reaktionsteil, der wiederum eigene, dem Aktionsteil entgegenkommende oder ihn hemmende Entwicklungsbedingungen mit sich bringt: so kann die Reaktion unmittelbar erfolgen und in eine eigene Aktion umschlagen, die das gesamte Entwicklungstempo der dargestellten Situation beschleunigt, oder die Reaktion erfolgt auch mit Verzögerungen oder bleibt ganz aus oder tritt an Stellen auf, die eine eindeutige Zuordnung zu ihrem Aktionsteil erschweren, wobei die Gesamtentwicklung verlangsamt wird. Man muß also unterscheiden zwischen der dem initiierenden Faktor inhärenten Eigendynamik und der tatsächlichen Dynamik der dargestellten Situation, die Resultante zweier Entwicklungsimpulse, des 'idealen' des initiierenden Faktors, und des diesen Impuls aufgreifenden und realisierenden des Reaktionsteils ist[8]. Da das Entwick-

lungsgesetz des initiierenden Faktors vor dem des Reaktionsteils rangiert, soll es als *immanenter Formimpuls* der gesamten
dargestellten Situation bezeichnet werden, der gegenüber der
tatsächlichen Entwicklung der gesamten dargestellten Situation den Charakter einer 'idealen' Entwicklungsanforderung
hat[9].

Die Phasen, innerhalb derer Aktion und Reaktion zu einem
jeweils vorläufigen (mit Ausnahme der Schlußphase) Ausgleich
ihres gegenseitigen Spannungsverhältnisses gelangt sind, tragen
als Teile das Entwicklungsgesetz des Ganzen, nämlich der
dynamisch sich entwickelnden Gesamtsituation, in sich. Dieses
sie umgreifende Gesetz bestimmt aber nicht nur ihr Verhältnis
zum Ganzen, das alle Phasen zusammen konstituieren, sondern
auch ihr Verhältnis untereinander: wie eine Phase an die vor-
aufgehende anschließt und die folgende vorbereitet, und mit
welcher Notwendigkeit die einzelnen Phasen gerade den Platz
in der Abfolge der einzelnen Phasen einnimmt, der ihr in der
Entwicklung des Dramas tatsächlich zukommt, ob also die einzelnen Phasen im Verhältnis zueinander umstellbar sind oder
nicht. Bei einem zeitlich-kausalen oder logischen Entwicklungsgesetz des Ganzen ist eine Umstellbarkeit der Phasen
nicht möglich, bei einer assoziativen Verkettung läßt sich
immer auch eine andere als die tatsächlich gegebene Abfolge
der Phasen denken.

Da die Phasen Teile des Ganzen der dargestellten Situation
bilden, gehen in sie nicht nur die Träger des Aktions-Reak-
tionspols in einer bestimmten Entwicklungsstufe ihres gegenseitigen Verhältnisses ein, sondern auch alle übrigen, von
diesem Spannungsverhältnis nicht unmittelbar erfaßten Komponenten der Gesamtsituation. Wenn z.B. initiierender Faktor
das Handlungsziel einer Person gegenüber einer andern ist, so
geht in die Phase außer dem Handlungsschritt der aktiven Person und der Reaktion der die Handlung 'erleidenden' Person
auch immer eine Bestimmung zu Zeit und Ort dieses Vorgangs
und zu den begleitenden Umständen mit ein. Die Phase spiegelt daher in ihrem inneren Aufbau das gesamte hierarchische
Verhältnis zwischen den Komponenten der dargestellten Situation wider, wie es durch den initiierenden Faktor als der

Dominanten bestimmt wird, und gleichzeitig trägt sie das Gesetz der dynamischen Fortentwicklung der Gesamtsituation in
sich. Sie ist insofern nicht nur ein Teil im Ganzen, sondern
auch das Ganze im Teil. Als ein solcher Teil soll sie *dramatische Situation* genannt werden, im Unterschied zur dargestellten Gesamtsituation, die einer Reihe dramatischer Situationen zu ihrer dynamischen Entfaltung bedarf.

Obwohl nun die Frage nach der Bezugsgröße der zu definie-
renden Teile beantwortet und die gesuchten Teile als dramatische Situationen, aus denen sich sukzessiv die gesamte im
Drama dargestellte Situation entwickelt, dingfest gemacht
sind, wissen wir noch nicht, wie die Textschnitte anzubringen
sind, die die dramatischen Situationen gegeneinander abgren-
zen. Hierzu muß geklärt werden, wie die dramatischen Situationen und ihre Bezugsgrößen im dramatischen Text existieren
und welches ihre Beziehung zum Text ist.

Alle die gesamte dargestellte Situation im Drama konstituierenden Komponenten wie Person, äußere gegenständliche
Situation, Ereignisse und Prozesse oder Gesprächsthemen sind
selbst wieder komplexe, aus Teileinheiten zusammengesetzte
Größen. Der Leser gelangt zu ihnen erst sukzessiv durch die in
den Texteinheiten vermittelten Informationen, die er verste-
hen, d.h. ihren zugehörigen Sinnkomplexen und deren gegenseitigen Beziehungen zuordnen muß. So baut sich erst aus dem
Prozeß des Lesens im Leser allmählich die Vorstellung davon
auf, wie die dargestellten Personen mit ihrer jeweiligen inneren
Situation und ihren gegenseitigen Beziehungen beschaffen
sind, in welcher äußeren Situation sie sich befinden, welche
Ziele und Zwecke sie verfolgen oder wodurch sie selbst determiniert werden. Im Text sind diese Sinnkomplexe, die wir im
folgenden als *thematische Komplexe*[10] bezeichnen wollen,
nicht unmittelbar gegeben, sondern hier finden sich nur Benennungen und Sätze sowie deren thematische Korrelate, die benannten Gegenstände und Sachverhalte. Der Leser muß, aus-
gehend von diesen Gegenständen und Sachverhalten, die
thematischen Komplexe, auf die sie sich aufgrund ihres Sach-
zusammenhangs beziehen, selbst gemäß der ihnen inhärenten
Ganzheitsgesetzlichkeit konstituieren. Neben der Verstehens-

fähigkeit erfordert dieser Vorgang vom Leser auch ein Abstraktionsvermögen, denn die die thematischen Komplexe konstituierenden Elemente sind einerseits in der linearen Abfolge des Textes gegeben, und anderseits sind sie in der Verquickung mit Elementen, die zu verschiedenen thematischen Komplexen gehören, gegeben, so daß der Leser die zu einem bestimmten thematischen Komplex gehörenden Elemente an verschiedenen, unzusammenhängenden Stellen in der Textlinie vorfindet: z.B. kann die Information über einen zusammenhängenden Ereignisstrang in der äußeren Situation unzusammenhängend, weil von dem Einschub von Teilen anderer thematischer Komplexe unterbrochen, übermittelt werden, oder ein Redethema wird, anstatt daß es bis zu seiner erschöpfenden Entfaltung den Redeprozeß beherrschte, ständig von eingeschobenen Hinweisen zur aktuellen äußeren Situation unterbrochen. Alle einen thematischen Komplex ausmachenden Elemente eines Textes sollen der *thematische Kontext* des zugehörigen Komplexes genannt werden, so daß es also Kontexte der Person, des Redethemas, der äußeren Situation usw. gibt. Diese thematischen Kontexte erscheinen dann in der tatsächlichen Textlinie als *projizierte Kontexte*[11]. Zwischen der Anordnung der Elemente eines thematischen Kontextes, die dem immanenten Formimpuls des thematischen Komplexes folgt, und der tatsächlichen Anordnung im dramatischen Text besteht oft eine Divergenz[12].

Der Leser muß also, um zu den thematischen Komplexen zu gelangen, einerseits abstrahieren von der tatsächlichen, im dramatischen Text vorgefundenen Reihenfolge der konstituierenden Elemente und abstrahieren von den mit diesen Elementen in unmittelbarer Nachbarschaft mitgegebenen, aber zu verschiedenen thematischen Komplexen gehörenden Elementen, zum andern aber muß er synthetisieren, und zwar einerseits die einzelnen thematischen Komplexe selbst gemäß ihrem immanenten Ganzheitsprinzip und anderseits die gesamte dargestellte Situation aus allen zu ihr gehörenden Einzelkomplexen nach dem sie prägenden Entwicklungsprinzip des Ausgleichs zwischen Aktion und Reaktion; hier muß er insbesondere den initiierenden Faktor ermitteln, der die hierarchische Beziehung

zwischen allen Einzelkomplexen der Gesamtsituation bestimmt. Erst wenn der Leser diese verschiedenen Verstehens-
aufgaben zumindest tentativ gelöst hat, kann er daran gehen,
dieses komplexe Ganze der dargestellten Situation wiederum
in Teile zu zerlegen, die die gesuchten dramatischen Situationen sind.

Die dramatischen Situationen sind also nicht unmittelbar
mit den von den Benennungen und Sätzen im Text gegebenen
thematischen Sinneinheiten mitgegeben, sondern zu ihnen gelangt der Leser erst, nachdem er verschiedene vom Text ge-
forderte Verstehensoperationen vollzogen hat. Die dramatische
Situation ist eine komplexe und zugleich auch abstrakte Sinneinheit, da sie sich auf das abstrakte Entwicklungsgesetz der
gesamten dargestellten Situation bezieht. Unterhalb dieser
schon komplexeren Ebene der dramatischen Situationen liegen
die Elemente der verschiedenen thematischen Komplexe, die
ihrerseits direkt von den thematischen Korrelaten der Benennungen und Sätze getragen werden. Diese Elemente stellen die
Verbindung her zwischen der Ausdrucks- und Bedeutungsseite
des Textes einerseits und der Schicht der thematischen und
damit außersprachlichen Bedeutungen anderseits. Kennzeichen
der thematischen, außersprachlichen Bedeutungen ist ihre Unabhängigkeit von einer bestimmten sprachlichen Gestaltung,
die sich darin äußert, daß man die thematischen Komplexe mit
einem andern als dem in einem Drama verwendeten Wortbe-
stand wiedergeben kann. Die tatsächlich in einem dramatischen Text auftretenden thematischen Elemente mit der
ihnen dort zukommenden Anordnung stellen gegenüber dem
thematischen Komplex, den sie konstituieren, Varianten dar
sowohl hinsichtlich der Art dieser Elemente als auch hinsichtlich ihrer Anordnung. Die Variierung ihrer Anordnung kann
in einem spürbaren Widerspruch und in einer Spannung zu der
'idealen' Anordnung münden. Entscheidend für die Wahl der
Elemente und ihrer Anordnung sind einerseits die Darstellungs-
bedürfnisse, anderseits künstlerische Gesichtspunkte.[13]

Die thematischen Elemente stellen die kleinsten, nicht
weiter teilbaren Einheiten der thematischen Ebene dar. Sie sollen als *Motive*[14] bezeichnet werden. Ebenso wie bei den thema-

tischen Komplexen und den dramatischen Situationen ist auch
bei ihnen nach den Bedingungen ihrer Existenz im dramatischen Text zu fragen. Daraus ergibt sich die Beziehung
zwischen ihnen und der dramatischen Situation.

In ihrer Funktion, die zugehörigen thematischen Komplexe
zu konstituieren, sind die Motive von dem sprachlichen Ausdruck, dessen Korrelat sie sind, unabhängig: dieselbe Funktion
könnte auch durch einen andern als den gerade gewählten Ausdruck erfüllt werden. Man könnte diese Funktion des Motivs
seine *thematische Funktion* nennen, da sie es mit den abstrakteren, vom Text wegführenden Sinnplanen des Werks verbindet. Neben seiner durch die thematische Funktion realisierten
Einbeziehung in größere und abstraktere Sach- und Sinnzusam-
menhänge vergegenwärtigt das Motiv durch seine konnotativen
Werte auch noch andere mögliche Sach- und Sinnzusammen-
hänge, und diese Zusammenhänge knüpfen sich sowohl an den
von ihm erfaßten Sachbereich als auch an den gewählten
sprachlichen Ausdruck. Die thematische Funktion wählt aus
den möglichen Konnotationen des Motivs die im Aufbau der
gemeinten dargestellten Welt nötigen aus, beschränkt damit die
sonst noch möglichen thematischen Funktionen und vermittelt
dem Leser die aktuellen Sinnbeziehungen des gegebenen Elements. Gegenüber dieser die aktuelle Sinnfunktion des Motivs
vermittelnden thematischen Funktion könnte man die unvermittelte, durch die Konnotationen ermöglichten Sinnfunktio-
nen des Motivs die *unvermittelte Bedeutungsfunktion*[15] des
Motivs nennen. Schließlich ist das Motiv aber auch noch durch
die Stelle, die es im sprachlichen Kontext eines Werks einnimmt, an den sprachlichen Ausdruck gebunden. Diese Stelle
ist nicht austauschbar, da das Motiv in einer begründeten Beziehung zu den vorangegangenen motivischen Einheiten und
den folgenden steht: es wird von dem vorangegangenen Text
vorbereitet und bereitet selbst die folgenden motivischen Einheiten, insbesondere aber die nächst folgende, mit vor. Die
Funktion, die das Motiv mit den vorangegangenen und den folgenden Motiven in einem Kontext verbindet, kann man als
seine *motivische Funktion* bezeichnen. Durch diese Funktion
ist das Motiv in die Gesamtheit aller Motive eines Textes in der

sprachlichen Gestalt und Abfolge, wie sie der Text gibt, gebunden. Innerhalb dieser Gesamtheit sind alle thematischen Kontexte eines Werks, projiziert auf den konkreten Text eines Werks, enthalten. Diese Gesamtheit aller projizierten thematischen Kontexte nenne ich den *Sujetkontext*. Der Sujetkontext hat eine eigene Entwicklungsdynamik, an der die einzelnen Motive mit der Weise, wie sie ihre motivische Funktion realisieren, teilhaben. Zwischen der Eigendynamik des Sujetkontextes und derjenigen der thematischen Komplexe, insbesondere des dominierenden thematischen Komplexes im Drama, kann ein Widerspruch entstehen, wenn sich die Anordnung der Motive im Sujet der Formierungsdisposition, die der dominierende thematische Komplex an die Gesamtheit der Motive weitergibt, widersetzt.

Wie der Leser von den im Sujetkontext enthaltenen Motiven zu den thematischen Komplexen gelangt, wurde mit der Darlegung der verschiedenen hierbei nötigen Verstehensoperationen schon angezeigt. Man kann nun präzisieren, daß die thematische Funktion der Motive zu den von ihnen konstituierten thematischen Komplexen und zu höheren Sinnebenen bis schließlich hin zum zentralen Thema des Werks leiten. Dieser Prozeß kann erschwert oder erleichtert werden durch die individuelle Konstruktion eines Textes, der die konnotativen Werte der Motive entweder beschränkt oder vermehrt. Je stärker der konnotative Druck der einzelnen Motive gegen ihre Bedeutungsbeschränkung durch die thematische Funktion in bezug auf die zugehörigen thematischen Komplexe und das zentrale Thema ist, desto stärker macht sich auch die Eigenwertigkeit und damit die Statik der einzelnen Motive gegen ihre Unterordnung unter die Entwicklungsdynamik der thematischen Komplexe geltend.[16] Diese Tendenz zur Statik der Motive wird noch bestärkt, wenn die dynamische Entfaltung des Sujetkontextes von der Entwicklungsdynamik der motivischen Komplexe spürbar abweicht, so daß das Auftreten einzelner Motive im Sujetkontext an der Stelle, wie sie der Text ihnen gibt, vom Gesichtspunkt der wesentlichen Entwicklungslinien der dargestellten Welt, die im Drama der Ausgleich von Aktion und Reaktion sind, bisweilen als unbegründet und unnötig erscheinen kann. Diese statischen, nicht unmittelbar in größere sich abzeichnende Sinneinheiten integrierbar erscheinenden Motive sind dann, bei einem künstlerischen Text, durch andere Bedürfnisse der Sinnkonstruktion begründet.

Mit dem Sujetkontext, innerhalb dessen die Motive als die kleinsten thematischen Einheiten dingfest zu machen sind, ergibt sich für die Segmentierung ein neuer Aspekt. Denn mit jedem Schnitt, der die Grenzen der dramatischen Situation festlegt, werden zugleich Abschnitte auf dem Sujetkontext und damit im dramatischen Text markiert, weil der Sujetkontext an die sprachliche Gestalt des konkreten Textes gebunden ist. Damit nähern wir uns wieder der zu Beginn dieses Kapitels gestellten Frage nach der Beschaffenheit der die dramatischen Teileinheiten, die dramatischen Situationen, ausdrückenden Textabschnitte.

Die Grundvorstellung, die die Textsegmentierung leitet, ist die, daß man in dem linearen Textverlauf Schnitte anbringen kann, die Textabschnitte markieren, welche Ausdruck zugehöriger abstrakterer Sinneinheiten, nämlich der dramatischen Situationen, sein sollen. Dieser Vorstellung liegt die Annahme zugrunde, daß der lineare Textverlauf der Entwicklungsdynamik der ausgedrückten abstrakten Sinneinheiten folgt. Da beim Drama die dargestellte ablaufende Zeit der Gesamtsituation mit der Zeit der Darstellung wenn nicht im Zeitumfang, so doch in der Richtung (Öffnung des dargestellten Jetztmoments auf die folgenden Jetztmomente) identisch ist, kann man mit einer Parallelität der beiden Entwicklungslinien (Entwicklung der dramatischen Situationen und Fortschreiten des dramatischen Textes) rechnen. Innerhalb der von 'oben', d.h. von den abstrakten dramatischen Situationen aus im Text vorgenommenden Schnitte finden sich nun einerseits die Motive, die die entsprechende dramatische Situation 'ausdrücken': Motive, die den gegebenen Entwicklungsstand des Aktionsteils beinhalten, Motive, die den Reaktionsschritt auf den Aktionsteil beinhalten, sowie Motive, die die übrigen, die dramatische Situation mitbestimmenden Faktoren bis zu dem für diese Situation nötigen Konkretheitsgrad vergegenwärtigen. Doch mit der Menge der für diese thematischen Funktionen nötigen

Motive erschöpft sich der Bestand an Motiven innerhalb eines
Abschnitts nicht unbedingt. Es können Motive darin enthalten
sein, die keine thematische Funktion in Hinblick auf die zuge-
ordnete dramatische Situation erfüllen, oder der Bedeutungs-
gehalt von Motiven, die thematisch an die dramatische Situation gebunden sind, kann über diese Funktion hinausgehen.
Solche Motive bringen z.B. 'überflüssige' Details, weisen auf
jetzt noch nicht Verstehbares hin oder eröffnen einen über die
Darstellung der dramatische Situation hinausgehenden Sinn-
aspekt des Ganzen des Werks usw. Die mit einem Textsegment
erfaßten Motive sind also einerseits thematisch an die auszu-
drückende dramatische Situation gebunden, zum andern aber
sind sie ihr gegenüber auch frei, da sie noch durch andere Bedürfnisse als die der dramatischen Situation begründet werden.
Auch hinsichtlich der linearen Abfolge sind die Motive auf der
Sujetebene einerseits an das Abfolgegesetz der dramatischen
Situationen gebunden, da sie deren Phasen wiedergeben müssen,
zum andern aber ist die Anordnung der Motive innerhalb der
die dramatische Situation ausdrückenden Menge von Motiven
von diesem Druck insofern auch wieder freigestellt, als die
Menge und Reihenfolge der statischen und 'überflüssigen' Motive
und ihre Verbindung mit den thematisch gebundenen und
dynamischen Motiven nicht von den Darstellungsbedürfnissen
der dramatischen Situation gelenkt werden.[17] Auch die Grenzen
zwischen den einzelnen Segmenten in der Sujetlinie können
anders gestaltet sein, als dies die immanente Entwicklungs-
gesetzlichkeit der Ebene der dramatischen Situationen verlangt.
    Trotz dieser möglichen Freiheit der Motive im Sujet hin-
sichtlich ihrer Zahl, Art und Abfolge von den Bedürfnissen der
dramatischen Situation nimmt die dramatische Situation, resp.
der sie dominierende initiierende Faktor auf die konkrete
sprachliche Gestaltung der Motive Einfluß. Zum sprachlichen
Ausdruck der Motive dienen beide den dramatischen Text bildenden Bänder, das der Anmerkungen und das der direkten
Reden. Diese beiden Bänder werden, in Abhängigkeit von dem
initiierenden Faktor eines Werks, in ganz unterschiedlichem
Maß funktional ausgenutzt. Dies hat, wie schon gezeigt wurde,
Folgen für die Gestaltung ihres gegenseitigen Verhältnisses und

für die Beziehung der Repliken der Personen untereinander, die entweder als Gegenrepliken direkt aneinander anknüpfen oder als bloße Folgerepliken sich 'räumlich' einander zuordnen. Man muß auch damit rechnen, daß eine bloße formale Aufeinanderfolge der Repliken Auswirkungen quantitativer Art hat: je weniger die Repliken einander inhaltlich bedingen, eine die andere provoziert und motiviert, desto stärker wird die Tendenz der Repliken aufzuschwellen, Reihungsverhältnisse, die beliebig fortsetzbar sind, einzugehen, oder sich selbst mit geringen Abweichungen zu wiederholen. Mit dem initiierenden Faktor ist damit eine Tendenz auch der Motive der jeweiligen, die dramatische Situation ausdrückenden Textsegmente zur Verbreiterung, Ausbuchtung und damit zur Statik vorgegeben oder die umgekehrte Tendenz zum knappen, fortstrebenden Entwicklungsgang der Motive auf der Sujetebene. Dieser durch die Dominante der dramatischen Situation vorgegebenen Tendenz in der textlichen Gestaltung kann dann die individuelle Textgestaltung entgegenkommen, es ist aber auch denkbar, daß die individuelle Textgestaltung von ihr abweicht, daß also eine mit einer vorwärtseilenden Situationsdynamik ausgestattete dramatische Konstruktion eine die Statik betonende Sujetgestaltung aufweist und umgekehrt.

Abschließend läßt sich zu der dramatischen Situation und dem sie ausdrückenden Textsegment folgendes feststellen: die dramatische Situation stellt eine Phase des Ausgleichs im gegenseitigen Verhältnis von Aktion und Reaktion dar, dessen gesamte Entwicklung die dynamische Entwicklung der im Drama dargestellten Welt, nämlich der umfassenden dargestellten Situation, bestimmt. Das Verbindungsgesetz zwischen den einzelnen dramatischen Situationen wird von dem initiierenden Faktor bestimmt. Wie sich der Aktions- und Reaktionsschritt im Innern der dramatischen Situation zueinander verhalten, hängt von der Beschaffenheit der Träger der Aktions-Reaktionspole in einem Drama ab. In die dramatische Situation gehen immer auch Bestimmungen der übrigen Komponenten der gesamten im Drama dargestellten Situation mit ein und zwar mit dem Konkretheitsgrad, wie dies ihr Verhältnis untereinander und zur Dominanten der thematischen Konstruktion im Drama, dem initiierenden Faktor, verlangt. Die dramatische Situation ist somit ein im wesentlichen dynamisch bestimmter Teil des Ganzen der im Drama dargestellten Welt, dynamisch, weil sie als Teil das Gesetz der Fortentwicklung zum Ganzen in sich trägt.

Die dramatische Situation wird ihrerseits durch Motive konstituiert, die sich den in sie eingehenden thematischen Komplexen zuordnen und diese in dem für die dramatische Situation gegebenen Entwicklungsstand und dem jeweils notwendigen Konkretheitsgrad bestimmen. Die Motive bringen eine von der Dynamik der Entwicklung der dramatischen Situationenkette unabhängige Eigenbewegung mit, die von der Eigenbewegung des Sujetkontextes bestimmt wird sowie von der individuellen sprachlichen Gestaltung eines dramatischen Textes. Diese Eigengesetzlichkeit kann sich gegenüber der dramatischen Situation als Statik geltend machen, wenn die Bedeutungsfunktion der Motive innerhalb eines Textsegments, das dem Ausdruck einer dramatischen Situation dient, mit der thematischen Funktion gegenüber dieser dramatischen Situation nicht erschöpft wird.

Trotz dieser möglichen Unabhängigkeit der Motive von den Anforderungen der durch sie konstituierten und ihnen gegenüber abstrakteren dramatischen Situation ist die sprachliche Gestaltung, von der Umfang und Art der Bedeutungsfunktion sowie die motivische Funktion der Motive abhängen, auch von dem Entwicklungsgesetz der gesamten dargestellten Situation berührt: der jeweilige initiierenden Faktor im Drama und der Verlauf der Aktions-Reaktionsachse bestimmen über die Art der Dialogizität, die quantitativen Tendenzen und das Folgeverhältnis der Repliken sowie über die Funktion der Anmerkungen und deren Verhältnis zu den Repliken. Die von den dramatischen Situationen aus im Text angelegten Schnitte erfassen somit solche Textteile, die ebenso wie die von ihnen ausgedrückten dramatischen Situationen – die Entwicklungsgesetze der gesamten thematischen Schicht – die wesentlichen Tendenzen der Textgestaltung zu erkennen geben. Sie sollen daher als *dramatische Kontexteinheit* bezeichnet werden. Der Beschreibung dieser dramatischen Kontexteinheit und der durch sie ausgedrückten dramatischen Situation dient die nachfolgende Textanalyse.

II. TEXT- UND BEDEUTUNGSAUFBAU IN ČECHOVS "TRI SESTRY"

DIE DRAMATISCHE KONTEXTEINHEIT

1. *Die intentionale Einstellung der Sprecher im Sprechakt*

Generell gilt für alle Sprechakte in dem Drama "Tri Sestry" eine nur schwache Aktualisierung der Kommunikationsspannung, da die Sprecher in der Mehrzahl ihrer Äußerungen den Sprechpartner in der gemeinsamen Situation nicht oder nur peripher wahrnehmen. Die schwache Orientierung der Sprecher aneinander gilt nicht nur für die häufigen Gruppengespräche[18], sondern auch für solche Reden, die in Anwesenheit zweier Personen in der gemeinsamen Situation geführt werden. Die Ursachen für diese generelle Schwächung der Einstellung der Sprecher aufeinander sind für die verschiedenen Sprechergruppen im Drama unterschiedlich:

A. Die Orientierung der Sprecher aneinander kann dadurch überflüssig werden, daß Sprecher und Adressat sich über die Bewertung des Redegegenstands von vornherein einig sind, so daß die Berücksichtigung der möglichen Haltung des Partners zu dem Gegenstand keine Spuren in der Wahl seiner Benennung zurückläßt. Bei einer solchen weitgehenden Identität von Sprecher und Adressat können beide Sprechpartner sich nacheinander äußern, ohne daß zwischen ihren Repliken eine Bedeutungswende[19] stattfindet, oder sie können zur gemeinsamen Aussage aus der Position eines 'wir' übergehen, oder die Äußerung kann auch ganz unterbleiben, so daß eine Pause eintritt. Zu einem solchen Austausch der Hörer- mit der Sprecherrolle kommt es im Einleitungsgespräch des Dramas zwischen Ol'ga und Irina, wo Irina als die zunächst Angeredete Ol'ga die Replik vor deren Beendigung abnimmt und sie im Sinne Ol'gas weiterführt: Ol'ga spricht von ihrem 'Traum', und Irina konkretisiert diesen als 'Traum, nach Moskau zu fahren'. Im Anschluß daran führt Irina dann die Ausführungen Ol'gas fort, ohne daß eine Veränderung in der Bewertung des Redegegenstands spürbar würde. Die Identität zwischen den Wertungspositionen der drei Schwestern zeigt sich deutlich am Schluß des Stücks, als sie nacheinander aus der Position des 'wir' sprechen. Ohne vorherige Verständigung reagieren die Schwestern in derselben Weise auf Vorgänge in der aktuellen Situation, wobei Außenstehenden nicht einmal klar gemacht wird, welches der Gegenstand der Reaktion ist: so bricht Maša im ersten Akt auf das sichtbare Gealtertsein Veršinins in Tränen aus, und Irina schließt sich ihr an, ohne daß ein eindeutiger Grund dieser Bestürzung genannt würde. Eine Verständigung über bloße, für Außenstehende nicht unmittelbar lesbare Anzeichen geht vor sich, als Maša sich weinend von den Festgästen verabschiedet, während Ol'ga versichert, sie 'verstehe' Maša, obwohl die übrigen in der Situation Anwesenden und auch der Leser noch nicht einsehen können, warum Maša sich so verhält (ebenfalls im ersten Akt). Im vierten Akt nach dem Abschied Veršinins sitzen die drei Schwestern schweigend da, weil eine Kommunikation zwischen ihnen mit Hilfe von Wörtern unnötig ist:

> *Irina.* Davajte posidim vmeste, chot' pomolčim. Ved'
> zavtra ja uezžaju... (IV).

Eine ähnliche Identität entwickelt sich im Verlauf des Dramas sonst nur noch zwischen Maša und Veršinin, die sich im dritten Akt durch bloße rhythmisierte Laute ohne Wortbedeutungen verständigen können:

Tram-tam-tam/Tam-tam//Tra-ra-ra?/Tra-ra-ta.

B. In den häufigen Konversationsgesprächen wird die aktive Orientierung der Sprecher aneinander dadurch gemindert, daß die Personen nur zufällig, ohne vorgegebenes Interesse aneinander, sich in derselben äußeren Situation vereint sehen. Das Gespräch kann sich dann in zwei Richtungen entwickeln: 1. Die Personen führen ein Gespräch über ein bestimmtes Thema, das für sie interessant ist, ohne daß sie sich aber für die Meinung des Partners hierzu speziell interessieren. Diese andere Meinung hat daher auch keine Rückwirkung auf ihre eigene, unveränderliche Bewertung des Themas. Solche themengesteuerten Konversationsgespräche führen vor allem Veršinin und

Tuzenbach; das zu verschiedenen durch die äußere Situation bestimmten Gelegenheiten behandelte Thema bleibt stets dasselbe: die Frage nach dem Sinn des Lebens und der Zukunft der Menschheit. Die Zufälligkeit des Zustandekommens dieser Gespräche und das Fehlen eines vorbedachten Interesses der Sprecher aneinander bei der Behandlung dieses Themas wird aufgedeckt, als Veršinin im zweiten Akt Tuzenbach den Vorschlag macht, gemeinsam zu 'philosophieren', da der Tee, auf den er in der aktuellen Situation wartet, ausbleibt. 2. Das Konversationsgespräch folgt den Sprechimpulsen der äußeren, aktuellen Situation, weil die Personen einander nichts Wichtiges mitzuteilen haben oder nicht in der Lage sind, miteinander über Dinge zu sprechen, die sie im Innern berühren. Die äußere, zumeist alltägliche Situation tritt hier als die Kraft hervor, die die Kommunikationsbewegung in Gang bringt und aufrechterhält, wobei die Personen selbst als bloße Erfüller der Situationsimpulse in den Hintergrund treten. An solchen situationsgesteuerten Gesprächen sind alle Personen beteiligt. Daneben gibt es Personen, deren Reden vornehmlich durch die Erfüllung der vorgegebenen, objektiven Situationsanforderungen bestimmt sind: die Diener Anfisa und Ferapont, die aufgrund ihrer sozialen Stellung zu 'Sprachrohren' der objektiven Situation werden, indem sie Berichte über die äußere Lage u. dergl. weitergeben.

C. In den Fällen, wo eine Person sich vorbedacht an die andere wendet und sich eine Reaktion auf ihre Sprechinitiative erhofft, wird die aktualisierte Kommunikationsspannung dennoch abgeschwächt, und dies auf zwei Weisen: 1. Die angesprochene Person vernimmt die auf sie einwirkende Rede nicht oder will sie nicht vernehmen, weil sie sie nicht interessiert oder weil sie sie stört. So verwehrt Irina Tuzenbach, über seine Liebe zu ihr zu sprechen, oder sie geht, wenn er sich darüber äußert, nicht auf ihn ein, als habe sie nichts gehört. Ihre Unfähigkeit zu einer angemessenen Reaktion wird offenkundig, als Tuzenbach sich von ihr verabschiedet, um zum Duell zu gehen: die erwartete Reaktion hätte hier Tuzenbach von dem unsinnigen Duell zurückgehalten (vierter Akt). 2. Die Adressatenseite einer Redeinitiative verweigert ausdrücklich jeden

Sprechkontakt und hört der an sie gerichteten Mitteilung nicht
zu oder tut, als höre sie nicht zu: die drei Schwestern verweigern Andrej die Aussprache über sein Verhältnis zu ihnen
(dritter Akt), und zwei von ihnen (Ol'ga, Irina) hören weg, als
die dritte (Maša) ihre innere Situation vor ihnen 'beichten' will
(dritter Akt). Eine Aufdeckung des Verfahrens, eine Kommunikationsspannung nur von einer Seite zu aktualisieren, liegt in
den Mitteilungen Andrejs an Ferapont vor: Andrej wendet sich
mit der Aussprache seiner inneren Situation ausdrücklich an
Ferapont, weiß aber, daß dieser schwerhörig ist und daß seine
Rede folglich ohne Reaktion bleiben wird (zweiter und vierter
Akt).

2. Die Abfolge der Repliken

Da die Intention der Sprecher, mit ihren Repliken Gegenrepliken bei den Kommunikationspartnern hervorzurufen, geschwächt ist oder, falls sie vorhanden ist, nicht den gewünschten Erfolg hat, haben die im Text aufeinanderfolgenden Repliken verschiedener Sprecher stärker den Charakter bloßer
Folgerepliken als tatsächlicher Gegenrepliken. Gleichzeitig besteht eine Tendenz zu einer Häufung gleichgerichteter Repliken verschiedener Sprecher, eine Tendenz, die durch die Konversation in der Gruppe gefördert wird.[20] So unterhalten sich
die drei Schwestern mit Veršinin über 'Moskau', wobei sich die
Repliken der Schwestern zu einer fortlaufenden Reihe fügen,
die auch von einer der Schwestern allein hätte geäußert sein
können. Gegen diese gleichgerichteten, einander fortsetzenden
und ergänzenden Repliken setzt dann Veršinin seine eine
gegensätzliche Sicht 'Moskaus' ausdrückende Gegenreplik
(erster Akt). Die absichtliche oder unabsichtliche Weigerung,
eine erwartete Gegenreplik zu geben, führt zu einem Aneinan-
der-Vorbeireden, wenn Tuzenbach zu Irina über seine Liebe
sprechen will, Irina aber in der darauf folgenden Replik über
ihre Müdigkeit redet, ohne erkennen zu geben, ob sie Tuzenbachs Äußerung überhaupt wahrgenommen hat (zweiter Akt).
Bloßgelegt wird das Verfahren des Aneinander-Vorbeiredens

wiederum in den Gesprächen zwischen Andrej und Ferapont, hier vor allem im vierten Akt, als Andrej seine gegenwärtige Lage und seine Zukunftsvorstellungen darstellt, Ferapont aber mit Hinweisen auf die Kältekatastrophe in Petersburg 'oder' Moskau antwortet.[21]

3. Die Ausnutzung der Replikenfolge als besonderes bedeutungsschaffendes Mittel

Die Aufeinanderfolge von Repliken verschiedener Personen suggeriert die Vermutung, daß sich die Folgerepliken auch inhaltlich aufeinander beziehen. Da die Personen aufgrund der schwachen Orientierung aneinander bei ihren Sprechakten das Moment der Beziehung einer Replik auf die vorangehende oder folgende der übrigen Personen aber häufig unbestimmt lassen, bietet sich hier dem abstrakten Autor eine Möglichkeit, Bedeutungseffekte über das Bewußtsein der sprechenden Personen hinweg zu schaffen. Hierbei bedient sich der abstrakte Autor verschiedener Verfahren:

A. Repliken aus verschiedenen Kommunikationssituationen folgen unmittelbar aufeinander. Zwischen ihnen besteht ein innerer Zusammenhang, der als oppositionelle Stellungnahme der folgenden zu der voraufgehenden Replik gewertet werden kann, ohne daß die sprechenden Personen von diesen, aus der äußeren Situation der Rede ihren Repliken zukommenden Bedeutungswerten etwas wissen oder ohne daß zumindest eindeutig wäre, ob sie hiervon etwas wissen[22]: im ersten Akt dringen in das Gespräch zwischen Ol'ga und Irina, das im Vordergrund des Raums geführt wird, Gesprächsfetzen aus dem im Hintergrund verlaufenden Gespräch zwischen Tuzenbach, Čebutykin und Solenyj ein, die – liest man sie linear ohne Berücksichtigung der unterschiedlichen Kommunikationssituationen – den Charakter einer oppositionellen Gegenreplik zu den Äußerungen der beiden Schwestern erhalten. So bezeichnet Tuzenbach eine nicht genannte Äußerung Solenyjs als 'Unsinn', als Ol'ga auf ihren Wunsch zu heiraten zu sprechen kommt. Gerade die Tatsache, daß von dem Hintergrundsge-

spräch außer diesen Replikenfetzen nichts mitgeteilt wird,
zeigt an, daß der abstrakte Autor diese Redeelemente benutzt,
um dem Gespräch der Schwestern einen zusätzlichen Bedeu-
tungsaspekt zu geben. Ähnlich ist der Hinweis auf das 'Lachen'
Tuzenbachs und Solenyjs zu werten, nachdem die Schwestern
ihren Traum 'Moskau' ausgesprochen haben. In diesen Zusammenhang gehören auch die nichtworthaften Äußerungen
Mašas, ihr Pfeifen bei der Beschäftigung mit einem Buch, das
bei ihr ein Zeichen der Trauer ist. Die Bedeutungsfunktion all
dieser durch ihre Stellung im Kontext der direkten Reden
Ol'gas und Irinas aktiv werdenden Äußerungen ist, einen negativen Aspekt auf die von den beiden Schwestern erörterten
Gegenstände zu werfen, der einem Vorverweis auf den weiteren Gang des Schicksals der Schwestern gleichkommt.

B. Im Kontext der direkten Reden folgen auch Repliken
aufeinander, die keinen unmittelbaren Bedeutungsbezug zueinander aufweisen. Die Reden erhalten dadurch scheinbar den
Charakter eines Unsinndialogs. Als Beispiel seien die aufeinander folgenden Repliken Solenyjs und Čebutykins im ersten
Akt genannt, die weder miteinander noch mit dem voraufgehenden und folgenden Kontext der direkten Reden einen
Sinnzusammenhang zu haben scheinen: im voraufgegangenen
Gespräch hat Tuzenbach Veršinin den Schwestern beschrieben; unmittelbar anschließend äußert sich Solenyj über das
Stärkeverhältnis zwischen einer Gruppe von Menschen und
einem Einzelnen, und Čebutykin liest anschließend ein Rezept
aus der Zeitung vor. Eine Bedeutungssynthese müßte sich aus
dem ergeben, was allen drei aufeinanderfolgenden Repliken gemeinsam ist: Tuzenbach hat Veršinin als schwachen, ent-
schluß- und handlungsunfähigen Menschen beschrieben.
Solenyj nennt als Bedingung der Stärke eines Menschen sein
Auftreten in der Gruppe. Čebutykin, der gescheiterte Arzt,
liest ein Rezept aus der Zeitung vor, das von niemandem verlangt wurde und niemandem hilft. Aus der Zusammenstellung
der auf den ersten Blick völlig beziehungslosen Repliken er-
gäbe sich dann ein Motto für das gesamte, die dargestellte
Situation dieses Dramas bestimmenden Geschehens: eine
Reihe talentierter Menschen geht unter dem Druck der un-

talentierten Umgebung zugrunde, weil sie nicht in der Lage sind, sich zu einer Gruppe zu fügen, und gemeinsam eine neue Lebenssituation zu schaffen und aufrechtzuerhalten. Der Arzt, der die Symptome des Übels deuten sollte, ist unfähig, seine Funktion zu erfüllen. Das Verfahren, aus 'zufällig' zusammengestellten Repliken Bedeutungssynthesen herzustellen, wird insbesondere im Kontext Čebutykins mit der Marotte dieser Person, ohne Berücksichtigung der aktuellen Gesprächssituation ständig aus der Zeitung laut vorzulesen, motiviert.

C. An Stelle einer erwarteten Replik kann auch eine Person in die aktuelle Sprechsituation eintreten, deren bloße Anwesenheit eine Bedeutungsergänzung zu der voraufgegangenen Replik einer anderen Person darstellt. So tritt Kulygin in dem Augenblick in die Gesprächsrunde, als Veršinin zu erkennen gibt, daß er unglücklich verheiratet ist (erster Akt). Kulygins Erscheinen macht eine Gegenreplik Mašas an Veršinin, in der sie ihm mitteilen müßte, daß sie ebenfalls unglücklich verheiratet ist, überflüssig. In ähnlicher Weise dringen Nataša (dritter Akt) und Andrej mit dem Kinderwagen (vierter Akt) in die Gesprächssituation ein und setzen durch ihr bloßes Erscheinen Bedeutungsakzente zu den Repliken der Personen in der aktuellen Situation. In dieser Funktion können außer Personen auch Klänge (das Geigenspiel Andrejs) oder Lärm (das Klopfen Čebutykins, der Feueralarm, das Geschrei der abziehenden Batterie, das Klingeln Protopopovs und das Klavierspiel im Haus) ausgenutzt werden.

Inmitten einer Textkonstruktion, die eine generelle Tendenz zum verweigerten Dialog zeigt, müssen stark impressive, am Kommunikationspartner orientierte Reden als besonderes Mittel erscheinen. In diesem Drama haben sie die Funktion, einzelne Personen, und zwar solche, die stark negativ charakterisiert sind, hervorzuheben. Ihre aktive, impressive Rede entspricht ihrer aggressiven Handlungsabsicht gegenüber bestimmten Situationspartnern. So ist Nataša, die gegenüber den Schwestern und Andrej zerstörerische Kräfte zutage treten läßt, in ihren Sprechakten stets initiativ und impressiv: sie beeinflußt Irina, ihr Zimmer aufzugeben, Ol'ga, die alte Dienerin Anfisa fortzujagen. Um ihre Absicht durchzusetzen, greift sie

zum Mittel des Gezänks und des offenen Kampfes. Solenyj dagegen steigert seine zunächst nur versteckt zutage tretenden
Aversionen gegen Tuzenbach (er reagiert auf Repliken Tuzenbachs, die nicht an ihn gerichtet sind, und äußert ohne sichtbaren Bezug zur Gesprächssituation dunkle Worte und literarische Zitate) bis hin zur offenen Morddrohung.

4. Der Aufbau der dramatischen Kontexteinheit

Die Bestimmung der Träger der Aktions-Reaktionsspannung
bereitet in diesem Drama Schwierigkeiten. Die geringe Aktualisierung der Kommunikationsspannung zwischen den Personen
weist darauf hin, daß die Aktions-Reaktionsspannung hier
nicht zwischen den Personen verläuft, obwohl es Personen gibt
(Nataša, Solenyj), deren Sprechverhalten von dem Ziel der
aktiven Einwirkung auf andere bestimmt wird. Die Redeakte
dieser beiden Personen werden noch speziell zu bewerten sein.
Man kann auch nicht sagen, daß die Personen oder ein Teil der
Personen von der Absicht geleitet werden, auf die äußere,
gegenständliche Situation einzuwirken. Die Personen sind, mit
Ausnahme der beiden genannten, nicht initiativ in ihren
Reden, sondern reaktiv, doch der eigentliche Aktionsträger zu
diesen Redereaktionen ist nicht auf den ersten Blick auszu-
machen. Ihre Beziehung zu der äußeren, vorgegebenen Situation kann verschiedene Gestalten annehmen: a) die Repliken
scheinen völlig situationsentbunden zu sein, insofern sie weder
an eine oder mehrere der anwesenden Personen gerichtet sind,
noch einen Bezug zu einem bestimmten Element der gegenständlichen Situation aufweisen. Von dieser Art ist das Zitat
aus "Ruslan i Ljudmila", das Maša im ersten Akt mehrere Male
vor sich hin spricht, oder die sporadischen, laut vorgetragenen
Zitate aus der Zeitung, die Čebutykin ohne Berücksichtigung
der aktuellen Situation um ihn herum in den Raum hinein
spricht; b) eine stärkere Bindung an die äußere Situation liegt
vor, wenn Veršinin sich den Blumen im Haus der Schwestern
zuwendet, dabei jedoch das aktuelle Konversationsthema auf-
gibt: oder wenn Ol'gas Erinnerungen durch den Schlag der Uhr

in der gegenwärtigen Situation weiterbewegt werden (beide Fälle im ersten Akt); c) eine Replik erscheint als Reaktion auf einen vorangegangenen Sprechakt einer anderen Person, wobei diese Person aber keine solche Reaktion intendiert hat: Irina greift Čebutykins Zitat aus seiner Zeitungslektüre auf ("Bal'-zak venčalsja v Berdičeve"), doch wird nicht ersichtlich, warum sie, die an dem um sie herum vor sich gehenden Konversationstreiben nicht teilgenommen hat, plötzlich dieses Zitat interessiert.[23]

Bei diesen Fällen einer scheinbar völlig fehlenden oder nur schwachen Bindung der direkten Reden an die äußere aktuelle Situation muß die eigentliche die Rede bewirkende Kraft im Innern der jeweils sprechenden Person zu suchen sein. Die Verbindung mit der äußeren Situation, da wo sie gegeben ist, wie etwa in der Hinwendung zu einem einzelnen Gegenstand (Blumen) oder dem Aufgreifen einer von einer andern Person geäußerten Replik, ist nur momentan. Die aktuelle äußere Situation erscheint als ein Reservoir möglicher Sprechimpulse für die einzelnen in ihr sich befindlichen Personen, man kann ihr jedoch nicht ohne weiteres die Rolle des initiierenden Faktors zusprechen, der die Reden dauernd lenken soll. Ein besonderes Licht werfen solche Fälle auf das Verhältnis zwischen den direkten Reden der Personen und der äußeren Situation, in denen von dieser äußeren Situation aktive Einwirkungen auf die Personen ergehen, sei es in Form von Vorgängen, die die Personen direkt angehen und betreffen, sei es in Form von Reden anderer Personen mit intendierter impressiver Wirkung. Solche Vorgänge sind z.B. das Klingeln Protopopovs, das eine Beleidigung des Hauses der Prozorovs bedeutet. Čebutykins Verhalten als Mitbewohner des Hauses — er hat seit acht Monaten 'vergessen', die Miete zu zahlen —, Andrejs Vertreibung aus dem Haus: als Protopopov kommt, wird Andrej hinausgeschickt, den Kinderwagen spazieren zu fahren. Auf all diese Fälle reagieren die direkt betroffenen Schwestern nicht oder nur inadäquat: Irina ignoriert das Klingeln Protopopovs im zweiten Akt, und erst Čebutykin thematisiert das Schweigen der Schwestern zu dem 'Roman' Natašas mit Protopopov (im dritten Akt); statt Čebutykin wegen der ausbleibenden

Miete zur Rechenschaft zu ziehen, dulden die Schwestern ihn und belächeln nachsichtig seine Schwächen (im zweiten Akt kommentieren sie lächelnd seine Weise dazusitzen und machen sich nicht bewußt, daß er als ein zerstörerischer Parasit in ihrem Hause sitzt); den ganzen vierten Akt durch promeniert Andrej mit dem Kinderwagen außerhalb des Hauses, aber nur Maša thematisiert einmal die sich darin ausdrückende Situation Andrejs. Aktiv einwirkende Reden führt Kulygin gegen Maša, als er ihr den Besuch beim Direktor aufzwingt (erster Akt), Nataša mit ihrem Einreden auf Irina und Ol'ga (zweiter und dritter Akt), Solenyj mit seinen dunklen Drohungen gegen Tuzenbach und Andrej, als er die Schwestern bittet, sich mit ihm auszusprechen (dritter Akt). In all diesen Fällen ist die Reaktion der Schwestern inadäquat: Maša bringt ihren Ärger über die Einladung nicht gegenüber Kulygin zum Ausdruck, sondern macht sich erst später gegenüber Tuzenbach und Čebutykin (erster Akt) Luft; Irina begegnet Natašas Vorschlag mit Schweigen; eine Reaktion erfolgt erst später, zum Schluß des zweiten Aktes, als sie nach eine Reihe von außen auf sie eindringender Ereignisse in den Ruf "V Moskvu!" ausbricht. Eine ähnlich verzögerte Reaktion nach einer ganzen Reihe von provozierenden Einwirkungen wiederholt sich zum Schluß des dritten Aktes an Irina.[24] Tuzenbach nimmt das drohende, feindliche Verhalten Solenyjs lächelnd, allenfalls leicht verärgert hin und verteidigt seinen späteren Mörder sogar noch, als Irina ihm gegenüber ihre Antipathie gegen Solenyj zum Ausdruck bringt.[25] Die Bitte Andrejs um Aussprache schließlich lehnen die Schwestern in ungewohnter Härte ab.

Für den Aufbau der dramatischen Kontexteinheit ergibt sich nun folgender Befund: die direkten Reden des größten Teils der Personen sind reaktiven Charakters. Die Hauptmotivation für diese Reden liegt nicht in der Kommunikationsspannung zwischen den Personen; diese wird vornehmlich als Konversation realisiert und hat allenfalls eine mitmotivierende Funktion für die Redeakte. Die Hauptmotivation kann aber auch nicht eindeutig der äußeren Situation zugesprochen werden, da die direkte Verbindung der Reden mit Elementen der äußeren Situation, soweit eine solche Verbindung überhaupt eindeutig nachweisbar ist, einen momentanen, zufälligen Charakter hat, so daß der äußeren Situation eher die Rolle eines Reservoirs augenblicklicher Sprechimpulse zukommt als die eines dauernden initiierenden Faktors.

Wo ist dann aber der initiierende Faktor zu suchen? Die Schwierigkeit, ihn ausfindig zu machen, liegt in der Weise der Darstellung der aktuellen Situation in diesem Drama. Der Reaktionsteil der Grundspannung in dieser Situation ist mit den Reden der Personen voll vergegenwärtigt, der eigentliche Aktionsteil wird jedoch in einer dem vergegenwärtigten Reaktionsteil nicht ganz entsprechenden Weise wiedergegeben: Träger dieser Aktion und damit initiierender Faktor ist zwar die äußere, vorgegebene Situation, jedoch handelt es sich dabei nicht allein um die den Personen im aktuellen Hier und Jetzt gegenwärtige äußere Situation, sondern man muß diese mit ihren perspektivischen Verlängerungen in die Vergangenheit (die Vorgeschichte der Prozorovs, die im ersten Akt mitgeteilt wird) sehen. Darüber hinaus gibt es in der äußeren Situation keinen eindeutigen Träger einer gegenüber den Hauptpersonen initiativ werdenden Kraft: die nur lose Verbindung der reagierenden Reden mit Einzelelementen der äußeren gegenständlichen Situation, vor allem aber das verschobene, uneindeutige und inadäquate Reagieren auf eindeutig aggressive Elemente in der äußeren Situation (Nataša, Solenyj, das Verhalten Protopopovs) machen deutlich, daß nicht die aktuell gegebenen Einzelelemente der äußeren Situation und auch nicht einzelne, z.T. sogar als 'Feinde' identifizierbare Personen voll verantwortlich für die gezeigten Reaktionen sind.

Erschwert wird die Suche nach den aktionsführenden Kräften zu den gezeigten Reaktionen der Personen auch noch durch folgenden Umstand: das geringe Interesse der Personen aneinander (bei dem themengesteuerten oder von der alltäglichen Situation gelenkten Konversationsgespräch), aber auch die Unnötigkeit einer gegenseitigen Mitteilung in Fällen einer Übereinstimmung der inneren Situation der Personen (bei den drei Schwestern, zwischen Maša und Veršinin) bewirken, daß auch die innere Situation der Personen als Teilkomplex dieser Personen nur indirekt und ausschnittsweise dargestellt werden.

Gerade die innere Situation könnte aber, da sie die jeweilige
Reaktion der Person neben der eigentlichen aktionsführenden
Kraft mitbedingt, Aufschluß geben über die Kräfte, die auf die
Personen von außen einwirken.[26]
Bei der Gestaltung des dramatischen Kontextes überwiegt
somit der Reaktionsteil, da er voll gegeben ist, während der
Aktionsteil und auch die innere Situation der Personen nur
unvollständig mitgegeben sind. Sie müssen einerseits aus den
direkten Angaben des Textes, anderseits aber auch indirekt
aus den dargestellten Reaktionen erschlossen werden. Da je-
doch der Reaktionsteil als das durch die Aktion Bedingte die
Aktion in sich enthält, kann diese in den für die Bedeutung des
Textes wichtigen Zügen vom Leser nachvollzogen werden.

DIE DRAMATISCHE SITUATION

1. *Die thematischen Komplexe*

A. Die thematischen Komplexe der Personen lassen sich in
zwei Gruppen einteilen, deren Gruppenmerkmal in dem einen
Fall der Aktionscharakter, in dem andern Fall der Reaktionscharakter der Reden ist. Aktionscharakter haben die wort- und
handlungsmäßigen Äußerungen Natašasa, Čebutykins, Solenyjs
und Kulygins, Reaktionscharakter die Äußerungen der drei
Schwestern, Andrejs, Tuzenbachs und Veršinins. Anfisa und
Ferapont sind durch ihre Dienerrolle auf die Erfüllung der objektiven Situationsanforderungen beschränkt und bleiben insofern außerhalb des Kreises der selbstverantwortlich sprechenden und handelnden Personen.
Die Personen der reaktiven Gruppe werden in ihrem Verhalten gegenüber der aktuellen Situation von ihrer inneren Situation bestimmt. Erst wenn diese innere Situation zu ihren
Äußerungen hinzugedacht wird, ergibt sich der eigentliche
Sinn all ihres Tuns und Redens. Innerhalb dieser Gruppe bestehen noch einmal Differenzierungen nach dem Merkmal der
Veränderlichkeit oder Unveränderlichkeit der inneren Situation einer Person. Der Veränderung im Sinne der Entwicklung

unterliegt die innere Situation jeder der drei Schwestern sowie
Andrejs, unverändert bleiben Tuzenbach und Veršinin. Die
innere Situation wird in den Reden der Personen z.T. direkt
thematisiert, z.T. muß sie aus Symptomen in der Rede und im
Gesamtverhalten erschlossen werden. Veršinin und Tuzenbach
verbinden die sie im Innern beschäftigenden Fragen mit allge-
meinen philosophischen Fragen, die sie in Konversationsgesprächen zum Ausdruck bringen.

Die Personen der aktionsausübenden Gruppe verfügen nur
ansatzweise über eine eigene innere Situation. Am stärksten
noch zeigt Čebutykin, daß er in seinem Verhalten gegenüber
der aktuellen Situation von einem Vergangenheitsbewußtsein
(seine Bindung an die Mutter der Schwestern, sein Versagen in
seinem Arztberuf) mitbestimmt wird. Die übrigen Personen
dieser Gruppe zeichnen sich vor allem durch einzelne dominierende Charakterzüge aus: Nataša ist herrschsüchtig und dumm,
Solenyj spielt den dämonischen Außenseiter, Kulygin ist
pedantisch und gutmütig. Diese isolierten Charakterzüge werden durch äußere Merkmale der Person unterstrichen: Nataša
erscheint im zweiten und dritten Akt mit der Kerze, um die
Räume zu kontrollieren; Solenyj trägt ständig ein Parfüm-
fläschchen mit sich herum, das, wie sich herausstellt, den
Mordgeruch seiner Hände überdecken soll; Kulygin wird durch
eine konstante Sprecheigentümlichkeit gekennzeichnet: er hat
ein Reservoir an lateinischen Schulbuchsprüchen zur Hand;
Čebutykin trägt die Zeitung in der Tasche oder in der Hand.
Die Adressaten der aktiven und bisweilen aggressiven Redeakte
und Handlungen dieser Personen sind: bei Solenyj Tuzenbach,
bei Kulygin Maša, bei Čebutykin Andrej (diese Einwirkung ist
allerdings versteckter als bei den übrigen Fällen), Nataša rich-
tet sich gegen Irina, Maša, Ol'ga und Andrej. Die zerstörerische
Wirkung Čebutykins und Kulygins wird in der letzten Szene
des ersten Aktes verdeutlicht. Hier veranlaßt Čebutykin Andrej
dazu, Nataša den Heiratsantrag zu machen, indem er durch
seine anzüglichen Reden Nataša in eine peinliche Situation
bringt, der Andrej als Natašas Beschützer dann gezwungen ist,
mit seiner Liebeserklärung zu begegnen. Čebutykin wird in
seinen provozierenden Reden von Kulygin unterstützt, der

seinerseits durch die Heirat mit Maša ja schon ein Mitglied der Familie Prozorov ins Unglück gebracht hat.

B. Der thematische Komplex der äußeren Situation wird durch verschiedene Einzelkomplexe konstituiert: 1. In der äußeren Situation geschehen Ereignisse, die alle Personen gemeinsam angehen. So wird im ersten Akt der Namenstag Irinas gefeiert, und Veršinin kommt an; im zweiten Akt ist das zentrale Ereignis das Maskenfest, zu dem sich alle zusammenfinden, das dann jedoch auf Intervention Natašas nicht stattfindet; im dritten Akt beherrscht der Brand das Geschehen; im vierten Akt zieht die Batterie mit Veršinin ab, und Irina bereitet ihre Abreise vor. 2. Die drei Schwestern und Andrej werden von Veränderungen ihrer räumlichen Lage betroffen, die sich von Akt zu Akt weiterentwickeln. Am Anfang des Stücks haben die Schwestern und Andrej das ganze Haus inne; im zweiten Akt vertreibt Nataša ihre Festgäste aus dem Haus; im dritten Akt ist Irina aus ihrem Zimmer verdrängt worden und lebt mit Ol'ga zusammen in einem Zimmer; das Kind Natašas hat ihr Zimmer beansprucht; im letzten Akt schließlich stehen alle Schwestern zusammen mit Andrej und den Freunden draußen vor dem Haus, während drinnen Nataša und Protopopov sich breit gemacht haben. Zwischen den Schwestern und Andrej besteht noch eine zusätzliche Differenzierung in ihrem Verhältnis zum Raum, denn Andrej ist immer nur punktuell mit den Schwestern in einem Raum vereint: am Anfang bemühen sich die Schwestern, ihn bei sich zu halten, während Andrej aus der Gesellschaft der Schwestern fortstrebt, am Schluß verweigern die Schwestern ihm die räumliche Gemeinschaft, die ein Gespräch erst möglich macht, indem sie die Bettschirme zwischen sich und Andrej schieben (dritter Akt). 4. Die Schwestern erleiden jede für sich eine Veränderung ihrer äußeren Situation: Irina wechselt von Akt zu Akt ihre berufliche Tätigkeit und entschließt sich im vierten Akt zur Heirat mit Tuzenbach; Ol'ga wird erst Vertreterin der Schulvorsteherin, dann selbst Schulvorsteherin und zieht infolgedessen mit Anfisa aus dem Haus; Maša verliebt sich in Veršinin und muß sich von ihm trennen. Andrejs Schicksal ist im Gegensatz zu dem der Schwestern, das im Verlauf des

Stücks zu keinem eindeutigen negativen Abschluß gelangt, sondern immer noch die Möglichkeit der Hoffnung offen läßt[27], mit dem Entschluß zur Heirat im ersten Akt besiegelt. In den drei darauf folgenden Akten wird sein Niedergang nur noch bekräftigt und verdeutlicht. Ihm bleibt keine Hoffnung, sondern nur ein utopischer Traum vom Leben künftiger Generationen (vierter Akt). 5. Neben den großen, die Akte tragenden Ereignissen spielen auch die alltäglichen, wiederkehrenden Ereignisse eine Rolle bei der Konstituierung des Gesamtkomplexes der äußeren Situation: das Teetrinken, die Konversationsgespräche, das grundlose Beisammensein. Zusammen mit den großen Ereignissen motiviert das Alltägliche das Zusammenkommen der Personen an demselben Ort zur selben Zeit und ersetzt damit das fehlende aktive Interesse der Personen aneinander, das sonst ihr Zusammensein begründen könnte.

Im Aufbau der äußeren Situation fehlt ein zentraler Entwicklungsstrang, der alle genannten Einzelmomente auf sich zuordnen könnte. Die auftretenden Veränderungen laufen einander parallel, statt sich zu einem Komplex zu verbinden. Die Vorstellung von dem, was in diesem Drama mit den einzelnen Personen geschieht, zerfließt in eine Reihe von Symptomen eines Prozesses, der in seinem ganzen Ausmaß nicht unmittelbar faßlich wird. Insbesondere wird die eigentliche Ursache zu diesem Prozeß nicht mit vergegenwärtigt, obwohl einzelne wirkende Kräfte (Nataša und alle übrigen 'schädlichen' Personen) dargestellt sind.

C. Zu relativ selbständigen Komplexen entwickeln sich auch die Redethemen der Konversationsgespräche. Hierzu gehören vor allem das Thema des Sinns des Lebens, der Möglichkeit des Glücks und das Thema der Arbeit. In der Weise der Stellungnahme, aber auch schon in der bloßen Tatsache der Anteilnahme an diesen Themen kommt einerseits etwas von der inneren Situation der jeweiligen Personen, aber auch etwas von ihrem Verhältnis zu den übrigen Personen zum Ausdruck, was direkt nicht benannt wird. So zeichnet sich etwa die Grundlage für die Beziehung zwischen Irina und Tuzenbach in ihrer Stellungnahme zu dem Thema 'Arbeit' ab, noch bevor ihre gegenseitige Beziehung im Stück problematisiert wird. Dasselbe ge-

schieht in Veršinins und Mašas Äußerungen zu dem Thema
'Sinn des Lebens'. Das oppositionelle Verhältnis Čebutykins
zu den Schwestern, Veršinin und Tuzenbach kündigt sich in
seiner betont negativen Sicht der 'Arbeit' an (erster Akt) und
wird durch sein Desinteresse (ausbleibende Stellungnahme) an
dem Thema 'Sinn des Lebens' bekräftigt. Als dieses Thema im
zweiten Akt aufkommt, liest Čebutykin Zeitung.

2. Das Verhältnis der thematischen Komplexe zueinander und der dominierende thematische Komplex

Innerhalb des thematischen Komplexes der Personen ist eine
Gruppe, nämlich die mit einer inneren Situation ausgestatteten
Personen, Träger der Reaktion. Diese Personen werden als Ziel-
objekte einer an ihnen ergangenen Einwirkung von außen dargestellt, die vor dem Beginn des Stücks eingesetzt hat, während
der dargestellten Zeit weiterwirkt und auch in der Zukunft
fortdauern wird. Die Reaktion der Personen schlägt niemals in
eine aktive Gegenwehr um, sondern bleibt weitgehend ein Erdulden und Erleiden. Insbesondere schließen sich die einzelnen
Betroffenen nicht zu einer Gruppe gemeinsam Handelnder zusammen, sondern jeder von ihnen versucht für sich, mit dem,
was an ihm geschieht, fertig zu werden. Ebenso wenig wie zu
einem gemeinsamen Handlungsentschluß kommt es zwischen
ihnen zu einer gemeinsamen Thematisierung des vor sich gehenden Prozesses, der sie alle betrifft; nur vereinzelt und im
Gespräch mit einem Nahestehenden äußern sich die Schwestern direkt zu dem Niedergang ihres Hauses: Irina gegenüber
Tuzenbach im ersten Akt, als sie ihr bisheriges Leben kommen-
tiert: "U nas, trech sester, žizn' ne byla ešče prekrasnoj, ona
zaglušala nas, kak sornaja trava ..."; Ol'ga gegenüber Veršinin
im vierten Akt: "Vse delaetsja ne po-našemu" usw.; Maša,
ebenfalls im vierten Akt, gegenüber Čebutykin: nachdem sie
sich über ihr eigenes Schicksal ausgesprochen hat, verweist sie
als Parallele dazu auf Andrej, den sie mit einer von vielen hoch-
gehobenen Glocke vergleicht, die plötzlich zu Boden fällt und
zerschellt. Ansätze zu einer Aktivität, die die bestehende Situa-

tion ändern soll, bringen nicht die gewünschten (bei Irinas wechselnden Berufen) oder keine dauernden Resultate (bei Mašas Liebe zu Veršinin).

Träger des Aktionspols ist die äußere, vorgegebene Situation, die man hier als Lebenssituation bezeichnen muß: nicht bestimmte Ereignisse und nicht bestimmte feindliche Personen wirken gegen die Schwestern und ihre Freunde, sondern das gesamte Spektrum der Lebensrealität. Diese Lebensrealität wird im Stück nur ausschnittsweise (in bezug auf die dargestellte Zeit) und auswahlweise gezeigt: die dargestellten negativen Personen, die willentlich oder unwillentlich den Niedergang des Hauses Prozorov bewirken, stehen für viele andere aus der Umgebung der Schwestern. Auf die Anonymität der eigentlichen wirkenden Kräfte weist das Darstellungsverfahren, das bei Protopopov, dem Nachfolger im Hause der Prozorovs, angewendet wird: Protopopov tritt niemals als Person auf, doch seine Gegenwart wird durch Geräusche und Gegenstände ständig bewußt gemacht.[28]

Wie verhält sich nun der Komplex der Redethemen zu den beiden Trägern der Aktion und der Reaktion in diesem Stück? Die Redethemen sind relativ selbständig, weil sie einerseits in Konversationsgesprächen, also weitgehend frei von den unmittelbaren Situationszwängen, aufgebracht werden, und weil sie andersseits mehrmals an verschiedenen Stellen im Verlauf des Dramas wiederkehren. Das Aufwerfen dieser Themen und die Stellungnahmen zu ihnen muß man als einen Bestandteil des reaktiven Verhaltens der Personen nicht nur gegenüber der aktuellen, dargestellten Situation, sondern auch dem zuvor schon Erlebten gegenüber bewerten. In der Behandlung und in der Wahl der Themen ergibt sich dabei eine Unterscheidung zwischen den Schwestern und Andrej auf der einen, Veršinin und Tuzenbach auf der andern Seite. Die Schwestern suchen nach einem Sinn des Lebens, und diese Suche manifestiert sich zunächst in dem Traum 'Moskau', dann in 'Arbeit' und schließlich im Leiden und Leben für andere. Bei jeder der drei Schwestern sowie bei Andrej nimmt diese Suche einen andern Verlauf, und jeder thematisiert sie in seiner Rede auf andere Weise (für Andrej ist insbesondere die scheinbare Mitteilung seiner innersten Gedanken an Ferapont, die eigentlich eine Aussprache vor sich selbst ist, charakteristisch). Die Veränderungen ihrer Themen und ihrer Stellungnahmen sind für die Schwestern und für Andrej Anzeichen für Veränderungen ihrer gesamten inneren Situation. Bei Veršinin und Tuzenbach besteht dagegen kein so enger Zusammenhang zwischen ihren Redethemen und der eigenen durchlebten Realität. Weder die sie interessierenden Themen noch ihre eigenen Bewertungen dieser Themen verändern sich im Verlauf des Stücks. Die Hinwendung zu diesen 'philosophischen' Themen kann bei ihnen fast als eine Ausflucht vor der aktuellen Wirklichkeit angesehen werden: dies zeigt sich besonders deutlich an Veršinin, der gerade in dem Augenblick, als Čebutykin den Vorwurf erhebt, alle im Hause sähen an dem 'Roman' Natašas mit Protopopov vorbei, einen langen Exkurs über das Glück der Menschheit in 'zweihundert, dreihundert' Jahren hält (dritter Akt). Ähnlich verhält sich Veršinin in der Abschiedssituation mit Ol'ga im vierten Akt. Den Charakter eines bloßen Konversationsthemas, das ohne Auswirkung für seine Lebensweise bleibt, erhält auch das Thema 'Arbeit' bei Tuzenbach: anders als Irina, die über 'Arbeit' nicht nur spricht, sondern bei der die Suche nach einer befriedigenden Tätigkeit die Hauptphasen ihrer im Stück gezeigten Entwicklung ausmacht, unternimmt Tuzenbach keinen ernsthaften Versuch, aus dem Redethema 'Arbeit' eine Lebensweise zu machen. Auch sein Entschluß im vierten Akt, in einer Ziegelfabrik zu arbeiten, ist nur eine Attitüde: er zieht der Ausführung dieses Entschlusses einen sinnlosen, einem veralteten Ehrbegriff entsprechenden Tod im Duell vor.

Für das gegenseitige Verhältnis der genannten thematischen Komplexe: äußere, vorgegebene Situation, Personen mit ihrer inneren Situation und Redethemen, ergibt sich nun folgendes Bild: zum Reaktionspol gehören die Prozorovs und ihre Freunde Tuzenbach und Veršinin, wobei ihre jeweilige innere Situation die Art der Reaktion bedingt. Die Hinneigung zu bestimmten in der Konversation aufgebrachten Redethemen muß als eine Komponente ihrer generellen Reaktion bewertet werden. Die äußere Situation ist Träger der Aktion, doch repräsentiert die im Stück vergegenwärtigte Situation mit ihren verschiedenartigen aktiven Kräften nicht das volle Ausmaß der eigentlichen gegen die reagierende Personengruppe gerichteten Aktion. Die Reaktionen sind nicht Reaktionen nur auf die gegenwärtig erlittenen Einwirkungen, sondern diese begründen sie nur zum Teil.

Wie ist nun die äußere Situation als dominierender thematischer Komplex und initiierender Faktor in der Lage, den Sujetkontext zu formieren, d.h. die Weise der sukzessiven Entfaltung dieser Komplexe in der Entwicklung des dramatischen Kontextes zu bestimmen? Dem Komplex der äußeren Situation fehlt ein zentraler Ereignisstrang, der der Entwicklung im gegenseitigen Verhältnis von Aktion und Reaktion eine von Anfang an einsichtige Richtung geben und im Leser die Erwartung eines bestimmten Abschlusses wecken könnte. Noch entscheidender wirkt sich jedoch die Tatsache aus, daß die gezeigten Aktionskräfte den Reaktionen nicht kongruent sind; dadurch befreien sich die Reaktionsmomente von der eindeutigen kausalen Bindung an die Aktionsmomente, und die zeitliche Zuordnung eines Reaktionsmoments zu den gegebenen Aktionsmomenten wird bis zu einem gewissen Grad willkürlich. Willkürlich, weil nicht eindeutig bedingt, erscheint neben der Art und der Zeit der Reaktion aber auch ihre Zahl: statt einer zentralen Person, die Träger und Mittelpunkt der Reaktionskräfte wäre, treten die drei Schwestern auf, deren Schicksale nebeneinander her laufen; ihnen wird das Schicksal Andrejs entgegengestellt. Die dem Reaktionspol zugeordneten Einzelkomplexe sind somit sowohl im Verhältnis zueinander als auch im Verhältnis zu den dargestellten Aktionskräften weitgehend selbständig, und die Stelle ihres Auftretens im Sujetkontext sowie ihre Eigenentfaltung sind nicht eindeutig von dem Aktionskomplex abhängig. Die Selbständigkeit der Einzelkomplexe des Reaktionspols aber ist wiederum eine Folge der inneren Konstituierung des Aktionspols, der äußeren Situation, die in sich nicht hierarchisiert und durch keine kausal-zeitliche Ordnung geformt ist und daher auch der Reaktion als der von ihr abhängigen Größe keine solche Hierarchie und Ordnung aufdrücken kann.

3. *Der Aufbau der dramatischen Situation und die Gliederung
   des dramatischen Textes*

Im folgenden soll keine Zergliederung des gesamten dramatischen Textes in die einzelnen dramatischen Situationen vorge-
nommen werden, sondern es werden nur die ersten drei dramatischen Situationen im Text untersucht. Aus ihnen läßt sich
das Prinzip des inneren Aufbaus aller dramatischen Situationen
und das Prinzips ihrer gegenseitigen Verknüpfung exemplarisch
gewinnen.

Die dramatische Situation stellt einen Entwicklungsschritt
im gegenseitigen Verhältnis der Aktions-Reaktionskräfte dar.
Träger der Aktion ist in diesem Drama die äußere vorgegebene
Situation mit bestimmten privilegierten aktionsführenden
Trägern aus dem Kreis der dargestellten Personen, Träger der
Reaktion sind die drei Schwestern, Andrej und die Freunde
des Hauses, Veršinin und Tuzenbach. Da die Reaktionsträger
jedoch keine gemeinsam handelnde Gruppe bilden, sondern
jede für sich oder auch in nicht dauerhaften Vereinigungen reagieren, brauchen auf dem Reaktionsteil in einer dramatischen
Situation nicht alle sechs genannten Personen zugleich zu erscheinen. Die Weise, wie in den drei Eingangssituationen des
Stücks der Reaktionsteil manifest zu machen ist, ist charakteristisch für die generelle Verbindung von Reaktion und Aktion
im Verlauf des gesamten Werks.

Der Textabschnitt, der die erste dramatische Situation umfaßt, beginnt mit der ersten Rede Ol'gas und endet mit Tuzenbachs Replik an Solenyj: "Takoj vy vzdor govorite, nadoelo
vas slušat'." Die zweite dramatische Situation setzt mit Tuzenbachs Ausführungen über Veršinin ein und endet mit Solenyjs
Replik über die Stärke des Menschen in der Gruppe und Čebutykins Verlesung eines Rezepts aus der Zeitung. Die dritte dramatische Situation setzt mit Irinas Hinwendung an Čebutykin,
die ihre Erörterungen des Themas 'Arbeit' einleitet, ein und
endet mit dem Klopfen gegen den Fußboden. In der ersten
Situation ist der Reaktionsteil allein realisiert, die Aktion
hierzu liegt in der 'Vorgeschichte' der dargestellten Jetztsituation: Ol'ga erinnert sich der Vergangenheit des Hauses Prozo-

rov und der Entwicklung ihres gemeinsamen Lebens seit dem Tod des Vaters. Anstoß zu diesen Erinnerungen liefert das Datum des heutigen Tages (Namenstag Irinas) und ein Einzelmoment in der gegenständlichen Situation: das Schlagen der Uhr. Die Reaktion kulminiert in Ol'gas und Irinas gemeinsamer Aussprache des Traums 'Moskau'. Die die erste dramatische Situation beschließende Replik Tuzenbachs an Solenyj weist auf die Aussichtslosigkeit dieses Traums, mit dem die Schwestern ihrer jetzigen Lage begegnen wollen, vorausdeutend hin und versieht auch Ol'gas Hoffnung auf eine Ehe mit einem negativen Vorzeichen. Damit ist zugleich ein mögliches Lebensziel aller drei Schwestern, die Erfüllung in einer auf Liebe basierenden Ehe, negativ vorbedeutet. Tuzenbachs anschließender Bericht über Veršinin ist unmittelbar durch die äußere Situation, nämlich die Ankunft der Batterie, motiviert. Die Weise, wie er das durch die objektive Situation aufgegebene Redethema 'Veršinin' behandelt, zeigt seine generelle Einstellung zur aktuellen Situation: er schildert Veršinins Charakter und knüpft an diese Schilderung eine allgemeine Bewertung aus seiner Sicht an, macht also aus dem aktuellen Thema ein generelles Konversationsthema. Der Abschluß dieser dramatischen Situation bringt mit den beiden, im Kontext der Rede Tuzenbachs unmotiviert erscheinenden Repliken Solenyjs und Čebutykins eine Bedeutungssynthese dieses Abschnitts, die an die Sinnsynthese des gesamten Stücks anknüpft (s.o.). Die dritte dramatische Situation zeigt keinerlei reaktive Verbindung mit der aktuellen äußeren Situation: Irina bringt ohne sichtbaren Zusammenhang mit den vorangegangenen Redethemen noch mit einem Gegenstand der äußeren Situation das Thema 'Arbeit' auf. Die Motivation ist hier in ihrer aktuellen inneren Situation zu suchen, die wiederum mit der in der Vergangenheit angelegten Gesamtsituation der Schwestern zusammenhängt. Das aufgeworfene Redethema wird als Konversationsthema weiterentwickelt, indem eine Reihe der anwesenden Personen (Ol'ga, Tuzenbach, Solenyj und Čebutykin) eine positive oder negative Stellungnahme abgeben.

Das Verhältnis der drei ersten dramatischen Situationen zueinander demonstriert das generelle Verknüpfungsgesetz der

dramatischen Situationen: die einzelnen Situationen gehen
nicht kontinuierlich ineinander über, sondern stehen einander
als selbständige Einheiten gegenüber. Ihre jeweiligen Inhaltskonzentrate (der Traum der Schwestern von 'Moskau' mit dem
ihm zugeordneten Thema der Liebe und Ehe, der Charakter
Veršinins, das Thema 'Arbeit') zeigen keine direkte innere Beziehung zueinander. Sie können statt in der gegebenen Reihenfolge auch in einer anderen Reihenfolge auftreten. Von den
ersten drei dramatischen Situationen aus ist nicht ersichtlich,
welcher Art die folgenden Situationsphasen sein werden: mit
Ausnahme der zweiten dramatischen Situation, die die Erwartung weckt, daß der angekündigte Veršinin irgendwann einmal
in der aktuellen Situation auftreten wird, gibt keins der genannten Inhaltskonzentrate einen konkreten Ausblick auf
seine eigene Weiterentwicklung in den kommenden Phasen.
Die einzelnen dramatischen Situationen bilden also relativ
selbständige, gegeneinander verschlossene Einheiten, die
keinen oder einen nur schwachen Ausblick auf ihre eigene oder
die Weiterentwicklung der Gesamtsituation, die sie konstituieren, geben. Das Bindeglied zwischen den unvermittelt nebeneinander stehenden einzelnen dramatischen Situationen bildet
die äußere, objektive Situation, die einen zeitlichen und räumlichen Rahmen für die in ihr vor sich gehenden Reden und Ereignisse liefert.

Ein eigentlicher Aktionsteil ist in keiner der drei Phasen
präsent. Er kann nur aus den die Phasen tragenden Reaktionen
rückermittelt werden. Aus der Weise, wie Personen, die später
zu Teilverkörperungen der aktiven Kräfte werden, hier einge-
führt werden (es handelt sich dabei um Čebutykin und Solenyj), läßt sich das generelle Verhältnis von Reaktion und dar-
gestellter Aktion in diesem Stück schon erkennen: Čebutykin
und Solenyj sind hier nur 'zufällig' anwesende Begleitpersonen,
die an einem aus ihrer Sicht 'zufällig' aufgeworfenen Konversationsthema ('Arbeit') teilhaben oder die ohne sichtbaren Zusammenhang mit dem vor sich gehenden Gespräch Repliken in
den Raum hineinsprechen, die erst im gesamten Sinnzusammenhang des Stücks eine von ihnen nicht erfaßte Bedeutung
erhalten. Mit den Aktionskräften, die das Verhalten der

Schwestern und Tuzenbachs in der Jetztsituation bewirken, haben sie keine direkte Verbindung. Ebensowenig werden ihre oder die der übrigen aktiven Personen für das Verhalten der von ihren Aktionen betroffenen Personen voll und direkt verantwortlich sein.

Die einzelnen dramatischen Situationen sind somit im Verhältnis zueinander statisch konstruiert. Statisch sind sie aber auch in ihrem inneren Aufbau. Diese innere Statik der dramatischen Situationen wird durch zwei Eigenschaften der Motive, die diese Situationen konstituieren, bedingt: 1. Die Motive innerhalb einer solchen Situationseinheit bringen von sich aus keine Tendenz zu einem Abschluß mit, so daß das Ende der Situation nicht vorhersehbar wird. Z.B. könnten die Erinnerungsmotive Ol'gas in der ersten dramatischen Situation beliebig fortgesetzt werden, und dasselbe gilt für Tuzenbachs Darstellung Veršinins und das Gespräch über 'Arbeit'. Der Abschluß wird jedesmal von außen, durch Eingriffe aus der äußeren Situation gesetzt: durch Repliken aus einer anderen Sprechsituation oder durch ein Ereignis in der äußeren Situation (das Klopfen zum Schluß der dritten dramatischen Situation, das den Weggang Čebutykins bewirkt). 2. Den einzelnen in die dramatische Situation eingehenden Motiven kommt ein Überhang an nicht vermittelter Bedeutungsfunktion zu: das deutlichste Verfahren hierbei ist das Symbolverfahren, das hier z.B. bei den Farben der Kleider der drei Schwestern angewendet wird: der Symbolwert der Farben Schwarz, Blau und Weiß – Trauer, Beständigkeit und Lebensfreude – entspricht der Grundstimmung der Schwestern, die mit Ausnahme Irinas die Schwestern bis zum Schluß durchhalten. Symbolische Details werden auch im weiteren Verlauf des Werks angewendet (der Gürtel, die Kerze, das Fotografieren[29], die Uhr u.a.). Bei diesen Details wird die Symbolbedeutung erst durch die Verwendung im Kontext des ganzen Stücks geschaffen, während die Farben schon von vornherein Symbolwert haben. Während bei den Symbolverfahren die genannten Gegenstände ihre thematische Funktion in bezug auf den thematischen Komplex, dem sie unmittelbar zugeordnet sind, überschreiten, gibt es auch ein umgekehrtes Verfahren: Elemente, die an der Stelle, an der sie im

Textzusammenhang auftreten, keine eindeutige Zuordnung zu
einem thematischen Komplex zu enthalten scheinen und als
überflüssige oder zufällige Details klassifiziert werden können,
erhalten im Bedeutungsaufbau des Werkganzen eine genau be-
stimmbare Bedeutungsfunktion: hierzu gehören die zufälligen
Repliken Tuzenbachs und Solenyjs, die innerhalb der ersten
dramatischen Situation auftauchen, und die 'Unsinnrepliken'
Solenyjs und Čebutykins, die die zweite dramatische Situation
abschließen. Durch dieses im Verlauf des Stücks häufig wieder-
kehrende Verfahren sowie durch das Symbolverfahren wird
eine Verkomplizierung des Verstehensvorgangs des Lesers er-
reicht: der Leser kann nicht nur der unmittelbaren Darstel-
lungslinie folgen, sondern muß gleichzeitig aus der Immanenz
der dargestellten Prozesse heraustreten und diese auf einen
'hinter' ihnen liegenden, vom abstrakten Autor intendierten
Sinn hin befragen. Die Tendenz zur Statik innerhalb der dramatischen Situation wird schließlich auch noch durch das ge-
wählte Darstellungsverfahren des Komplexes der inneren Situation der Personen bestärkt: diese innere Situation wird nicht
oder nur vereinzelt direkt dargestellt, sie wird vornehmlich
durch ein symptomhaftes Sprechverhalten der Personen mit-
dargestellt. Die Symptome lassen sich ihrerseits beliebig reihen
und häufen und projizieren keine kontinuierliche Entwicklung
von einem Symptom zum andern. Das in ihnen angezeigte
Ganze, nämlich die innere Situation, kommt auch nicht gleich
mit dem ersten Symptom zur Erscheinung, sondern läßt sich
erst in nachhinein, nach Vorliegen einer bestimmten Menge
von Symptomen, genauer bestimmen. Sie verlangen somit statt
eines nach vorn gerichteten Lesens ein regressives Lesen, das
immer wieder auf die schon erfaßten Details des Textes zu-
rückgreifen läßt, um ihre Bedeutung von dem später Gelesenen
aus korrigierend zu bestimmen.

Über das Verhältnis der einzelnen dramatischen Situation
zum Gesamtaufbau des Stücks läßt sich zusammenfassend folgendes sagen: das generelle Verhältnis von Aktion und Reaktion spiegelt sich in der dramatischen Situation als dem Teil
des Ganzen wieder, insofern einerseits die Aktionskraft nicht
(bei später folgenden dramatischen Situationen muß man

sagen: nur zum Teil identisch ist mit der in der dramatischen Situation dargestellten äußeren Situation und deren Bestandteilen; die eigentliche Aktionskraft muß aus der dargestellten Reaktion rückerschlossen werden. Die geringe Eigendynamik des Aktionsträgers spiegelt sich anderseits auch in der Gestaltung der Reaktion wider, die ihrerseits als das explizit Dargestellte für die Statik der einzelnen dramatischen Situationen im Verhältnis zueinander verantwortlich ist. Statisch sind schließlich auch die dramatischen Situationen in ihrem inneren Aufbau aus den einzelnen Motiven, die weder auf einen Abschluß der dramatischen Situation hinzielen, also eine geschwächte motivische Funktion haben, noch stets eindeutig den thematischen Komplexen zuzuordnen sind: sie überschreiten entweder ihre thematische Funktion, wenn sie zusätzliche symbolische Bedeutung mitbringen oder durch den Kontext erhalten, oder sie unterschreiten die motivische Funktion, wenn sie als überflüssig oder unsinnig erscheinen. Auch die regressive Bedeutungsfunktion der Symptome trägt zur Statik des gesamten Sujetkontextes bei.

Für die Auswahl und Zusammenstellung der Einheiten der thematischen Bedeutungsschicht sowohl auf der Ebene der Motive als auch auf der Ebene der dramatischen Situationen läßt sich schließlich dasselbe Prinzip feststellen, das auch für die Ebene des dramatischen Textes gilt: ebensowenig wie die Repliken verschiedener Sprecher sich wechselseitig in ihrer Aufeinanderfolge bedingen – die einzelnen Sprecher provozieren nicht direkt die Rede des andern und werden selbst nicht eindeutig und in für den Leser vorhersehbarer Weise von den Reden der andern provoziert –, ebensowenig bedingen sich die einzelnen Motive innerhalb einer dramatischen Situation eindeutig gegenseitig, und dasselbe gilt auch für die dramatischen Situationen: auch sie rufen nicht die ihnen folgenden zwingend hervor und folgen ihrerseits nicht notwendig aus den ihnen vorhergehenden. Die Zufälligkeit und Unvorhersehbarkeit der Aufeinanderfolge gilt auch auf der Ebene der größten Teileinheiten des Dramas, der Aktschritte: die hier eintretenden aktbildenden Ereignisse (Namenstag, Fest, Brand, Abschied) sind willkürlich gewählt und könnten (mit Ausnahme

des letzten) auch umgestellt werden oder durch andere denk-
bare ersetzt werden.

Da weder Einheiten von der Größenordnung der Motive
noch solche von der Größenordnung der dramatischen Situationen noch schließlich die Akteinheiten die Abfolge und die
Art der Einheiten ihrer eigenen Ebene zwingend bestimmen,
bedarf die tatsächliche Zusammenstellung dieser Einheiten im
dramatischen Werk einer zusätzlichen Begründung, wie dies
auch schon für die Abfolge der Repliken der Personen gegolten
hat. Hier lassen sich zwei Prinzipien feststellen: 1. Das Prinzip
des Kontrasts oder der Übereinstimmung des Stimmungswerts
einer Einheit. Dieses Prinzip gilt für die Motive ebenso wie für
die dramatischen Situationen. So besteht zwischen den beiden
ersten dramatischen Situationen ein Kontrast der Stimmung,
da Ol'gas und Irinas Ausführungen vornehmlich ernst gestimmt
sind (wobei sich auch hier Schattierungen der Stimmungen der
beiden Schwestern ergeben, denn Ol'ga ist wehmütig, Irina versucht dagegen, ihren Lebensmut durchzusetzen), während
Tuzenbachs Darstellung von Veršinins Charakter einen anek-
dotisch-heiteren Ton hat. Auf der Ebene der Motive besteht in
der dritten dramatischen Situation zwischen den ernstgemein-
ten Reflexionen Irinas und Tuzenbachs zum Thema 'Arbeit'
und den Meinungen Solenyjs und Čebutykins ein komischer
Gegensatz. Eine Übereinstimmung der Grundstimmung kann
man der Gesamtheit der dramatischen Situationen zusprechen,
die jeweils eine Akteinheit ausmachen; die Stimmungswerte
dieser Akteinheiten lassen sich jedoch nur ungefähr angeben:
der erste Akt wäre demnach in der Grundstimmung heiter,
während die bedrohlichen Anzeichen noch verborgen bleiben;
der zweite Akt stellt ein Aufeinanderprallen zweier Prinzipien
dar, des Versuchs der Schwestern, ein heiteres Fest zu veran-
stalten, und der Unterdrückung dieses Versuchs durch eine
dumpfe, kleinliche Macht; der dritte Akt zeigt die Zerstörung
durch den Brand und der vierte schließlich Bewegung und Auflösung der bisherigen Lebensordnung der Schwestern und
einen unbestimmten Aufbruch zu Neuem. Im vierten Akt hat
das Lachen und die Musik seine Trägerpersonen gewechselt:
nicht mehr die Schwestern und ihre Gäste lachen und feiern,

sondern diejenigen, die an der Auflösung ihrer ehemaligen
Lebensweise mitgewirkt haben (Čebutykin, Kulygin, Nataša).
Verfolgt man den Wechsel der Grundstimmung von Akt zu
Akt, so zeigt sich, daß hier eine stufenweise Entwicklung vor
sich geht, die im vierten Akt zu einer Umkehrung der Aus-
gangssituation im ersten Akt gelangt. Die Einheit der Grundstimmung, die jeden Akt trägt, kann als ein Hinweis für die Gesamtentwicklung im Ausgleich von Reaktion und Aktion angesehen werden, und ein solcher Hinweis ist um so nötiger, als
die Lektüre des Werks von Motiv zu Motiv entlang der Linie
des Sujetkontextes und von dramatischer Situation zu dramatischer Situation aufgrund der statischen Konstruktion des Kontextes auf jeder dieser Ebenen nur schwach das Bewußtsein
einer dynamischen Fortentwicklung dieser beiden Größen auf-
kommen läßt. Als Hinweise, die einzelnen aufeinanderfolgenden Teile in Hinblick auf dieses Ganze, nämlich die dynamische Gesamtheit der Reaktions-Aktionsphasen, zu betrachten,
müssen schließlich auch die symbolischen Elemente des Stücks
gewertet werden. Dieses Symbolverfahren wird nicht nur, wie
schon erwähnt, auf der Ebene der Motive angewandt, sondern
betrifft auch die dramatischen Situationen und ganze Akte:
symbolisch ist z.B. die letzte Situation im ersten Akt, die dreizehn Festtagsgäste um den Tisch herum vereint zeigt. Der symbolische Gehalt dieser Situation ist folgender: die Schwestern
laden diejenigen, die ihnen Zerstörung und Mord ins Haus
tragen, nichtsahnend (wie im Fall Čebutykins) oder auch
ahnend (wie im Fall Solenyjs, den Irina nicht mag, und
Nataša[30], die alle Schwestern nicht mögen) zu sich ein. Die
Fotografenszene weist auf diesen Symbolgehalt der Situation
hin. Auf der Ebene der Akte hat den dichtesten Symbolgehalt
der dritte Akt: hier wird die Gesamtsituation von dem Brand
der Stadt beherrscht, dem die Schwestern durch tätige Hilfe
für die Betroffenen zu begegnen versuchen. Den 'Brand' (d.h.
die Zerstörung) und den Raub in ihrem eigenen Haus jedoch
bemerken sie nicht, oder sie tun doch, soweit sie ihn wahrnehmen, nichts dagegen, sondern dulden die 'Brandstifter' und
Räuber. Diese Symbolverfahren bewirken, daß die Statik der
Gesamtkonstruktion auf den einzelnen Ebenen (Sujetebenen,

Ebene der dramatischen Situationen), die das Erfassen des thematischen Zusammenhangs der jeweiligen Teile erschwert, ein Gegengewicht erhält: denn der Symbolgehalt weist immer auf den Sinnzusammenhang des symboltragenden Elements (Motiv, dramatische Situation oder Akt) mit dem Ganzen hin.

ANMERKUNGEN

[1] Den Begriff des Textbandes und später auch den der Äußerungsebene entnehme ich dem grundlegenden Werk zur Analyse der Erzählung von Lubomír Doležel, 1960, *O stylu moderní české prózy* (Praha).

[2] Mit dem Begriff der Wechselrede ist eine minimale, weil nur formale Bestimmung der dialogischen Rede gegeben, weil dieser Begriff sich nur auf die Tatsache des alternierenden Sprechens verschiedener Sprecher bezieht.

[3] Neben der Rede sind auch andere Arten der Kontaktaufnahme zwischen Personen möglich, doch für das Drama ist die Rede die wichtigste Art der Kommunikation zwischen den Personen.

[4] Zur Semantik des Worts in der dialogischen Rede s. insbesondere Jiří Veltruský, 1942, "Drama jako básnické dílo", in: Bohumil Havránek, Jan Mukařovský (Hrg.), *Čtení o jazyce a poesii*, Bd. 1 (Praha), S. 401-502; dt. (gekürzt): "Das Drama als dichterisches Werk", in: Aloysius van Kesteren, Verf. (Hrg., 1975, *Moderne Dramentheorie* (Kronberg/Ts.), S. 96 bis 132.

[5] Die maximale Opposition zwischen den dialogisierenden Personen ist dann eine solche, die auf einander ausschließenden Gegensatzpositionen zu demselben Gegenstand beruhen. Solche Gegensätze müssen dann in einem 'Kampf' um die Oberhand ausgetragen werden.

[6] Damit ist das Monodrama, das nur eine sprechende Person vorsieht, eine vollständige Realisierung der Gattung des Dramas.

[7] Zum Problem der Typisierung der dramatischen Struktur s. Verf., 1973, *Strukturalistische Dramentheorie – Semantische Analyse von Čechovs "Ivanov" und "Der Kirschgarten"* (Kronberg/Ts.)

[8] Man kann in dem Ausgleich zwischen dem Aktionsimpuls und der Reaktion im Drama eine dramenspezifische Variante der Fabel-Sujetopposition sehen, wie sie L. S. Vygotskij, 1968, *Psichologija iskusstva* (Moskva) im Anschluß an die russischen Formalisten formuliert hat. Dabei wird in den Sujetbegriff jedoch nicht, wie dies weiter unten geschieht, die Gesamtheit aller in einem literarischen Werk zur Entfaltung gebrachten thematischen Komplexe aufgenommen.

[9] Das hier als immanenter Formimpuls bezeichnete Entwicklungsgesetz des Aktionsteils kann man mit der 'Disposition' Vygotskijs, op. cit., ver-

gleichen. Die 'Disposition' meint dort aber nur den der Fabel inhärenten Formimpuls.

[10] Felix Vodička, 1948, *Počátky krásné prózy novočeské* (Praha), hier S. 113 ff., spricht von 'thematischen Reihen', die das ganze Werk durchziehen und zusammenhängende Kontexte bilden; sie konstituieren die 'Plane' des thematischen Aufbaus. Als solche thematischen Plane sieht er die Handlung, die Hauptpersonen und die äußere Welt an. Vgl. dazu auch Mojmír Grygar, 1969, "Sujetová výstavba básnické prózy", *Problémy sujetu – Litteraria XII* 1971, S. 135-168.

[11] Zum Begriff der Projektion von Motiven und thematischen Komplexen vgl. Josef Heidenreich, 1943, "O tvaru motivô", *Slovo a slovesnost*, Jg. 9, S. 69-96.

[12] Diese Divergenz gilt nicht nur für das dramatische, sondern für jedes literarische Werk, das thematische Komplexe zur Entfaltung bringt, insbesondere für Erzählwerke.

[13] Vygotskij, op. cit., sieht in der Abweichung des Sujets von der Fabeldisposition ein Hauptmittel zum Erzeugen der künstlerischen Spannung.

[14] Zum Problem des Motivs vgl. Boris V. Tomaševskij, 1927, *Teorija literatury* (Moskva/Leningrad), S. 136, und Heidenreich, op. cit.

[15] Diese unvermittelte Bedeutungsfunktion umfaßt sowohl die sprachlichen Konnotationen als auch Denotationen im Bereich der außersprachlichen Bedeutungen. Die Konnotationen können durch bestimmte sprachliche Verfahren wie lautliche Instrumentierung usw. vermehrt werden, die Denotationen (als potentielle oder unbestimmte Denotationen) sind dann eine Folge der vermehrten Konnotationen.

[16] Zum Begriff der Statik und Dynamik vgl. Jan Mukařovský, 1973, "Über die Dichtersprache" (O jazyce básnickém), in: J.M., *Studien zur strukturalistischen Ästhetik und Poetik* (München), S. 142-199.

[17] Neben der Möglichkeit, daß ein Text 'überflüssige' Motive enthält, besteht auch die umgekehrte Möglichkeit, daß ein Text zuwenig Motive enthält, als daß skizzierte thematische Komplexe voll bestimmt würden. Dadurch kann das Moment der Offenheit und Unbestimmtheit in einem Werk begründet sein.

[18] Generell gilt für Gruppengespräche eine Schwächung der Kommunikationsspannung, da hier keine Intention auf einen bestimmten Partner mit dessem individuellen Kontext beim Sprecher vorausgesetzt werden kann.

[19] Zum Begriff der Bedeutungswende im Dialog s. Jan Mukařovský, 1967, "Zwei Studien über den Dialog", in: J.M., *Kapitel aus der Poetik* (Frankfurt/M.), S. 108-149.

[20] Die Tendenz zur Häufung und Reihung von Repliken wird in der Konversation dadurch gefördert, daß die Intention der Sprecher auf die Reaktion eines bestimmten Redepartners mit einer festgelegten und vorherberechenbaren Einstellung zum Redegegenstand geschwächt ist. Die Gegenreplik kann daher zur bloßen 'Ergänzungsreplik' werden.

[21] In einem vordergründigen Sinn ist dieses 'unsinnige' Wechselgespräch

zwischen Andrej und Ferapont, bei dem Andrej über seine Schwestern und sich selbst spricht, Ferapont über entfernte Katastrophen, komisch. Die Zusammenstellung dieser auf den ersten Blick nicht zusammenpassenden Repliken ergibt aber einen bestimmten 'Sinn': Andrej ist so von seinem persönlichen Unglück gefangengenommen, daß er, als von gesellschaftlicher Not die Rede ist, nicht einmal hinhört. Damit wirft der abstrakte Autor einen kritischen Aspekt auf das gesellschaftliche Bewußtsein Andrejs, der sonst nirgends direkt ausgesprochen wird.

[22] Gerade die Ungewißheit darüber, ob eine Person das um sie her Gesprochene und Geschehene wahrgenommen hat oder nicht, macht eine nur psychologisierende Deutung des Stücks unmöglich; die psychologische Zeichnung der Personen ist den semantischen Verfahren untergeordnet. Mit diesen semantischen Verfahren 'setzt' der abstrakte Autor die Bedeutungen zusammen, die er braucht, und dabei benutzt er die sprechenden Personen als ein Mittel der Bedeutungsschaffung unter anderen.

[23] Im dritten Akt im Gespräch zwischen Irina und Ol'ga wird deutlich, warum sich Irina für Čebutykins Zitat interessiert: sie offenbart Ol'ga, daß sie von einer Liebesheirat in Moskau geträumt hat.

[24] Irina hatte zuvor nacheinander die Beichte Mašas und die Aussprache Andrejs anhören müssen. Scheinbar unmotiviert bricht sie, als sie mit Ol'ga allein ist, in den Ruf nach Moskau aus.

[25] Im ersten Akt erklärt Irina, daß sie Solenyj 'fürchtet'. Tuzenbach dagegen verteidigt ihn, weil er in ihm einen eher mitleidswerten als furchtbaren Menschen sieht.

[26] So begleitet Čebutykin Andrej zur Spielbank, obwohl er weiß, daß Andrej schon hoch verschuldet ist (vgl. ihrer beider Flucht aus dem Haus im zweiten Akt).

[27] Vgl. dazu bes. die Schlußszene des Stücks.

[28] Gleich im ersten Akt wird Protopopov durch die Torte, die er Irina zum Geschenk überreichen läßt, vertreten. Irina reagiert mit Unwillen auf dieses Geschenk, wobei dem Leser aber noch nicht klar ist, warum sie so unwillig ist.

[29] Der Gürtel spielt zweimal eine Rolle, im ersten Akt als Natašas Gürtel, dessen Farbe Ol'ga befremdlich findet, und im vierten Akt als Irinas Gürtel, den nun Nataša kritisiert. Natašas Kerze steht in Zusammenhang mit dem Brand: die Schwestern (Maša) vermuten in ihr die Brandstifterin. Als Maša diese Worte ausspricht, weiß nur der Leser, der die symbolische Bedeutung des Brandes verstanden hat, da Maša hier unwissentlich die Wahrheit getroffen hat (dritter Akt). Das Fotografieren im ersten Akt hält die symbolische Szene der Dreizehn am Tisch fest. Im dritten Akt ist die Rede davon, daß alle Fotos zerstört worden sind. Die Bedeutung dieses Details ist nicht sicher interpretierbar. Möglich ist eine solche Deutung, die in den Fotos ein Dokument von dem Eindringen der Zerstörer in das Haus und bis an den Tisch der Prozorovs sieht, daß zerstört werden muß, um die Spuren zu verwischen. Die Bedeutung der Uhr ist

ie des Erinnerungsstücks an die Liebe Čebutykins zur Mutter der
hwestern. Mit der Uhr verlöscht seine Erinnerung an sie (er kann sich
cht mehr erinnern, ob die Mutter ihn auch geliebt hat), und seine Akte
r aktiven Zerstörung nehmen ihren Lauf: er betrinkt sich, verführt
ndrej zum Spiel, dient als Sekundant beim Duell, obwohl er weiß, daß
r Baron gegen Solenyj keine Chance hat.

Mit dem zweiten Akt setzen die Aktionen Natašas ein, die sich bis
um Schluß des vierten Akt steigern.

S
n
de
A
de
3

z